PIERRE FRANEY'S
LOW-CALORIE GOURMET

OTHER BOOKS BY PIERRE FRANEY

Classic French Cooking (with Craig Claiborne)
Veal Cookery (with Craig Claiborne)
Craig Claiborne's The New New York Times Cookbook
(with Craig Claiborne)
Craig Claiborne's Gourmet Diet (with Craig Claiborne)
The New York Times 60-Minute Gourmet
The New York Times More 60-Minute Gourmet
Cooking with Craig Claiborne and Pierre Franey (with Craig Claiborne)
The Seafood Cookbook (with Bryan Miller)
Cuisine Rapide (with Bryan Miller)

Other Books by Pierre Franey and Richard Flaste
Pierre Franey's Kitchen

PIERRE FRANEY'S
Low-Calorie Gourmet

by
PIERRE FRANEY
RICHARD FLASTE

TIMES BOOKS

RANDOM HOUSE

Copyright © 1984 by Billi-Bi Enterprises
All rights reserved under International and Pan-
American Copyright Conventions. Published in the
United States by Times Books, a division of Random
House, Inc., New York.

Originally published in hardcover by Times Books
in 1984.

The calorie content of the recipes was computer
analyzed by Hill Nutrition Associates, Inc.

Library of Congress Cataloging-in-Publication Data
Franey, Pierre.
Pierre Franey's Low-calorie gourmet/
Pierre Franey, Richard Flaste.
p.   cm.
Includes index.
ISBN 0-8129-1836-3
1. Low-calorie diet—Recipes.   I. Flaste,
Richard.   II. Title.   III. Title: Pierre Franey's Low-
calorie gourmet
RM222.2.F692   1989
64.5′635—dc19   89-4419

Coordinating Editor: Rosalyn T. Badalamenti

Designer: Janis Capone

Manufactured in the United States of America

9   8   7   6   5   4   3   2

First Paperback Edition

For Claudia, Diane, Jacques, Becky, and Jordan

ACKNOWLEDGMENTS

Many people have contributed to the creation of this book: researchers, editors, family members. A few people have loomed over it: the chefs of today and yesterday, to whom we owe a great deal—Escoffier, Paul Bocuse, Roger Vergé, the Troisgros Brothers, and Michel Guérard. And although he did not contribute directly to this book, Craig Claiborne, the food editor of *The New York Times*, has served as an abiding example of how things ought to be done.

CONTENTS

Introduction

I have changed my mind.

To put it another way, many of the values and approaches to cooking that were mine decades ago are no longer mine. My approach to food—which has its foundations in the *haute cuisine* that reigned in the 1930s—has evolved from one that was heavily laden with the silken fats and oils of traditional French cuisine to one that tends to use them only at a minimum. I like it better that way now. And I offer no apology for allowing myself to change over the years. In some ways, my cooking has evolved toward approaches to food that are mine alone. In other ways I have changed with the times.

French cooking and the appreciation of it have been in flux ever since the eighth century, when Charlemagne demonstrated, in all his majesty, that food was worth the adoration of man. Today, however, few would adore Charlemagne's meals, which were often long, crude and gluttonous experiences. By the time Antonin Carème, the founder of the grand cuisine of France, came along, in the early nineteenth century, although the dining was still excessive by today standards, it had been elevated to an art. (A *science* is what Carème liked to call it.) The French took to good, sumptuous food so completely that by the end of Carème's reign, a clergyman from Bavaria, Sebastian Kneipp, issued a stern warning: "Frenchmen, you have created the finest cuisine in the world, but you abuse it. . . . Your food is not healthy: your dishes are too highly seasoned, too spicy or too alcoholic. You are shortening your lives."

Moderation began to take hold by the turn of this century. The chef Prosper Montagne wondered then how the men and women of the generation before his could have possibly eaten so much— dozens of courses at a single sitting—and he prepared some "modern menus." One of those modern, lighter menus was offered on February 4, 1899, at the Hôtel de Paris, Monte Carlo: hors d'oeuvres, an omelette with morels and cream decorated with asparagus tips and surrounded with a chateaubriand sauce, frogs' legs in cream sauce, roast quail, pâté de foie gras, salad, and apple fritters.

Still a bit much.

When Escoffier arrived, a few years later, he made his own contributions to a lighter cuisine. These days, Escoffier's *haute cuisine* often sounds like the villain, but the truth is that Escoffier was the first to banish the heaviness of *espagnole,* a kind of burnt *roux* (a mixture of butter and flour), which was used constantly in French cooking until then. He preferred arrowroot as a thickener, and he was indeed trying to achieve greater lightness. But he still used the flour and butter of the *roux,* blended with stock, in a *velouté* that was the base of a great many sauces. It was at that time, when Escoffier's thinking influenced every fine kitchen, that I first came into the business, as an a apprentice at the Drouant in Paris.

By the time the now-famous *nouvelle cuisine* took hold, I was ensconced in the United States as chef at Le Pavillon, a restaurant that expired in the late 1960s after spawning much of the great French cooking in America. It was hard not to notice the *nouvelle* as it grew. It expelled flour-based sauces altogether. It insisted on fresh ingredients, deplored overcooking, and maintained that every dish should look exquisite. *Nouvelle* also reached out to regional dishes and to the cuisines of other countries.

One reason for *nouvelle*'s popularity (which is waning rather dramatically now) was that it was touted in its early days as a low-calorie approach to food. This it was not. The sauces were often built around reduced stocks thickened with cream or egg yolks or hollandaise sauce. Often the cream itself was reduced through the rapid evaporation of its moisture, as is frequently the case in more traditional approaches, too. The result of that reduction is that all the calories of a cup of cream will reside in a half cup of liquid or less. I believe that a steady diet of *nouvelle cuisine* would immobilize anyone in a matter of weeks or months.

Nevertheless, the tendency was there: The French, who had been making their cuisine ever lighter over the decades, now had accelerated the trend. One saw, for instance, the sudden popularity of *cuisine minceur,* the invention of Michel Guérard at his spa, Eugénie-les-Bains. His was a strictly dietetic approach to food, exploring complicated subsitutes for conventional ingredients to achieve a refined sense of flavor despite the absence of calories. It is a very difficult regime to follow at home, in my opinion.

Others have come up with a variety of approaches to lighter dishes or to explicitly dietetic food. André Guillot cut down on the butter and the cream and the frying in his *Cuisine Legère.* Guillot's is far from the dietetic approach of Guérard, but it is in fact lighter than the cooking of many of his contemporaries. Even the team of Henri Gault and Christian Millau, the writers and reviewers who are the high priests of *nouvelle cuisine,* have come out with their own approach to eating fewer calories.

As I say, I've been observing all this happen for more than 40 years, and I think I understand how the collective sense of taste has evolved. Today, we desire food that punishes the body less. It is, after all, an age when most of us will live as long as the rarest of our luckiest ancestors did—if we're careful. And we are vain too; we want our long-lived bodies to be svelte and attractive and strong even when we are in a period of our lives that used to be thought of as old age.

I believe that I have something to contribute—with a bow in the direction of Escoffier and yet another in the direction of *nouvelle cuisine*—to the satisfaction of that desire for lighter food.

For several years, I have been the author of the ''60-Minute Gourmet,'' which appears weekly in *The New York Times,* and I am the author of two books by the same name. The column has been a major force in urging me toward new, simpler ways of cooking that sacrifice little or nothing in taste. It has also made me many new friends. Often, as I have traveled around the country, those who use my books have urged me to create recipes that are not only simple and quick to prepare but also less fattening.

In this new book, I have combined the tactics of the ''60-Minute Gourmet'' column with my own approach to the lighter dishes that have increasingly emerged from France and elsewhere, including my own kitchen.

In doing so, I have *not* created a dietetic collection of recipes, nor have I used any gimmicks. My method, which I will expand upon in the first chapter of this book, uses no cream, no flour-based sauces, relatively little butter and, in accordance with modern sensibilities, only a touch of salt. It emphasizes small portions beautifully presented (I've included a separate chapter on presentation). The sauces are, each and every one of them, light, although intense with flavor. And, with a few exceptions, the recipes here fit within the requirements of the 60-minute format, which is to say they are simple and fast.

The steps I have taken to create these lighter dishes are not meant to be proprietary information. It is important, I think, for the cook at home to understand how one dish grows out of another one. An awareness of the kinship all good dishes have with each other is indispensable to one's growth. Thus, with the major recipes here, I have included a discussion that often explains how a dish qualified for this book. It describes the changes that had to be made in its traditional character, significant or otherwise. Sometimes, I grant you, I have so altered a classic dish that it resembles the original only slightly.

But despite the great distances traveled, I think you will still recognize that all of these dishes are without question the progeny of Carême's "science."

PIERRE FRANEY'S
LOW-CALORIE GOURMET

THE FRANEY APPROACH TO

Lightness

The creation of this book required more than a little discipline. I put all of my skills into the service of designing dishes that are as low in fat and thus as low in calories as I could make them without doing violence to my sense of how food ought to taste. I applied the techniques I developed as the "60-Minute Gourmet" to creating light dishes that could, for the most part, be completed within an hour. Even those few that can't be prepared quickly—the light stews in the book, for instance—are nevertheless geared for speed.

To stay within the rigid guidelines I set up for myself, I eliminated heavy cream, and I believe the dishes do not suffer for the lack of it. There are no sauces made heavy by the addition of flour or starch or egg yolk, either.

All the ingredients are selected with lightness in mind. Ingredients that are similar in their uses and perhaps equally satisfying can vary enormously in caloric content: Beef cooked in some simple fashion will deliver about twice as many calories as chicken will. Veal and seafood are also relatively low in calories. In this book I respect that caloric hierarchy and have created recipes for chicken, veal, and seafood that take advantage of their natural lightness.

Sometimes I use chicken or veal or both in dishes where beef is more familiar, as in meatballs or a meat loaf. In the relatively few instances in which I do choose to use beef or pork, I stipulate that the meat must be extremely lean and cooked in a manner that diminishes the fat.

In fact, as part of the disciplined approach to this book I have tended to diminish the fat even in recipes that call for the use of the leaner meats (as long as I am certain that moistness will not be sacrificed). The browning of chicken pieces before moving on to any other cooking step helps burn away much of the fat near the skin, for instance. And some of the lamb dishes offered here are prepared in a fashion that at first looks merely decorative—the fat is trimmed entirely from the bone, leaving it gracefully arched and totally naked—but beyond terrific looks I had in mind, of course, reducing the calories of this relatively lean meat (3 ounces of roast lamb has 230 calories compared with the 300 in a similar quantity of roast beef) as much as possible.

Many cookbook writers, trying to make their recipes seem lower in calories, have dispensed with butter in favor of margarine (the invention of a Frenchman, for crying out loud!). I won't do it. Margarine has the same number of calories as butter (about 100 to the tablespoon), so any idea that it is dietetic is entirely false. It is, however, less harmful than butter on the cholesterol front. Butter supplies the body with some cholesterol. Margarine, if it is made from polyunsaturated fats, helps to rid the body of it. If you are among those who are extraordinarily concerned about cholesterol, it is not for me to dissuade you. But it is my own certain belief (and it is one that a great many in the scientific community would support) that no harm will come from a teaspoon of butter per serving every now and then, whereas margarine, with its phony taste and very unpleasant aftertaste, does real harm to one's appreciation of food.

My approach to butter here has been, therefore, to use it wherever its flavor is central to the character of a dish (it is often central, because butter is a cornerstone of French cooking), but I use it in such small quantities—often a third or less of the volume that I would have employed in the past—that very little damage is done to the calorie count of a dish. I can get away with the small amount of butter because I frequently add it at the very end of the preparation of a dish to be sure that the flavor will hold on. You'll notice my proclivity for tossing vegetables in a bit of butter at the end of cooking or for softening a sauce meant to serve four with a tablespoon of butter just before serving (after all the other fat has been discarded). Thus a mere 25 calories per serving has been contributed by the butter, which is trivial when you realize that the total daily intake of a grown man is something like 3,000 calories (2,500 for a woman).

The sauces, in any event, are all of the lightest sort. They are primarily condensations of the natural cooking liquid combined with wine, stock, vinegar, or even water. The liquid intensifies as it condenses (a lesson well learned by those of us who in years past became accustomed to employing demiglaces—stocks condensed to a glaze—to enrich sauces). Reduction sauces, as they are called, often still require some binding agent. In the absence of cream or a starch, I find that simply chopping tomatoes or other vegetables into a sauce will give it body. Puréeing those vegetables in the sauce will give it smoothness. Mushrooms, especially, puréed into a sauce with an electric blender will yield an exquisite smoothness, much the same body, in fact, that one obtains through the use of cream, because the mushrooms are spun into an airy emulsion.

Oils are unavoidable in cooking, but I have kept the calories to a minimum here, too. Not only do I discard all cooking oil before a dish is served in most cases, but I also employ as little as possible to start with.

As for salt, which is a matter of concern these days, I have never used much in my own cooking, and perhaps I was remiss in the past when I created recipes that had the instruction, "Salt to taste." In the recipes for this book, I stipulate exactly how much salt is required to suit my taste. That might be as little as ½ teaspoon for four to six servings. The reason I continue to use the ingredient at all is that I believe salt is an important catalyst for the flavors of food. Although I have worked with salt-free recipes and find some of them produce worthwhile dishes, there is no question in my mind but that they are inferior to dishes that use some salt, an ingredient that man has craved since the beginning of time. And for the record, I should say that the case against salt's moderate use in the diets of healthy people has, in the view of many, been vastly overstated. (Obviously, those who are predisposed to salt-linked illnesses or who actually suffer from them should not use even the small amounts stipulated in this book without the approval of a doctor.)

I manage to keep the salt use to a minimum because my cooking tends to be richly flavored by herbs and spices. In addition to the traditional French accents provided by thyme, bay leaf, parsley, tarragon, garlic, and the like, I have gone out of my way to recognize some of the current international trends. Thus, I make wide use of ginger, imparting an Oriental flavor to some of the dishes, and there is the cumin of North Africa, the coriander of Mexico, and the curry of India.

This low-fat, high-flavor approach of mine has one other requirement: no funny business. I am not in the habit of assailing you with gimmicky flavor combinations or with yogurt-based everything. There's no righteousness here.

There is a good measure of inventiveness, though. An example of my principles at work is the recipe for steamed chicken stuffed with spinach. What I had in mind at the outset was a Chicken Florentine, a classic dish that, if I had been following the traditional approach, would have involved placing the breast of chicken (with its skin intact) on a bed of spinach and covering it with a sauce of cream and cheese. In my invention for this book, I chose to omit the cream, to skin the chicken—and thus remove most of its fat—and to steam the breasts so that no additional fat would be added in the cooking. Thus the chicken breasts are stuffed with the spinach and cheese before being steamed. The melted cheese becomes, in effect, an internal sauce for the chicken. The dish can be recognized and admired for its Florentine heritage. But, my goodness, it is light!

All of my efforts to reduce calories in my own approach to cooking have resulted in a great many dishes that, by any measure, are practically "dietetic." The Cod with Vegetables, for instance, is virtually a complete meal totaling 160 calories. But, after reducing the fat content of these dishes as much as I could in good conscience, I found that a few worthy dishes insisted on residing in the vicinity of 500 calories, and I decided, in these rare instances, to allow that caloric level to remain in the book. For one thing, the dishes that reach that caloric height tend to be those that contain vegetables as well as meat and are, in effect, two dishes. For another, in the pressure to move toward ever fewer calories, one tends to forget that 500 calories isn't really all that much for a main course. Keep in mind that a cup of lowfat yogurt with jam totals 260 calories or so. In these recipes, then, the very highest calorie counts for the day's main dish, usually with a vegetable accompaniment, will assault you with about the same number of calories as two cups of yogurt. Not bad, in my book.

A Note on Equipment

Appropriate equipment is essential to this low-fat approach. In a great many recipes in this book, I use nonstick skillets and pans. The nonsticking quality of the pans allowed me to add just as much oil or butter as the flavor of the dish required and not a drop more, since I was confident the food could be removed from the pot in the end without damage.

Nonstick pans seem to be sold everywhere, and at casual glance there appears to be very little difference among them. But there are important differences. Some pans are much better than others and, as with every other piece of equipment you buy, high quality will pay for itself over and over again.

Ironically, the element that is advertised most—the coating of the pans—seems to me to matter least. Most brands of nonstick coating work pretty well these days; none scratches and peels as readily as the first pans on the market did (although all still damage more readily than standard pans will). The differences are in the thicknesses and sturdiness of the pots. Be sure that your nonstick pans are as heavy as possible. Usually, they are made of aluminum, an excellent conductor of heat when it is thick but a poor conductor when it is thin.

Another piece of equipment that is mentioned often in this book is the electric blender. I know that the food processor displaced the blender in many home kitchens. But now I think you need both. The blender is far better at incorporating air into a liquid. Thus, when the instructions tell you to blend the mushrooms thoroughly into a sauce, the blender will bring an airiness, a lightness to the sauce that the food processor cannot achieve.

... 2 ...

THE ART OF

Presentation

Home entertaining these days very often involves an effort to emulate restaurant cooking and presentation at home. Everyone, skilled or not, knows enough to concentrate on the cooking part of the proposition. It's the presentation part that often proves elusive. The fact is that just about any food at all can be repulsive or alluring, depending on how it looks.

Professional chefs, those of us who have put our livelihoods on the line each time we positioned a pork chop on a plate, have had to have the wit to develop an advanced sense of showmanship. Much of that showmanship can, in fact, be transported directly into the home with no great effort. Thus, I offer here a set of rules for the presentation of food at home. I do not expect nor want them to be followed blindly. Like the presentation suggestions that follow most of the recipes in this book, these rules are meant to serve as guidelines, insights into how it's done. But, in the end, it's your show.

Rule #1.
Serve on individual dishes.

Serving platters can ruin the day. They come to the table looking fine, but then a great deal of reaching and groping has to go on. The host may try to act as a waiter, serving everyone a little of this and that while the guests all sit there being polite, but then the heat drifts away from the food. The food transferred to the dish, unless the host is in truth an accomplished waiter, never looks as good as the food on the platter did. The illusion is gone, just as quickly as that. All of this can be even worse if everyone around the table is invited to help himself. No, it is far better here to arrange all the food on individual plates first and then gently slide it, in all its planned beauty, in front of each guest. There is really no more time spent at arranging the plates away from the table than arranging them on the table. The food will be no colder. But the effect will be far grander and more precise. A pitfall in this approach is that you are in danger of having guests at the table with neither plate nor food in front of them, while they await a serving. I avoid that, as restaurants do, by always having the table set and then removing the empty plates as I arrive with the full ones.

Rule #2.
Serve on warm plates for hot food and chilled plates for cold food.

Presentation is important, but not at the expense of taste. And food tastes better if it is served at the desired temperature. If you simply place the plates in the oven for as few as five minutes at a temperature between 100 and 150 degrees, you will find that they will indeed hold their heat—and thus the food's heat—admirably well. If you have a shelf above the stove, rest the plates there while cooking. To chill plates for cold food place them in the refrigerator an hour or so before they will be needed for serving. For ice cream or sherbet, place the plates in the freezer for half an hour. This cooling of plates should be done just as routinely as you would chill the wine, as part of standard preparation before the guests arrive.

Rule #3.
Don't overcrowd the plate.

Once it was good form to pile a dish high, but that practice eliminates any chance of achieving the good looks one hopes for. It is better to serve several portions than to fill a plate with food. Moreover, by offering small portions to start with you give guests a better opportunity to eat only a little, if that's what they want. I find that some plates are too large and some too small for the usual needs of the home cook. A 10-inch plate will turn out to be just right for most main courses. (My own preference is for the simplest patterns possible—a white plate, for instance, with no more than a band of color around its periphery so that the colors of the food are not diminished.)

Rule #4.
Strive for striking color combinations.

Even if *nouvelle cuisine* sinks into oblivion, as some predict—and hope—it will, it will have left us with a greater appreciation of the importance of colors to a dish's looks. I always avoid monochrome effects; white on white looks bland even if the food isn't. Instead, I tend to go for bright colors that help make the dish look fresh and alive. I try to blend them as a painter would, looking for harmony and proportion. (The presentation suggestions that follow many of the recipes in this book attest to this effort.) The "paints" of this art are most often supplied by vegetables. The only reason to combine yellow squash with green zucchini is the ability those two vegetables give you to create an interesting pattern. Sometimes a bit of tomato or tomato paste is added to a dish with no other intention than reddening the sauce. In any event, it is hard to go wrong unless you start to use ingredients that blend well for the sake of color but whose flavor does not harmonize with the dish. Beware of the kiwi fruit!

Rule # 5.
Strive for precise patterns.

Sometimes, with a stew or a soup, for instance, there's little point in worrying about the pattern on the plate. But in the great majority of dishes you can achieve a startlingly handsome effect with a little planning and some deft arrangement. The most common approach used in restaurants and by me is to look for some kind of symmetry, some balance. This is done, say, by placing thin overlapping slices of a roast in the center of a plate and positioning bright vegetables so that they radiate out from the meat, like spokes of a wheel. If there is more than one vegetable, the second should be part of the pattern, too, perhaps alternating with the first. If you have a relatively large portion of some vegetable, such as broiled tomatoes, it is better to divide the portion and employ it as part of the pattern than to place it in a single position; thus, one half of a tomato might go above the meat and one half below. You will find, with practice, that you can move very rapidly while arranging these plates. If you are serving string beans, place no more than five or six on each plate at a time; that will make it possible to move faster from plate to plate as well as to enhance the precision of the design.

Rule #6.
Be aware of textures.

Textures are like colors. Not only do I choose the accompaniments to a particular dish's centerpiece according to their color, but I try to look for textures that will make the experience of eating more interesting. It is not especially dainty to discuss it, but the truth is that food is masticated—chewed—and different components of a dish tend to be masticated together. It is boring to have, say, a mouthful of a soft steamed fish joined by a soft purée of spinach. What you want to do is offer something that has resistance to it to go with the fish. Once you know to do this sort of thing, it becomes almost intuitive. Sharp contrasts in texture are not necessary, but a sense of counterpoint is.

Rule #7.
Learn the three fundamental presentation techniques.

In this book the saucing and slicing of food are critical, and a frequent accompaniment to many dishes is molded rice. Thus I want to focus briefly on each technique.

Saucing. Sometimes I suggest placing the sauce underneath the food, in a pool that serves as a kind of canvas for the remaining colors and textures, and sometimes I suggest putting it over the food. I don't recommend one or the other simply according to whim. Generally speaking, if a sauce has been prepared with the food it will accompany and is an integral part of the preparation, it will be spooned over and around the food it goes with. One would not extract the gravy from a veal stew and spoon it out first, for instance. On the other hand, if a sauce is prepared separately, as a creole sauce for a steamed fish might be, then it is a strong candidate to go on the plate first, providing an explosively colorful backdrop to the fish, which will be allowed to remain in a kind of pristine whiteness on top of the sauce. Even when I do stipulate placing the sauce over chicken or veal or fish, it is with the understanding that the sauce is usually very light and will not obliterate the food it accompanies.

Slicing. Now that small portions are valued over large ones, I always slice meat as thinly as possible and on the bias, so that there appears to be more of it than there is. I would much prefer two small slices to one thick one; not only will it give the appearance of more to the serving but it gives you latitude in arranging the food in a pattern. Sometimes, because I like that freedom to create patterns, I will even slice meats ordinarily left alone, such as chicken breast.

Molding rice. Rice is usually very difficult to incorporate into some precise pattern, so I often recommend molding it. This, like so many other techniques, takes practice and planning. The molding can be done in almost any attractive container you like, from a demitasse coffee cup to a fluted pastry mold. Unless the rice already contains a good deal of butter, you will need to butter the mold or brush it with vegetable oil. Then pack the rice into it tightly. You can do this ahead of time, using several molds, cover them and keep them warm near the stove. Just when you are ready to serve the rice, invert it onto the plate. It should slide out easily. Molded rice, you will discover, is often precisely the neat element required to achieve that quickly formed symmetrical pattern you are looking for.

A few last thoughts. Since the beautiful presentation of food requires care—and demonstrates that you really *do* care—you don't want the whole show lost on your guests. I never present them with so much to drink before a meal that they will miss the nuances of the main act, and I never serve any food at all with the drinks, for fear of killing their appetites. Then I keep the number of courses to a minimum. My usual approach is to serve an appetizer, main course, and dessert. If I choose to go right for the main course, as I sometimes do, I will follow it with cheese and salad and then dessert.

...*3*...

Soups

When soup recipes are wisely conceived, they can manage to satisfy the appetite while supplying incredibly few calories. Not only that, but a magnificent soup does not necessarily require hours of preparation and hours of simmering. There is in this chapter, for instance, a Carrot and Dill Soup that is smooth, sweet, and elegant, but the preparation is so straightforward and fast that the soup is liable to leave you feeling guilty, as if you didn't work hard enough to achieve something so remarkable. (You'll get over it; I did.)

In this chapter, too, there are two vegetable soups that include chicken. Both are so quick to prepare that I found myself picturing them in some kind of race. The one called Chicken Vegetable Soup seemed the faster. One soup here that does require a good deal of preparation is the Gazpacho. Despite the tedium, the effort is unavoidable. A good Gazpacho is marked by the variety of its ingredients. But then, of course, once you've done the preparation, you're finished. There's no cooking.

A number of these soups require the use of stock. If you are going to make your own stock rather than use the canned variety—as we strongly suggest—that procedure will take time. The best approach is to do it well in advance and store it, frozen in the form of cubes.

This is a versatile soup that can be served in summer or winter. It contains very little fat.

BORSCHT À LA RUSSE

1 tablespoon butter
1 cup chopped onions
1 tablespoon chopped garlic
4 cups shredded red cabbage
1 cup peeled and grated beets
1 cup chopped sweet green pepper
1 teaspoon caraway seeds
1 teaspoon sugar
2 cups chopped, peeled and seeded ripe tomatoes
4 tablespoons fresh lemon juice
10 cups beef stock (see recipe page 31)
Salt, if necessary
Sour cream for garnish, optional

1. Melt the butter in a kettle and add the chopped onions and garlic and cook briefly. Stirring, add the red cabbage, beets, green pepper, caraway seeds, sugar, tomatoes, lemon juice, and beef stock. Simmer for 1½ hours. Taste for saltiness and add a touch of salt, if necessary.

2. Serve hot or cold, with sour cream on the side, if desired.

YIELD: 8 servings.   CALORIES PER SERVING: 83.

One of the simplest and fastest soups I know is a purée of carrots combined with broth and given a creamy texture by a touch of ricotta.

CREAMY CARROT SOUP WITH DILL

2 tablespoons butter
1 cup finely chopped onions
1½ pounds carrots, cleaned and sliced (about 5 cups)
½ teaspoon salt
Freshly ground black pepper (4 turns of the pepper mill)
4 cups chicken stock (see recipe page 30)
¼ cup ricotta
2 tablespoons port wine
2 tablespoons chopped fresh dill

1. Melt the butter in a saucepan and add the onions. Cook until

they are wilted. Add the carrots, salt, pepper, and chicken stock. Cook over low heat for 30 minutes.

2. Strain the carrots over a saucepan. Purée the solids in a food processor along with the ricotta and 1 cup of the cooking liquid. Reserve the rest of the liquid. Transfer the purée to a saucepan and add all of the remaining cooking liquid, blending it in well. (These contortions involving removing the liquid and returning it are designed to overcome a flaw in the Cuisinart, which leaks if there is too much liquid. If you are using a food processor that does not leak, or a food mill, purée the carrots with all the liquid.) Bring the purée to a boil and add the port and dill. Serve hot or cold.

YIELD: 6 servings.   CALORIES PER SERVING: 139.

This rich version of Gazpacho, in which I have altered the ingredients to include more tomatoes than usual and also some shrimp and crab meat, can be a first course or a main course. All of the vegetables should be chopped coarsely, and the food processor will do it well enough. The crab meat, unlike the shrimp, is cooked when you buy it.

GAZPACHO WITH SHRIMP AND CRAB

3 cups ripe tomatoes, peeled, seeded, and chopped
½ cup chopped red onion
¼ cup chopped celery
½ cup chopped sweet green or red pepper
1 tablespoon chopped hot pepper, such as
jalapeño pepper
2 teaspoons chopped garlic
½ cup chopped fresh coriander leaves
1 cup tomato juice
2 tablespoons olive oil
2 tablespoons fresh lemon juice
2 tablespoons red wine vinegar
½ teaspoon salt
Freshly ground black pepper (10 turns of the pepper mill)
1 pound cooked and peeled shrimp (see recipe page 99)
1 pound lump crab meat

1. Combine all the ingredients, except the shrimp and crab meat, in a mixing bowl. Cover with plastic wrap and refrigerate until cold.

2. Add the shrimp and crab meat at the last minute and stir them in. Serve in a chilled bowl with Garlic Croutons (see recipe page 264)

YIELD: 10 servings.   CALORIES PER SERVING: 146.

The vegetable soup Gazpacho is a virtually fat-free, cool, and spicy staple of Spanish and Latin American cuisine. It can be either smooth or coarse. My own preference is for coarseness. All the chopping done in this recipe, incidentally, can be done, well enough and quickly, with a food processor. Slice each vegetable thickly by hand and then place it in the processor with the chopping blade in position. Pulse the blade carefully so as not to chop the vegetables too fine.

GAZPACHO À LA MEXICAINE

*1½ pounds ripe tomatoes, peeled, seeded,
and chopped (about 2 cups)
¼ cup chopped red onion
¼ cup chopped celery
3 tablespoons chopped scallion
¼ cup chopped sweet green pepper
½ cup cucumber cut into ¼-inch cubes (or very coarsely
chopped in a food processor)
2 tablespoons chopped green hot or mild chilies
1 tablespoon chopped garlic
¼ cup chopped fresh coriander leaves
2 tablespoons chopped Italian parsley leaves
1 cup tomato juice
1 tablespoon olive oil
2 tablespoons red wine vinegar
2 tablespoons fresh lime juice
½ teaspoon salt
Freshly ground black pepper (8 turns of the pepper mill)*

Combine all the ingredients in a mixing bowl, cover the bowl with plastic wrap, and refrigerate until cold.

YIELD: 6 servings.   CALORIES PER SERVING: 68.

PRESENTATION: Serve the soup in large chilled bowls with Garlic Croutons (see recipe page 264) in the center of the table.

Fish broth is, by its nature, light. With this soup, I've done nothing to double cross the intentions of nature. It is a very fast soup to prepare, as well.

LIGHT FISH SOUP

1 tablespoon olive oil
1 cup coarsely chopped onions
1 tablespoon chopped garlic
4 pounds fresh fish bones, including the head
but with gills removed
1 cup coarsely chopped celery
1 cup coarsely chopped leeks, green portion only
1 cup chopped ripe tomatoes
3 tablespoons tomato paste
½ teaspoon saffron stems
1 teaspoon fennel seed
1 cup dry white wine
6 cups water
½ teaspoon salt
Freshly ground black pepper (6 turns of the pepper mill)
6 drops Tabasco sauce

1. Heat the olive oil in a kettle and add the onions, garlic, and fish bones. Cook, stirring, for about 5 minutes. Add the celery, leek greens, tomatoes, tomato paste, saffron, fennel seed, wine, water, salt, pepper, and Tabasco. Stir and bring to a boil.

2. Simmer the soup for 20 minutes, skimming the scum that forms on top. Pour the soup through a strainer and reheat in a clean saucepan before serving.

YIELD: 6 servings.   CALORIES PER SERVING: 69.

Although one doesn't usually think of it as low in calories, the shellfish soup (usually clams or mussels) originated by the Italians seems to me to qualify admirably. A look at the ingredients for the clam soup offered here will immediately give you the sense of a nutritious first course that has a great deal of flavor and only a little fat. The only problem with making this otherwise simple soup is in the cleaning of the soft-shell clams.

SOFT-SHELL CLAM SOUP

3 pounds soft-shell clams
2 tablespoons olive oil
½ cup finely chopped onion
2 teaspoons chopped garlic
1 cup dry white wine
2 cups canned Italian plum tomatoes
1 cup water
½ teaspoon dried oregano
⅛ teaspoon cayenne pepper
¼ cup chopped Italian parsley leaves
½ cup chopped fresh basil leaves, or
2 tablespoons dried basil
Freshly ground black pepper (8 turns of the pepper mill)

1. Soak the clams for several hours in several changes of cool water. Scrub the clams thoroughly and drain them well.

2. Heat the oil in a saucepan or kettle. Add the onion and garlic and cook, stirring, for 45 seconds. Add the clams, wine, tomatoes, water, oregano, cayenne, parsley (reserve a little of the parsley for garnish), basil, and pepper. Cook, covered, for about 20 minutes.

YIELD: 6 servings.   CALORIES PER SERVING: 117.

PRESENTATION: Serve the soup in deep bowls that can easily hold an ample portion of the clams and liquid. Place a plate of Croutons (see recipe page 264) or plain crusty bread in the center of the table. The idea is to dip the bread in the broth.

When I go fishing, I very often prepare a soup with the catch. The version presented here, with a bow to Marseilles, the home of bouillabaisse, is of my own devising (although others no doubt have done something similar). It combines the elegance of saffron and Pernod with the crude heat of Tabasco sauce. An aspect of this soup bound to be appreciated by some is that it is very easy and very neat to eat, because all the fish are skinless and boneless.

FISH SOUP MARSEILLAISE

3 tablespoons olive oil
½ cup finely chopped onion
½ cup finely chopped leek
1 tablespoon finely chopped garlic
½ teaspoon saffron stems
2 cups fresh or canned peeled tomatoes
3 cups **fumet de poisson** *(fish stock, see recipe page 29)*
or water
1 cup dry white wine
1 bay leaf
½ teaspoon dried thyme
6 drops Tabasco sauce
Freshly ground black pepper (10 turns of the pepper mill)
1½ pounds nonoily fish fillets, such as monkfish,
cod, or tilefish
½ pound mussels, well cleaned
¾ pound shrimp (about 24), peeled and deveined
2 tablespoons Pernod or Ricard
¼ cup chopped fresh parsely leaves for garnish

1. Heat the oil in a saucepan or kettle. Add the onion, leek, garlic, and saffron and cook until wilted. Do not brown. Add the tomatoes, fish stock, wine, bay leaf, thyme, Tabasco, and pepper. Stir and cook over medium heat for 15 minutes.

2. Cut the fish into 1-inch cubes. Add the fish to the pot along with the mussels and shrimp and cook for about 5 minutes, or until the mussels have opened and the shrimp have turned pink. Stir in Pernod, garnish with the parsley, and serve.

YIELD: 8 servings.   CALORIES PER SERVING: 202.

PRESENTATION: Serve the soup in large bowls with rounds of Garlic Croutons (see recipe page 264) or crusty bread in the center of the table. A good idea is to put a tablespoon of Aïoli or Rouille (see recipes pages 236 and 240) on top of each portion of soup.

The kidney bean soup presented here may surprise you with its smoothness—a silken texture derived from puréeing the soup after it's cooked. The ham hocks will, of course, add something in the way of calories, but they also add a lot in the way of character. You can eliminate them from the recipe if you like.

RED KIDNEY BEAN SOUP

1 pound red kidney beans
1 tablespoon butter
1½ cups chopped onions
1 cup chopped celery
1 tablespoon chopped garlic
2 smoked ham hocks (about 1¼ pounds)
8 cups water
2 cups chicken stock (see recipe page 30)
1 teaspoon ground cumin
¼ teaspoon freshly ground black pepper
1 teaspooon chili powder
¼ teaspoon salt
1 bay leaf
¼ teaspoon dried thyme
1 tablespoon fresh lemon juice
2 tablespoons red wine vinegar

1. Wash the beans in cold water and drain them.

2. In a soup kettle, melt the butter and add the onions, celery, and garlic. Sauté for 2 minutes, stirring constantly. Add the ham hocks and all the remaining ingredients, except the lemon juice and vinegar. Bring to a boil, cover, and simmer for 1½ hours.

3. Remove the ham hocks from the soup, and cut the meat away from the bone in slices; you will need about ½ cup of meat.

4. Purée the soup coarsely. (A food mill will do this better than a food processor.) Add the lemon juice, vinegar, and meat from the hocks. Reheat the soup gently.

Yield: 10 servings.   Calories per Serving: 213.

Potato and leek soup is among the most common of soups. It became rather distinctive in my kitchen one day when I happened to be working with a series of curried dishes. I tried some of the curry in the soup. And then, to both add the fruit that is typical of curries and also to give some crunch to the smoothness of the liquid, I topped it with diced apples (they should be cut into firm, distinct little cubes, perhaps an eighth of an inch in thickness). Personally, I thought it was a marvelous little invention.

POTATO-LEEK SOUP WITH CURRY

1 tablespoon butter
4 leeks, washed, trimmed thoroughly, and sliced thickly
(about 4 cups)
2 teaspoons Oriental Curry Powder (see recipe page 265)
1½ pounds potatoes, peeled and diced (4 cups)
½ teaspoon salt
4 cups chicken stock (see recipe page 30)
4 cups water
Diced apple for garnish

1. Melt the butter in a saucepan. Add the leeks and cook over low heat for about 5 minutes. Add the curry powder and stir it in well, but do not let it brown. Add the potatoes, salt, chicken stock, and water. Bring to a boil and simmer for 30 minutes.

2. Purée the mixture in a food mill or processor. Blend until very smooth. Return to the saucepan. Bring to a boil and serve, garnished at the last minute, with the apple.

YIELD: 10 servings.   CALORIES PER SERVING: 104.

PRESENTATION: Serve in large soup bowls as a first course. (A variation is to serve this soup cold, but, after it is chilled, you must thin it with the addition of chicken stock and then garnish it with apples as before.)

I usually don't use yogurt, but in a cold soup, it provides just the right tanginess.

ZUCCHINI SOUP WITH YOGURT AND DILL

6 small zucchini (about 2½ pounds)
1 tablespoon butter
3 cups coarsely chopped onions
1 teaspoon finely chopped garlic
1 cup coarsely chopped ripe tomatoes
3 cups chicken stock (see recipe page 30)
½ teaspoon salt
Freshly ground black pepper (6 turns of the pepper mill)
¼ teaspoon Tabasco sauce
2 cups plain yogurt
¼ cup chopped fresh dill

1. Wash the zucchini and trim off the ends. Cut them into ¼-inch rounds.

2. Melt the butter in a deep saucepan and add the onions and garlic. Cook, stirring, until the onions are wilted and golden. Add the zucchini and tomatoes and cook for 2 minutes.

3. Add the chicken stock, salt, pepper, and Tabasco. Simmer for 5 minutes. Pour the mixture into a food mill or processor and purée. Refrigerate the purée. When it is chilled, stir in the yogurt. Serve cold (or reheat to serve hot) with a sprinkling of chopped fresh dill.

YIELD: 6 servings.   CALORIES PER SERVING: 157.

This tomato soup achieves smoothness through a ploy that I have used in lobster bisques as well: Soft rice is puréed into the soup to thicken and bind it, as cream might do in some other recipe. Carolina rice is specified because converted rice tends to be too firm for this purpose. Since the heart of this dish is the tomato, be sure to obtain the very best tomatoes possible.

TOMATO BISQUE

3 tablespoons butter
3 cups coarsely chopped onions (¾ pound)
2 teaspoons chopped garlic
3½ pounds ripe tomatoes, cut into large cubes
1 bay leaf
1 teaspoon dried thyme
4 cups chicken stock (see recipe page 30)
¼ cup Carolina rice
1 teaspoon salt
Freshly ground black pepper (8 turns of the pepper mill)
1 cup diced, peeled and seeded ripe tomatoes
2 tablespoons chopped fresh dill for garnish, optional

1. Melt 1 tablespoon of the butter in a saucepan and add the chopped onions and garlic. Sauté them briefly without browning. Add the large chunks of tomato, bay leaf, thyme, chicken stock, rice, salt, and pepper. Bring the mixture to a boil and simmer for 30 minutes.

2. Transfer the liquid to a food mill or processor and purée. Strain the purée through a very fine strainer. Pour the liquid into a pan and bring it to a boil. Add the remaining butter and diced tomatoes. Stir and serve hot with chopped dill, if desired.

YIELD: 8 servings.   CALORIES PER SERVING: 147.

The problem with my usual minestrone, in the context of this book, anyway, is that it requires bacon and salt pork, and sometimes a paste of lard and herbs added at the last minute. I like it a lot, but it's obviously high in calories. So the recipe here has no lard and it is predictably lighter and less fattening. Perhaps less predictably, it's marvelous tasting, a wonderful winter soup, with a satisfying richness despite its diminished calories.

THICK VEGETABLE SOUP

1 tablespoon olive oil
1 cup chopped onions
1 tablespoon chopped garlic
2 cups diced ripe tomatoes
2 cups zucchini cut into ½-inch cubes
1 cup carrots cut into ¼-inch cubes
1 cup white turnips cut into ¼-inch cubes
1 cup chopped celery
1 pound dried navy beans
Freshly ground black pepper (8 turns of the pepper mill)
10 cups chicken stock (see recipe page 30)
¼ cup chopped fresh basil leaves
Salt, if necessary

1. Heat the oil in a kettle and add the onions and garlic. Cook them briefly and add the tomatoes, zucchini, carrots, turnips, and celery. Cook, stirring, for about 10 minutes. Add the beans, pepper, and stock. Bring to a boil and simmer for 1 hour and 45 minutes. Add the basil and salt, if desired.

2. Serve with Parmesan cheese on the side.

YIELD: At least 12 servings.   CALORIES PER SERVING: 197.

One usually thinks of soup as a time-consuming, laborious thing to make. What I offer here is a relatively quick, yet thick, chicken soup (quick, that is, after all the vegetables are chopped) much like a favorite soup of my boyhood. The difference is that I've used only skinless chicken breast as the meat. Until very recently, I would certainly have used the whole chicken, but that would have resulted in a dish with considerably more fat. Incidentally, this soup will work well enough if you use a good canned chicken broth, but homemade stock is far better.

VEGETABLE SOUP WITH BREAST OF CHICKEN

1 tablespoon butter
1 onion (about ¼ pound), cut into ¼-inch cubes (1 cup)
4 leeks (about 1 pound), cut into ¼-inch cubes (3 cups)
3 carrots (about ½ pound), cut into ¼-inch cubes (1½ cups)
1 parsnip (about ¼ pound), cut into ¼-inch cubes (1 cup)
3 potatoes (about 1 pound), cut into ¼-inch cubes (2 cups)
½ teaspoon salt
Freshly ground black pepper (8 turns of the pepper mill)
4 cups chicken stock (see recipe page 30)
4 cups water
2 whole skinless and boneless chicken breasts (about 1 pound), cut into ½-inch cubes
2 tablespoons chopped fresh parsley leaves for garnish

1. Melt butter in a saucepan and add the onion, leeks, carrots, parsnip, and potatoes and cook, stirring, until wilted, about 5 minutes. Add the salt, pepper, chicken stock, and water. Bring to a boil and simmer for 30 minutes.

2. Add the chicken breast cubes and cook for 10 minutes. Garnish each serving with fresh parsley.

YIELD: 8 servings.   CALORIES PER SERVING: 197.

PRESENTATION: Soup like this always looks better with a sprinkling of herbs, such as the parsley suggested here. This soup can be served as a first or main course. If it's a main course, serve it with crusty French bread.

The essence of a good vegetable soup is the stock. Since in this case we make the stock first, it is possible to cook the vegetables and chicken so that they are not rendered into mush, but are rather crisp and still retain their individual flavors. Moreover, it is the stock that takes time; the rest is a breeze, so the soup can be made quite quickly for entertaining. In the chicken soup race, this one is even quicker than the chicken soup offered above.

CHICKEN-VEGETABLE SOUP

6 cups chicken stock (see recipe page 30)
1 pound skinless and boneless chicken breasts,
cut into ½-inch cubes
1 cup zucchini cut into ¼-inch cubes
1 cup cucumber cut into ¼-inch cubes
1 cup peeled and chopped ripe tomatoes
½ teaspoon salt
Freshly ground black pepper (6 turns of the pepper mill)
¼ cup chopped fresh coriander leaves for garnish

1. Heat the chicken stock in a kettle and add the chicken. Bring it to a boil and simmer for 3 miniutes. Add the zucchini and simmer for 3 minutes more. Add the cucumbers and tomatoes and simmer for 3 minutes more. Season with the salt and pepper.
2. Serve the soup garnished with the coriander at the last minute.

YIELD: 8 servings.   CALORIES PER SERVING: 104.

This is the traditional fish stock. Unlike other stocks, beef or chicken, for instance, it takes very little time to prepare and so there is little reason to use substitutes such as bottled clam juice. Clam juice is good in a pinch, but it simply doesn't have the right flavor: It's too clammy, if you will, and it's not gelatinous enough. This stock can be used to prepare a variety of sauces for steamed or baked fish or for soups. The stock should be made in a large quantity, frozen in an ice cube tray and then transferred to a plastic bag, which will protect the stock against odors. It can then be defrosted and used as necessary.

FUMET DE POISSON (FISH STOCK)

**3 pounds fresh fish bones, including the head
but with gills removed
6 cups water
1½ cups dry white wine
1½ cups sliced celery
1 cup sliced leeks, green portion only
4 sprigs fresh parsley
1 bay leaf
½ teaspoon dried thyme
6 whole black peppercorns**

1. Chop the fish bones.
2. Combine all the ingredients in a kettle or saucepan. Bring the mixture to a boil and simmer for 20 minutes. Strain and discard the solids. Leftover stock can be frozen.

YIELD: 6 cups.   CALORIES PER CUP: 34.

The two basic stocks below, chicken and beef, are far better than any canned broth would be. I like to prepare them on days of leisure, freeze them in ice cube trays, and then transfer the cubes to a plastic bag to keep them fresh for use during rapid cooking on some other day.

CHICKEN STOCK

4 pounds chicken bones
8 cups water
4 whole black peppercorns
1 cup quartered onions
½ cup coarsely chopped carrots
½ cup coarsely chopped celery
4 sprigs fresh parsley
1 bay leaf
½ teaspoon dried thyme
1 whole clove
1 garlic clove

1. Put the bones in a kettle and add the remaining ingredients. Bring to a boil and simmer, uncovered, for 1 hour. Skim from time to time to remove the fat and foam or scum from the top.

2. Strain the stock through a very fine piece of cheesecloth or through a fine-screened strainer, such as a *chinois*. Leftover stock can be frozen.

YIELD: 6 cups.　　　　　CALORIES PER CUP: 38.

BEEF STOCK

*4 pounds shin bones (If possible, it is best to ask
the butcher for bones with some meat on them.)*
1 cup thinly sliced onions
1 cup coarsely sliced carrots
1 cup coarsely sliced celery
1 bay leaf
½ teaspoon dried thyme
4 whole black peppercorns
2 sprigs fresh parsley

1. Put the bones in a large kettle and cover them with cold water.
Bring to a boil for 2 minutes and drain. Return the bones to the kettle and add 3 quarts of water, the onions, carrots, celery, bay leaf,
thyme, peppercorns, and parsley. Bring to a boil and simmer for 4
hours, skimming the fat and scum from the surface.

2. Strain the stock and discard the solids. Use as a base for Borscht
à la Russe (see recipe page 16), or serve alone or with cooked diced
vegetables. Leftover stock can be frozen.

YIELD: About 10 cups.   CALORIES PER CUP: 18.

...4...

Salads

The tradition for warm salads mostly embraces the likes of potato salad, bean salads, and dandelion salads. In recent years, however, there has been a welcome expansion of this kind of thinking. The technique can be applied to a great many foods and some of those applications will be suggested below, along with a selection of cool salads. Although salads are usually regarded as simple dishes, in this book they are among the most complicated and a few may take well over an hour to prepare (at least until you become practiced or find shortcuts of your own).

The first of the warm salads, the sweetbread salad, with the tart sweetness of strawberry vinegar is extraordinary. In this salad, as well as the other warm salads, the secret to the presentation is in the most beautiful arrangement of salad ingredients that you can devise. The meat is transferred hot to the salad, wilting the greens somewhat, with the deglazed sauce serving as the dressing. Because the deglazing takes place in a nonstick frying pan the result is, in fact, more like a dressing than a gravy (few particles stick to the pan to darken the sauce). Incidentally, it may seem that a large quantity of oil is being used in the cooking, but keep in mind that this is the oil that will convert to a dressing later on. In fact, there is less oil than I would ordinarily use for a dressing— chicken stock has been included to make up for the relatively small amount of oil.

WARM SWEETBREAD SALAD WITH STRAWBERRY VINEGAR DRESSING

4 very fresh sweetbreads, about 1¾ pounds
½ teaspoon salt
Freshly ground black pepper (about 8 turns of the pepper mill)
3 to 4 scallions

VEGETABLES
4 endives (¾ pound)
32 small radiccio leaves
3 cups red leaf lettuce
6 loosely packed cups field lettuce (in French, mâche) or some other salad green, such as arugola
8 plum tomatoes
3 tablespoons olive oil
2 tablespoons finely chopped shallots
½ teaspoon garlic
¼ cup chicken stock (see recipe page 30)
4 tablespoons strawberry vinegar
8 tablespoons chopped chives

1. Trim the sweetbreads of much of the membranous tissue and fat. Soak them overnight in water in the refrigerator.

2. Place the sweetbreads in a pot, cover with cold water and bring to a boil, blanching them in boiling water for 5 minutes. Place them on a rack set over a pan and weight them down with a plate and something heavy on it (anything that's at least 2 pounds will do). Let sit for about 1 hour. The intention is to remove all the liquid.

3. Slice each of the sweetbreads on the bias, producing pieces that

are as uniform as possible, about ¼ inch thick. There should be about 30 small pieces. Sprinkle the sweetbreads with half the salt and pepper.

4. Wash and trim the scallions, removing only the wilted green portion. Slice the scallions into small rounds, about ⅛ inch thick. There will be about ½ cup.

5. Prepare the salad plates. Cut the endives in half. Separate the leaves from the top halves. Trim the ends of the endive bottoms. Hold the bottom half of an endive perpendicular to a cutting board and cut down on it in crossing horizontal and vertical strokes to create spears resembling julienne strips. Repeat with the remaining bottom half.

6. Place the strips of endive in a mound in the center of each plate. Take 4 leaves for each plate and place them so they are evenly spaced, radiating outward from the strips in the center.

7. Between the endive leaves place a radiccio leaf. There will be 4 leaves for each plate. If a leaf is too large, overlapping an endive leaf, cut it to fit.

8. Cut the red leaf lettuce into manageable pieces and drape 1 piece over each of the radiccio leaves.

9. Field lettuce comes in small bunches. Trim and wash each bunch, allowing the grouping of leaves to remain intact. Place about 3 bunches of leaves over the center of each plate.

10. Quarter the plum tomatoes and place 1 quarter on each of the endive leaves.

11. Heat the oil in a nonstick skillet and sauté the sweetbread pieces for 5 minutes on each side over medium heat so that the pieces are evenly and lightly browned. Add the shallots, scallions, and garlic. Add the vinegar along with the stock, stirring them in with a wooden spatula. With a slotted spoon remove the sweetbreads to the plates and spoon the dressing over the top. Garnish each salad with a tablespoon of chives.

NOTE: If this salad is to be used as an appetizer rather than a luncheon main course, the recipe should be cut in half.

YIELD: 8 servings.   CALORIES PER SERVING: 290.

The following version of a warm salad has much in common with the sweetbread recipe above but in this instance there's a Chinese touch. Some of the liquid required for the dressing is contributed by the soy sauce. In addition there are ginger and scallions. The key to the success of this dish is the freshness of the salmon. I am frequently asked whether canned salmon can replace the fresh in this or that recipe. Here, it will not adequately replace the fresh salmon.

WARM FRESH SALMON SALAD WITH GINGER AND DILL

VEGETABLES
2 endives
24 small leaves radiccio
½ pound red leaf lettuce, cut into 2-inch pieces (6 cups)
¼ pound arugola, cut into manageable pieces (4 cups)

THE SALMON
1½ pounds salmon fillets, skin removed
3 tablespoons olive oil
Freshly ground black pepper (8 turns of the pepper mill)
4 scallions, sliced into ⅛-inch rounds (about ½ cup)
½ teaspoon chopped garlic
2 tablespoons finely chopped fresh ginger
⅓ cup red wine vinegar
2 tablespoons soy sauce
2 tablespoons chicken stock (see recipe page 30)
6 tablespoons chopped fresh dill

1. Cut the endives in half. Trim away the hard bottom of each lower half. Separate the leaves from the top halves. Arrange 4 leaves on each plate, radiating out from the center. Place 4 of the radiccio leaves around the edge of each plate.

2. Distribute the red leaf lettuce over each of the plates. Place the arugola over the lettuce.

3. Chop the bottom halves of the endives very coarsely and sprinkle over the center of the mound on each plate.

4. Cut each salmon fillet in thirds, lengthwise. Then cut the strips, on the bias, into 2-inch chunks.

5. Heat the oil in a nonstick frying pan. Place the salmon in the pan and sprinkle with pepper. Cook briefly. Add the scallions, garlic, and ginger. Sauté the salmon on both sides for a total of about 2 more minutes. Be careful not to overcook it. Add the vinegar and then the soy sauce and finally the chicken stock. Stir the liquid in with a wooden spatula. Remove from the heat.

6. Place the salmon pieces over the salad. Evenly distribute the sauce from the pan over the salmon and the greens. Garnish each plate with a tablespoon of dill.

YIELD: 6 servings.　　　　CALORIES PER SERVING: 336.

As the other warm salads in this book suggest, the possibilities are incredible in their variations. One of the most appealing certainly is to use game: partridge, pheasant, and mallard among them. A good representative of that clan is quail, a delicate and elegant bird. To make this dish especially memorable, go out of your way to find the quail eggs suggested in the presentation section below.

QUAIL SALAD

1 bunch watercress, large stems removed (about 4 cups)
2 cups romaine lettuce, cut into 2-inch pieces
2 endives (½ pound), cut in julienne strips 1½ inches long
(about 3 cups)
2 tablespoons raspberry vinegar
1 tablespoon coarse French or Dijon mustard
1 teaspoon chopped garlic
3 tablespoons olive oil
1 teaspoon salt
Freshly ground black pepper (12 turns of the pepper mill)
8 oven-ready quails
4 to 5 scallions, chopped (¾ cup)

1. Preheat the oven to 475 degrees.
2. Rinse and dry the watercress, romaine, and endives.
3. With a whisk, blend 2 tablespoons of the vinegar, the mustard, and garlic in a mixing bowl. Continue to whisk, gradually adding 2 tablespoons of the olive oil. Add ½ teaspoon of the salt and 4 turns of the pepper mill.
4. In a shallow metal roasting pan large enough to hold the quails, arrange the birds breast side up. The birds should not be touching. Brush them with the remaining tablespoon of olive oil and sprinkle them with the remaining salt and pepper.
5. Heat the pan on top of the stove. When the fat starts to sizzle beneath the quails, transfer the pan to the oven. Cook for about 7 minutes, basting.
6. Remove the pan from the oven. With a knife, remove the meat from each side of the breasts. Remove the legs, separating the thighs from the drumsticks. Remove the bone from the thighs.
7. In a large mixing bowl, place the romaine, watercress, endive, scallions, sauce, salt, and pepper. Toss well. Distribute the salads on each plate and serve with the quail over them.

YIELD: 8 servings.   CALORIES PER SERVING: 196.

PRESENTATION: The handsomest presentation involves cutting the breasts on the bias into 3 or 4 slices. Place the breast slices, overlapping, in the center of the salad. Radiating out from the breast meat, like spokes, should be the drumsticks. Between the drumsticks should go the thighs. An added, worthwhile touch is provided by quail eggs (sometimes available in specialty stores). Place them in cool water on the stove, bring to the boil and then simmer for 4 minutes. Peel the eggs and place 4 of them around the periphery of each dish.

The duck salad here will take a good deal longer than 60 minutes and is somewhat higher in calories than the other salads, but it is worth it on both counts; it is a startling construction in the end.

DUCK SALAD WITH STRING BEANS AND MANGOES

1 5-pound ready-to-cook duck
½ teaspoon salt
Freshly ground black pepper (8 turns of the pepper mill)
¾ cup Ginger Vinaigrette (see recipe page 243)
24 small radiccio leaves or red leaf lettuce
4 cups loosely packed arugola, or any salad green
½ pound string beans, trimmed and
cut into 3-inch lengths
2 mangoes, peeled and sliced (2 cups)
⅓ cup pecan halves

1. Preheat the oven to 450 degrees.

2. Place the duck breast up in a roasting pan. Season with salt and pepper, and roast for 1¼ hours. Remove the fat from the pan as the duck roasts.

3. Remove the duck from the pan. Discard all the fat. Pour ¾ cup of water into the pan. Bring the water to a boil on top of the stove. Scrape the bottom of the pan to dissolve any solids. Reduce the liquid and strain it. There should be ¼ cup. Put it aside to be mixed with the vinaigrette.

4. Cut the breast and legs away from the carcass. Remove the skin and discard it. Carve the meat away from the bones and slice it very thinly on the bias.

5. Add the pan liquid to the vinaigrette.

6. Place the radiccio leaves in a bowl and toss with 1 tablespoon of the vinagrette. On each plate, place 4 evenly spaced leaves.

7. Toss the endive leaves with 1 tablespoon of the vinaigrette. Alternate them with the radiccio.

8. Toss the greens with 2 tablespoons of vinaigrette. Distribute the greens over the center of each plate in flat circles. Take care to keep the greens from covering the other colors entirely. Some of the red of the radiccio, in particular, should still show through toward the edge of the plate.

9. Put the string beans, mangoes, and pecans in a bowl, along with salt and pepper, and toss with 2 tablespoons of the vinaigrette. Distribute this mixture in the center of the greens, but in a smaller circle so that the green forms a frame around it.

10. Place the slices of duck in a small mound in the center of the plate. Spoon the remaining vinaigrette over the top. The whole construction should ascend to a peak, like a hill.

YIELD: 6 servings.   CALORIES PER SERVING: 456.

The salad here is a bit trendy, using some of the stars of the current approaches, namely radiccio (the startling red chicory) and goat cheese. Sun-dried tomatoes, which look like red prunes, come from Italy and are also ballyhooed a lot these days. Trendy or not, I'm glad these combinations have come to the forefront. In this instance, the result is a gorgeous piece of work. It makes a handsome light lunch.

GREENS WITH GOAT CHEESE AND SUN-DRIED TOMATOES

2 teaspoons Dijon mustard
2 tablespoons red wine vinegar
6 tablespoons vegetable oil
Freshly ground black pepper (6 turns of the pepper mill)
2 cups radiccio, washed and dried
4 cups Bibb lettuce, washed and dried
¼ pound goat cheese
4 sun-dried tomatoes, diced (available in specialty stores)

1. To make the dressing, place the mustard in a bowl and add the vinegar. Start beating with a wire whisk and add the oil slowly as you do. Add the pepper.
2. Divide the dressing evenly between 2 bowls. Put the radiccio leaves into one of the bowls and coat them well. Place the Bibb lettuce leaves in the other and coat them well.
3. Arrange a ring of radiccio around the outer edge of each plate. Place the Bibb lettuce in the center. Crumble the goat cheese over the lettuce. Distribute the tomatoes evenly over the goat cheese on each plate. Serve as an appetizer or as the cheese course.

YIELD: 6 servings.   CALORIES PER SERVING: 239.

A combination of shrimp with feta cheese, orange sections, and onion slices is a marvel of food chemistry. The ingredients result in a sense of lightness and freshness.

COLD SHRIMP SALAD WITH FETA CHEESE

1 bunch watercress, trimmed, washed, and dried
36 poached shrimp, peeled and deveined
(see recipe page 99)
2 cups orange sections
1½ cups thinly sliced red onions
3 hard-boiled eggs, coarsely chopped
¾ cup feta cheese
¼ cup chopped fresh coriander leaves
1 tablespoon Dijon mustard
3 tablespoons fresh lemon juice
1 tablespoon red wine vinegar
1 teaspoon chopped garlic
4 tablespoons olive oil
Tabasco sauce to taste
Freshly ground black pepper (8 turns of the pepper mill)
½ teaspoon salt

1. Place a portion of the watercress in the center of a serving plate or salad bowl. Take 6 shrimp and position them so that there are two groups of 3 shrimp each radiating away from the watercress on opposite sides. In the spaces between the portions of shrimp, place an evenly divided amount of the orange sections. Around the periphery of the plate, arrange the onion slices. Distribute the chopped egg over the onions. Sprinkle the feta cheese over the shrimp and the orange slices. Distribute the coriander over that.

2. Combine the remaining ingredients in a bottle or jar and shake well. Pour the dressing over the salad and serve. (The dressing can be mixed with a whisk, too, but I find a jar more effective.)

YIELD: 6 servings.   CALORIES PER SERVING: 314.

SHRIMP AND AVOCADO SALAD

1 sweet red pepper
½ cup olive oil
½ cup red wine vinegar
1¼ pounds shrimp, peeled and deveined
½ cup chopped red onion
1 tablespoon chopped candied ginger
1 teaspoon salt
Freshly ground black pepper (10 turns of the pepper mill)
1 avocado (about 1 pound), peeled and sliced (1½ cups)
2 tablespoons chopped fresh dill

1. Cut the pepper in half and remove the seeds. Blanch it in boiling water for 2 minutes. Cool the pepper and slice it, crosswise, into strips.

2. Heat the olive oil and vinegar in a nonstick frying pan. Add the shrimp, onion, ginger, salt, and ground pepper. While stirring, cook the mixture for 1 minute. Add the avocado and red pepper. Mix the ingredients well and transfer the salad to individual plates. Sprinkle with the dill and serve immediately.

YIELD: 6 servings.   CALORIES PER SERVING: 344.

If some salads are subtle string quartets, this one is a full orchestra with so much going on in it that it is, to use an overused word, exciting. The sharp flavoring and the many textures are the key, and it can't be done without a lot of preparation. In its favor is that, while there is a good deal of work to do, it all can be done well in advance. By the way, the salad can be made without the squid or, perhaps, with firm-cooked monkfish substituted for the squid. But I do like the squid here for the chewiness it adds to the salad and also because it is almost impossible to gain weight eating squid.

MUSSEL, SHRIMP, AND SQUID SALAD

¼ pound fine ("angel hair") noodles
1 teaspoon salt
1 pound small squid
1 pound shrimp, cooked (see recipe page 99)
3 pounds mussels
1 bay leaf
6 whole black peppercorns
2 whole cloves
4 sprigs fresh parsley
5 tablespoons red wine vinegar
¼ cup fresh lemon juice
¼ cup olive oil
Freshly ground black pepper (12 turns of the pepper mill)
4 fresh mint leaves, finely chopped
¼ teaspoon hot red pepper flakes
1 cup thinly sliced red onions
2 cups sliced, peeled and seeded cucumber
3 plum tomatoes (½ pound), cut into cubes
1 tablespoon chopped garlic
¼ cup chopped fresh basil leaves
¼ cup chopped fresh parsley leaves
2 endives
1 large bunch watercress

1. Place the noodles in 2 quarts of boiling water with ½ teaspoon salt. Cook for about 3 minutes, or until they are al dente. Allow the pasta to cool briefly and then cut the strands into 2-inch lengths.

2. To clean the squid, twist and pull off the heads, pulling out much of the interior of the body and the ink sac along with it. Discard. Pull out and discard the semihard, sword-shaped pen. Cut off the tentacles from the head of the squid, just in front of the eyes. Cut them in half and set aside. Pop out the hard round beak in the center of the tentacles and discard. Rub off the brown skin of the

squid under cold water. Rinse and drain the squid. Cut the squid into ½-inch slices. Boil 2 cups of water in a saucepan and add the squid, including the tentacles, and return to the boil. Remove the squid immediately, drain, and allow to cool.

3. Slice the shrimp in half lengthwise, so they retain their arched shape; there should be 2½ cups.

4. Remove the beards and barnacles from the mussels. Place them in a large mixing bowl and cover them with cold water. Swirl the mussels about vigorously so they rub against each other until they are clean. Place the mussels, along with the bay leaf, peppercorns, cloves, parsley sprigs, and 2 tablespoons of the vinegar in a large saucepan. Cover tightly and cook over high heat, shaking the pan a bit. Remove the mussels as soon as they open. Drain the mussels and allow them to cool. Remove the meat from the shells; there should be about 2 cups.

5. Put the noodles, seafood, and all the remaining ingredients in a large salad bowl. Toss, blend well, and serve with a garnish of endive leaves and watercress.

YIELD: 8 servings.   CALORIES PER SERVING: 304.

PRESENTATION: Place a mound of the seafood salad in the center of a chilled plate. Around the periphery, radiating away from the center, place several endive leaves. Between the leaves, place little bunches of watercress.

I do enjoy a can of tuna fish every now and then, especially when there's nothing else in the house for a quick lunch. What I can't stand is the pedestrian bottled mayonnaise and chopped celery that many people mash into it. So let me suggest a variation.

TUNA SALAD VINAIGRETTE

2 large radiccio leaves, quartered
Vinaigrette (see recipe page 243)
16 endive leaves
4 cups loosely packed greens, such as arugola
4 plum tomatoes, quartered
4 hard-boiled eggs
½ cup chopped scallions
2 8-ounce cans water-packed tuna fish, drained
2 teaspoons Oriental Curry Powder (see recipe page 265)

1. Place the radiccio leaves in a mixing bowl. Add 1 teaspoon of the vinaigrette dressing and toss the leaves. Place two leaf sections opposite each other on 4 plates.

2. Cut the endive leaves in half and slice the upper half into strips. Place all the endive in a mixing bowl with 1 teaspoon of the dressing and toss. Remove the bottom halves and place them between the radiccio leaves.

3. Place the greens in the bowl with the strips of endive, along with another teaspoon of dressing. Toss. Distribute in the center of each plate.

4. Arrange the tomatoes around the edge of the salad. Quarter the eggs and arrange and alternate them with the tomatoes, over the radiccio.

5. Mix the scallions into the tuna fish, along with 4 tablespoons of dressing and the curry powder. Do not mash the fish; allow it to remain in chunks. Place a portion of fish in the center of each plate.

YIELD: 4 servings.   CALORIES PER SERVING: 320.

In the heat of Morocco, the people know how to make a light salad. This is a typical approach.

MOROCCAN-STYLE CARROT AND ORANGE SALAD

6 large carrots (about 1 pound), shredded (3 cups)
4 seedless oranges, peeled and membranes removed,
sectioned (about 2 cups)
1 medium-sized onion, sliced and cut into 2-inch lengths
(about 2 cups)
½ cup currants, soaked in water for 10 minutes
and drained
¼ teaspoon hot red pepper flakes
3 tablespoons olive oil
Juice of 1 lemon
¼ cup chopped walnuts
½ teaspoon salt
Freshly ground black pepper (8 turns of the pepper mill)

Put all the ingredients in a bowl and toss. Refrigerate for ½ hour or more before serving.

YIELD: 6 servings.   CALORIES PER SERVING: 211.

For years now, I've been sure to take Guacamole with me on most picnics. Like Gazpacho, a spicy Guacamole manages to fit perfectly with fresh air. An important tip: Be sure to mash the avocado with a fork, as suggested here, rather than some mechanical method of puréeing. The fork technique provides a coarse Guacamole that is head and shoulders above the smooth baby food versions. When selecting an avocado be sure it is ripe, not too green, but not mushy either.

GUACAMOLE

2 large ripe avocados
Juice of 1 lime
¼ cup finely minced onion
2 tablespoons rinsed and finely chopped seeded serrano
chilies, canned or fresh
¾ cup peeled, seeded, and coarsely chopped ripe tomatoes
¼ cup finely chopped fresh coriander leaves
½ teaspoon salt
Freshly ground black pepper (10 turns of the pepper mill)

1. Halve and peel the avocados. Remove the pits and any brown tissue, such as fibers clinging to the flesh. Place the avocados and the lime juice in a mixing bowl.

2. With a knife in one hand, slice the avocado into chunks. At the same time, with a fork in the other hand, mash the avocados coarsely. Add the chopped onion, chilies, tomatoes, coriander, salt, and pepper. Mix well.

YIELD: 6 servings. CALORIES PER SERVING: 180.

PRESENTATION: For a Guacamole appetizer, take a whole leaf of lettuce (the red radiccio is my favorite) and use it as a cup for 4 tablespoons of the Guacamole. The Guacamole can, of course, also be served as a dip.

Here I offer what is essentially a string bean vinaigrette. There is a large proportion of mustard and vinegar in it to provide the tanginess that might be muted by the mushrooms.

STRING BEAN AND MUSHROOM SALAD

1 quart water
1 pound string beans, trimmed
½ pound fresh mushrooms
1 tablespoon Dijon mustard
2 tablespoons red wine vinegar
½ teaspoon chopped garlic
1 teaspoon salt
Freshly ground black pepper (4 turns of the pepper mill)
4 tablespoons olive oil
¼ cup chopped fresh parsley leaves
¼ cup chopped scallions

1. Bring the water to a boil and cook the string beans in it, uncovered, for 8 to 10 minutes. Drain and cool.

2. Wash and dry the mushrooms. Slice them thinly.

3. Prepare the sauce by whisking together the mustard, vinegar, garlic, salt, and pepper. Slowly add the olive oil while whisking.

4. Put the string beans, mushrooms, parsley, and scallions in a salad bowl. Pour the sauce over the vegetables and toss gently.

YIELD: 6 servings.   CALORIES PER SERVING: 122.

I have never been to Lebanon, but came to appreciate the food of that nation through the work of Lebanese restaurants in Paris. A refreshing appetizer is Tabbouleh. It also happens to be light and nutritious.

TABBOULEH

½ cup fine bulgur wheat
1 cup finely chopped onions
1 cup finely chopped fresh Italian parsley leaves
¾ cup seeded and chopped ripe tomato
½ teaspoon finely chopped garlic
⅓ cup fresh lemon juice
½ teaspoon salt
Freshly ground black pepper (8 turns of the pepper mill)
3 tablespoons olive oil
2 tablespoons finely chopped fresh mint leaves, or
1 tablespoon dried mint

1. Place the bulgur wheat in a bowl and cover with cold water. Let it soak for the period of time indicated on the package. Then drain it and place the bulgur in a piece of cheesecloth to vigorously squeeze out the extra water.

2. Put the bulgur, onions, parsley, tomato, garlic, lemon juice, salt, and pepper in a bowl. With a fork, toss the mixture gently but thoroughly.

3. Stir in the olive oil and mint before serving.

YIELD: 6 servings.   CALORIES PER SERVING: 138.

PRESENTATION: Like the Guacomole, this can be served as an appetizer in a cup formed from a lettuce leaf; in this instance, romaine or radiccio would do especially well.

...5...

Fish

For a long time, it seemed to me, large parts of this nation were burdened by a kind of cultural aberration in which people were raised to despise fish (spinach, for some reason, is another public enemy). As the interest in food—and calorie-counting—has widely grown, however, fish has come to be admired here much the way it is elsewhere in the world.

Now, however, I sense a new feeling about fish that is almost as bad as the old one. In many a fine restaurant you can hear weight-conscious diners, even sophisticated ones, routinely order broiled fish "dry." It's always the same, broiled and dry. It is as if fish represents diet medicine more than one of nature's gifts.

This chapter will demonstrate that there are an incredible number of lively, alluring approaches to fish. I have coated some fillets with toasted sesame seeds and others with pepper, like steak au poivre. I have baked fish with an intricate design of summer squash and zucchini, so that the result resembles a painting. I have poached it, and I have steamed it. I have braised it in red wine and marinated it in white. I have served it raw with lime and hot pepper and broiled it with grapefruit. None of it is dry.

This recipe employs a venerable trick: poaching in both milk and water. Most flat, white-fleshed fish benefits from the approach, which not only preserves its attractive whiteness, but seems to enhance it, almost like a bleach. An important role of the vegetables is, of course, to lend color to the bare white of the fish. Here, we have the familiar orange of the carrots and green of the asparagus, punctuated by the return of the white theme in the turnips.

POACHED COD WITH VEGETABLES

3 carrots (about ¾ pound)
2 white turnips (about ½ pound)
12 asparagus (about ¾ pound)
¾ teaspoon salt
4 ¼-inch-thick codfish steaks (about ¼ pound each)
¼ cup milk
1 bay leaf
2 whole black peppercorns
1 sprig fresh parsley

1. Peel the carrots, quarter them, and cut them into pieces about 3 inches long.

2. Peel the turnips, cut them through the middle and cut the halves into 4 pieces so that there are 16 pieces.

3. Peel the asparagus, using a vegetable peeler, and cut off the tough ends to make spears that are each 5 inches long.

4. Place the carrots in a saucepan and cover them with water. Add ¼ teaspoon of the salt. Bring the water to a boil and cook the carrots for about 5 minutes. Add the turnips and cook about 4 minutes. Add the asparagus and cook 3 minutes longer. Remove the vegetables from the heat, drain them, and keep them warm.

5. Put the fish in a saucepan and cover it just barely with the milk and water. Add the remaining salt, bay leaf, peppercorns, and parsley. Bring the liquid to a boil and simmer for 4 minutes.

6. Transfer the fish to warm plates, allowing it to drain. This is best accomplished with a skimmer. Serve with the vegetables.

YIELD: 4 servings.   CALORIES PER SERVING: 160.

PRESENTATION: Place a single cod steak toward the top of a plate and remove the skin. (It is better to do this in the serving plate because the skin will be useful in holding the fish together on its way to the plate.) The bone can be removed, but I don't advise it, since you run the risk of destroying the looks of the fish. Place a tablespoon of Aïoli (see recipe page

236) at each side of the steak. In lieu of Aïoli, plain or flavored melted butter drizzled over the top is marvelous. The vegetables should be arranged in an alternating pattern radiating out from the steak.

Nouvelle cuisine, *when it is executed sensitively, has done us the favor of inspiring the use of much more fruit in cooking. A broiled fish is accompanied here by what is in fact a beurre blanc in different dress. Instead of combining the butter with wine and vinegar for acidity, I tried a reduction of orange juice as the acidic component. It was marvelous. The dish has a tart sweetness to it and leaves you feeling refreshed.*

BROILED FISH FILLETS WITH ORANGE-BUTTER SAUCE

¼ cup orange juice
2 tablespoons butter at room temperature
½ cup diced ripe tomatoes
4 skinless and boneless white-fleshed fish fillets, such as
fluke, red snapper, striped bass, or lemon sole
(about 1½ pounds)
2 teaspoons olive oil
½ teaspoon salt
Freshly ground black pepper (8 turns of the pepper mill)
¼ cup chopped fresh coriander leaves

1. Preheat the broiler, but remove one tray to keep it cool.
2. Pour the orange juice into a saucepan and reduce it by half over high heat. Add the butter and tomatoes and cook just until the butter is well blended with the tomatoes.
3. Brush the fish on both sides with olive oil. Sprinkle with salt and pepper. Arrange the fish on the unheated broiler tray. Put the fish 2 to 3 inches from the heat source.
4. Broil for 3 to 4 minutes, or just until the fillets are cooked through. Remove from the heat and serve with the orange sauce. Garnish with the coriander.

YIELD: 4 servings. CALORIES PER SERVING: 364.

PRESENTATION: Place a fish fillet in the center of each plate. Arrange Sautéed Sweet Red or Yellow Peppers (see recipe page 227) horizontally in 4 rows radiating out from the fish like spokes. Spoon the sauce over the fish. Sprinkle the fillets with coriander.

The use of mustard in the United States tends to be extraordinarily limited, a relish for pastrami, salami, and the like. In France, it is so common that it is served with French fries and countless other dishes. That's why, if you've ever wondered about it, the French felt compelled to be so creative in producing a variety of mustards. Nouvelle cuisine, *especially, has made wide use of it. A delightful use for mustard, one that until recently has been rare in America, is to season fish. By placing it on flounder, as this recipe requires, a surprisingly delicate flavor is imparted to the fish, although it has some bite at the same time. The mustard also browns quickly under the broiler, giving the fish a rich color.*

BROILED FLOUNDER À LA MOUTARDE

4 skinless and boneless flounder fillets, about 1½ pounds
Freshly ground black pepper (7 turns of the pepper mill)
1 tablespoon olive oil
2 tablespoons Dijon mustard
2 tablespoons chopped chives
4 lime wedges

1. Preheat the broiler.
2. Arrange the fillets on a baking sheet or in a baking dish and sprinkle them with pepper. Then brush them with the oil.
3. Using a pastry brush, spread the mustard evenly over the fish.
4. Put the fillets into the broiler, about 3 inches from the heat source. Broil for about 2 minutes, or until golden brown. Do not overcook. Place on individual dishes, sprinkled with chives and accompanied by a wedge of lime.

YIELD: 4 servings. CALORIES PER SERVING: 178.

PRESENTATION: Since this dish so light and fast to make, I suggest preparing accompaniments that are equally light and fast, but that differ enough in the flavors they bring along to make the dish adventurous. Zucchini Bordelaise (see recipe page 233) and Broiled Tomatoes Provençale (see recipe page 232) fill the bill and will also bring marvelous color to the presentation. Place a flounder fillet off center toward the top of the plate. On the rim of the plate, just above the flounder, place a wedge of lime. Below the fish, center a whole Baked Tomato Provençale. Flank it with zucchini strips radiating away from the fish.

In the muddy bayous of Louisiana, there is a lowly fish in the perch family—they call it a redfish—that has become the pride of the state. To mask its overpoweringly fishy taste, the locals tend to coat it with pepper. The chef Paul Prudhomme has taken this redfish and coated it with several kinds of pepper. He fries it in very hot butter, blackening the fish. Prudhomme's fish from the bayous is now known coast to coast. But Prudhomme's redfish do not reside in East Hampton, where I live. So what I have done is to adapt his recipe, with some of my own touches, for a number of similarly firm fish. The following is one of the easiest and most memorable of dishes.

FILLETS OF FISH AU POIVRE

½ teaspoon sea salt or Kosher salt
1 teaspoon whole white peppercorns
1 teaspoon whole black peppercorns
4 fish fillets, such as fluke, perch, black fish, or lemon sole (about 1½ pounds total weight)
2 tablespoons olive oil
2 tablespoons chopped fresh coriander leaves, or ¼ cup chopped fresh parsley leaves

1. Grind the salt and peppers together in a mill or grinder. Coat the fish thickly with the seasonings, almost as if the salt and pepper were a breading.

2. Make a black iron pan very hot, virtually red hot. (If you have an exhaust fan be sure it is on.) Pour 1 teaspoon of the olive oil into the pan and coat the bottom quickly. (The oil will begin to smoke and burn at once.) Place 2 fish fillets in the pan and cook them about 1½ minutes. Turn and cook them about 1 minute on the other side. (You turn the fish when the rim of the raw side begins to whiten.) Transfer the fish to a warm platter.

3. Remove any particles of fish that might remain in the pan and then repeat the cooking process with the remaining fish. Transfer the fish to the platter. Brush the fillets with the remaining olive oil and sprinkle them with coriander before serving.

YIELD: 4 servings.   CALORIES PER SERVING: 266.

PRESENTATION: This dish cries out for a very simple accompaniment. My preference is for a sliced tomato with oil, vinegar, and basil, arranged alongside a single fillet on each plate.

Fricassee, of course, is a term most often applied to meat and poultry, specifically a stew with a lean meat and a light sauce. It shows up here because I was struggling for a term that captured my intentions with this recipe, which was to create a fish stew that has a flavorful and thick, yet light, sauce. You'll find that this is an easier to eat fish concoction than most, too. There are no bones; everything is bite-sized.

SEAFOOD FRICASSEE

3 tablespoons olive oil
½ cup finely chopped onion
1 tablespoon finely chopped garlic
½ cup chopped fennel (do not include the leaves)
½ cup chopped carrot
½ cup chopped leek
1 dried hot red pepper, crushed
1 bay leaf
½ teaspoon dried thyme
1 cup dry white wine
1 cup chopped ripe tomatoes (or canned, if necessary)
2 cups water
½ teaspoon salt
Freshly ground black pepper (8 turns of the pepper mill)
1 pound boneless white-fleshed, nonoily fish, such as
halibut, monkfish, striped bass, red snapper, or tilefish,
cut into ¾-inch cubes
½ pound bay scallops
½ pound shrimp, peeled and deveined
¼ cup finely chopped fresh parsley leaves

1. Heat the olive oil in a kettle and add the onion, garlic, fennel, carrot, and leek. Cook the vegetables until they wilt.

2. Add the crushed hot pepper, bay leaf, thyme, wine, tomatoes, and water. Bring the mixture to a boil and add the salt and pepper. Cover the kettle tightly and simmer for 15 minutes.

3. Add the fish and cook for 2 minutes. Add the scallops and shrimp and cook for another minute. Do not overcook or the fish will fall apart. Sprinkle the stew with parsley and serve it with Croutons (see recipe page 264).

YIELD: 6 servings.   CALORIES PER SERVING: 239.

PRESENTATION: Serve the fricassee in large soup bowls, portioning out the seafood first so that each serving has its due. Then surround the seafood with vegetables and liquid. The croutons should be served on the side. A caution: Handle the fricassee carefully; you don't want to break up the fish.

Mackerel is an inexpensive, widely available fish that, in this preparation, is flavorful and light. This is an excellent dish to prepare well ahead of time, since it improves over two or three days. In France, it is commonplace. In the United States, it certainly deserves to be better known.

MACKEREL MARINATED IN WHITE WINE

1 cup dry white wine
1 cup water
1 carrot, peeled and sliced (½ cup)
2 medium-sized white onions, sliced (½ cup)
Bouquet garni of 5 sprigs fresh parsley, 1 bay leaf, 1 sprig fresh thyme (or ½ teaspoon dried), tied together or enclosed in a piece of cheesecloth
2 whole cloves
2 garlic cloves, peeled and crushed
8 mackerel fillets, about 1½ pounds
12 whole black peppercorns
1 teaspoon salt
1 lemon, peeled and cut into 8 slices
½ cup white wine vinegar

1. In a saucepan, bring the wine and water to a boil. Add the carrot, onions, bouquet garni, cloves, and garlic. Boil over moderate heat for 15 minutes.

2. Put the mackerel in a deep serving dish or gratin pan and sprinkle with the peppercorns and salt. Lay the slices of lemon on top of each fillet.

3. Add the vinegar to the saucepan containing the vegetables, bring back to a boil, and pour it immediately over the fish. (Speed is required here to be sure that the liquid retains enough heat to cook the fish.) Cover the fish tightly, perhaps with plastic wrap, and refrigerate overnight. Serve cold.

YIELD: 8 servings, as   CALORIES PER SERVING: 193.
an appetizer.

PRESENTATION: When the mackerel is a luncheon main course, rather than an appetizer, it can be served with string bean salad and wedges of tomato. Arrange the fillets on the plate so that there is enough space between them for the string beans. Place a single tomato wedge at each end, enclosing the string beans. Be sure to serve the fillets on a chilled plate.

In the south of France, where fish are so abundant, they are combined with great exuberance, most notably in the bouillabaisse. It's not so much that the flavors blend—although that happens to some degree—but rather that the widely varying textures turn out to be delightful and the looks of the dishes are invariably spectacular. I call this version a ragout because it is more like a stew, richer in meat and vegetables in relation to the liquid, than a soup. The most important considerations are these: The fish should be fresh and it should not be overcooked.

RAGOUT OF FISH MEDITERRANÉE

2 tablespoons olive oil
1 tablespoon finely chopped garlic
1 cup finely chopped onions
1 cup finely chopped celery
1 cup finely diced sweet green pepper
½ teaspoon saffron stems
⅛ teaspoon cayenne pepper
2 cups finely diced leeks
½ teaspoon fennel seeds
¼ teaspoon freshly ground black pepper
2 cups canned tomatoes with juice
1 cup dry white wine
3 cups fumet de poisson (fish stock, see recipe page 29)
1½ pounds skinless and boneless fillets of monkfish,
cut into ¾-inch cubes (Black fish, striped bass, sea bass,
or red snapper fillets can also be used.)
1 pound bay or sea scallops
1 pound shrimp (30 to the pound), peeled and deveined
2¼ pounds mussels, cleaned
½ cup chopped fresh parsley leaves

1. In a large shallow saucepan, heat the olive oil and add the garlic, onions, celery, green pepper, saffron, cayenne pepper and leeks. Sauté over medium heat for 5 minutes. Add the fennel seeds, black pepper, tomatoes, white wine, and fish stock. Bring to a boil and simmer for 20 minutes.

2. Add the monkfish and scallops and cook for 3 minutes. Add the shrimp and mussels and cook for 3 minutes longer. Add the parsley and serve very hot.

YIELD: 8 servings.   CALORIES PER SERVING: 439.

PRESENTATION: Serve in big soup plates with Garlic Croutons and Rouille (see recipes on pages 264 and 240) on the side.

Red snapper is not a delicate fish. It can stand a lot of seasoning, and often benefit from it. Here, I've used some typically Cajun ingredients, and added some capers to give it even a little more punch. Ordinarily, I would have used two or three times as much olive oil, but I was delighted to see how well the dish turned out with a more moderate touch.

BAKED RED SNAPPER FILLETS

2 pounds skinless and boneless red snapper fillets
2 tablespoons olive oil
1½ cups thinly sliced onions
2 cups mixed, sliced sweet red and green peppers
1 tablespoon chopped garlic
1 cup sliced celery
2 cups chopped ripe tomatoes
¼ cup drained capers
¼ cup chopped fresh parsley leaves
½ teaspoon salt
Freshly ground black pepper (8 turns of the pepper mill)
¼ teaspoon Tabasco sauce
2 tablespoons butter

1. Preheat the oven to 425 degrees.
2. Cut the fish into 6 portions.
3. Heat the olive oil in a saucepan and add onions, peppers, garlic, and celery. Cook, stirring, for about 5 minutes, or until the vegetables are wilted. Add the tomatoes to the pan along with the capers, parsley, salt, pepper, and Tabasco. Cover the pan and cook for 10 minutes.
4. Put the fish in a baking dish. Spoon the sauce over the fish and dot it with the butter.
5. Place the baking dish on top of the stove and bring the sauce to a boil. Move the dish to the oven and bake for about 12 minutes.

YIELD: 6 servings.   CALORIES PER SERVING: 266.

PRESENTATION: Place a fillet in the center of each plate. Mold Creole Rice (see recipe page 213) by pressing it into a coffee cup and place it to one side of the fish. With a slotted spoon extract the vegetables from the sauce and surround the fish with them. Spoon the remaining liquid over the top of each fillet.

The way I often prefer to buy salmon steaks is to have them cut from the fillet (which looks like the familiar side of smoked salmon) so that there is no bone and so that there is a coat of skin on the bottom of each steak. The result is salmon that is more moist and more tender. It will flake as you touch it with the fork. To be sure that it does stay moist, notice that I recommend that the meat should be only barely cooked in the center of the steak. Also, it is best, by far, if you cook the salmon at the last minute. What I usually do is serve the first course and then leave the table to quickly cook the salmon.

BROILED SALMON WITH FRESH DILL

4 salmon steaks, 6 ounces each (preferably boneless)
½ teaspoon salt
Freshly ground black pepper (8 turns of the pepper mill)
4 tablespoons chopped fresh dill
1 tablespoon olive oil
2 tablespoons fresh lemon juice

1. Place the salmon on a platter or in an au gratin pan and sprinkle it with salt, pepper, and dill.

2. Blend the olive oil and lemon juice and pour the mixture over the salmon. Cover the fish with plastic wrap and allow it to marinate in the refrigerator for 2 hours.

3. Preheat the broiler.

4. Place the salmon in a broiler pan skin side down, about 3 to 4 inches from the source of the heat. Broil for about 5 minutes without turning the fish. The meat in the center should be just barely cooked.

YIELD: 4 servings.   CALORIES PER SERVING: 434.

PRESENTATION: The salmon can be served simply with a bit of fresh lemon juice and steamed vegetables. It has more character when served with Ginger-Butter Sauce (see recipe page 238). To serve it with the sauce, place a single steak in the center of a plate and spoon the sauce over it, 1 tablespoon per serving, reserving some sauce for those who want more. Arrange Asparagus with Mushrooms and Fresh Coriander (see recipe page 219) around the fish so that it radiates away from the center. Or try Snow Peas with Sesame Seeds (see recipe page 228).

The making of this book has led me into some unfamiliar territory.
I knew that I wanted steamed salmon here, but I wished to stay clear of
oil-laden and butter-laden sauces this time. So I decided to try it with a
yogurt-based sauce. I believe that yogurt has been used in excess lately.
Moreover, it tends to separate when heated. But here, bound with
mustard, it stood up to heat very well, and infused with dill, it was an
attractive, flavorful low-calorie dressing.

STEAMED SALMON WITH
YOGURT-DILL SAUCE

3 tablespoons prepared yellow mustard
½ cup plain lowfat yogurt
2 tablespoons olive oil
1 tablespoon chopped fresh dill
¼ cup chopped scallions
Freshly ground black pepper (6 turns of the pepper mill)
1 tablespoon white wine vinegar
16 sprigs fresh dill
4 salmon steaks (6 ounces each)

1. Put the mustard, yogurt, olive oil, chopped dill, scallions, pepper, and vinegar in a small saucepan. Blend well with a whisk.

2. Press 2 sprigs of dill onto the bottom of each salmon steak. Place the salmon in a steamer and press 2 more sprigs of dill on top of each steak. Cover, bring the water in the bottom of the steamer to a boil, and steam for about 6 minutes. The fish is done when the bone in the center loosens (try moving it with a long-handled fork). Turn the heat off and let the fish rest in the covered steamer for 3 minutes.

3. Meanwhile, gently heat the sauce until it is warmed through.

4. Transfer the fish to serving plates. Nudge the bone loose and remove it. Peel away the skin. Serve the fish with the sauce.

YIELD: 4 servings.   CALORIES PER SERVING: 463.

PRESENTATION: Spoon the sauce all around the fish but not over it. Place a small boiled potato at the closed end of the fish. Alongside the fish place 2 or 3 pieces of cucumber, scraped and cut into 1½-inch lengths (to refine them a bit, the cucumbers can be shaped into an oblong with a knife so they resemble large olives).

If the point about variation in raw fish hasn't already been made, take a look at how different this marinated salmon is from the next one.

MARINATED SALMON WITH MUSHROOMS

½ pound large white mushrooms, washed, dried,
and sliced
1 teaspoon sea salt
Freshly ground black pepper (18 turns of the pepper mill)
6 tablespoons fresh lemon juice
3 tablespoons olive oil
1 pound skinless and boneless salmon fillets
2 tablespoons chopped fresh dill

1. Chill 4 serving plates.

2. Put the mushrooms in a mixing bowl and sprinkle them with ½ teaspoon of the salt and 6 turns of the pepper mill, 2 tablespoons of the lemon juice, and 1½ tablespoons of the olive oil. Toss well, cover with plastic wrap, and refrigerate.

3. Slice the salmon very thinly (it should resemble the familiar slices of smoked salmon) and place on chilled plates. Arrange the slices in a fan pattern. The slices should overlap only slightly.

4. Sprinkle the salmon with the remaining salt, pepper, lemon juice, and oil. Distribute the dill over the salmon. Refrigerate, covered with plastic wrap, for at least ½ hour.

YIELD: 4 servings.   CALORIES PER SERVING: 360.

PRESENTATION: When ready to serve, place a portion of the mushrooms at the base of the fan pattern arranged on each plate. Take care not to cover more than a little of the salmon.

Raw fish may not seem as though it allows for much variety in
preparation. But even small changes in preparation can yield
very different dishes. Although we marinate salmon in another recipe,
in that instance it is sliced thinly, like smoked salmon. Here, it is offered
in chunks, along with the chunky scallops and its own combination of
seasonings. The texture is its own, too, as well as the marvelous marriage
of colors. It is a light and tangy appetizer.

MARINATED SALMON AND SCALLOPS

¾ pound skinless and boneless salmon
½ pound bay or sea scallops
⅓ cup fresh lemon or lime juice
12 large fresh basil leaves, or ¼ cup coarsely chopped
fresh coriander leaves
4 tablespoons olive oil
4 drops Tabasco sauce
½ teaspoon salt
Freshly ground white pepper (12 turns of the pepper mill)

1. Cut the salmon into ½-inch cubes. If sea scallops are used, they
will have to be cut, too, into ¼-inch-thick slices.

2. In a mixing bowl, combine all the ingredients and blend well.
Cover with plastic wrap and refrigerate for 4 hours.

YIELD: 6 servings.   CALORIES PER SERVING: 240.

PRESENTATION: Serve on a chilled platter garnished with a sprig of
fresh coriander or small fresh basil leaves.

The heart of this recipe is the sauce, a rich, deep red sauce with a red pepper purée base. It has very few calories. The few that do exist come from the tablespoon of oil. (There is also a tablespoon of oil in sautéeing the fish, but if you are especially calorie-conscious dispense with it and just trust your nonstick pan not too stick.) But mostly it is the way the sauce accompanies salmon in flavor and, especially, in color that appeals to me.

SCALOPPINES OF SALMON WITH TOMATOES

2 sweet red peppers (½ pound), halved, seeded, and boiled
for 7 minutes
2 tablespoons olive oil
1 teaspoon chopped garlic
1½ pounds ripe tomatoes, peeled, seeded, and cut into
½-inch cubes (3 cups)
1 teaspoon salt
Freshly ground black pepper (8 turns of the pepper mill)
1 bay leaf
1¼ pounds skinless and boneless salmon fillets, cut into
12 ½ inch-thick-strips, about 2 ounces each
3 tablespoons butter
1 cup chopped scallions
2 tablespoons red wine vinegar or strawberry vinegar

1. In a food mill or processor, purée the peppers. There should be about ¾ cup.

2. Heat 1 tablespoon of the olive oil in a frying pan and add the garlic. Cook briefly but do not brown the garlic. Add the tomatoes, pepper purée, and ½ teaspoon of salt, along with 4 turns of the pepper mill and the bay leaf. Sauté over high heat, stirring, for about 5 minutes. Keep warm.

3. Sprinkle the fish with salt and pepper. Heat the remaining tablespoon of oil in a nonstick frying pan and add the fish. Cook for about 1 minute on each side. Do not overcook. Keep warm.

4. Place the sauce on the bottom of a platter or dish and position the fish over it.

5. Put the 3 tablespoons of butter in a clean nonstick skillet and when it foams add the scallions. Cook briefly and add the vinegar. Pour the mixture over the fish.

YIELD: 6 servings.   CALORIES PER SERVING: 335.

PRESENTATION: Place enough of the tomato sauce on each plate to cover the bottom. Position the fish over it and then pour the vinegar and butter sauce over it as described in steps 4 and 5. Serve immediately with Dilled Potatoes (see recipe page 212).

Poaching fish poses some small perils. You have to be careful to reduce the heat immediately after the liquid comes to a boil to bring it to a simmer, or else the turbulence may break the fish apart. It is hard to tell when a poached fish is done, other than by following the guidelines in recipes. The reason is that you see it so poorly in the water. One method is to remove it from the water and press on it with a fork; if it's springy, it's not done yet. The flavoring of the fish offered here is meant to be noticeably different. There is a powerful taste of thyme, and I ordinarily would not add the cloves. If you wish to poach any fish at any time and give it the standard flavoring, just revert to only 1 sprig of thyme and forget about the cloves.

POACHED SALMON FILLETS WITH THYME

*1¼ pounds skinless and boneless salmon, in 4
equal pieces
6 sprigs fresh thyme, or 1 tablespoon dried thyme
enclosed in cheesecloth
1 bay leaf
2 whole cloves
4 whole black peppercorns
½ teaspoon salt*

1. Put the fish fillets in a shallow saucepan with enough water to cover them. Add all the remaining ingredients. Bring the water to a boil and cover the pan. Simmer for 5 minutes.
2. Drain and serve hot with Ginger Vinaigrette (see recipe page 243).

YIELD: 4 servings. CALORIES PER SERVING: 312.

PRESENTATION: Place the salmon in the center of each plate, with a ring of asparagus around it (see the recipe on page 219, but do not use the butter). Spoon the vinaigrette over the salmon amply so that it runs down the sides and moistens the asparagus, too. Garnish the fish, if you like, with a sprig of fresh thyme.

Of course, fish is almost always accompanied by white wine. It is usually thought to be too delicate for the robust reds. The exception, a delightful one, is salmon. A classic is Saumon Chambord, salmon in red wine. The fact is that salmon, which is so rich in flavor, can handle the reds. And the recipe here is a version I designed for this book, inspired by a salmon dish prepared for me by André Genin at the restaurant Chez Pauline in Paris.

BRAISED SALMON WITH RED WINE SAUCE

3 tablespoons butter
½ cup chopped shallots
½ cup chopped onion
½ cup chopped celery
1 cup diced carrots
1 pound fish bones and head, saved from the filleting of the salmon
3½ cups dry red wine
2 cups water
½ bay leaf
¼ teaspoon dry thyme
4 sprigs fresh parsley
2¼ pounds skinless and boneless salmon fillets, cut into 8 pieces
½ teaspoon salt
Freshly ground black pepper (6 turns of the pepper mill)

1. In a saucepan, put 1 tablespoon of the butter, ¼ cup of the shallots, the chopped onion, celery, and carrots and cook, stirring, for 1 minute. Chop the fish bones and head coarsely and add them to the pan. Cook and stir for 2 minutes. Pour 3 cups of the wine and the water into the pan, and add the bay leaf, thyme, and parsley. Cook, allowing the liquid to reduce, for 45 minutes. Strain the sauce and set aside in a saucepan. There should be about 1 cup.

2. Preheat the oven to 425 degrees.

3. Select a baking dish large enough to hold the fish in one layer. Rub the bottom of the dish with ½ teaspoon of the butter and sprinkle the remaining shallots over the bottom of the dish. Arrange the fish skin side down in the dish. Sprinkle it with salt and pepper. Add the remaining ½ cup of wine. Dot the fish with 2 teaspoons of the butter.

4. Place the dish on top of the stove and heat it thoroughly, then transfer it to the oven. Bake the fish for 5 minutes. Do not overcook.

5. Transfer the fish to a serving dish, cover it with foil, and keep it warm.

6. Add the cooking liquid from the baking dish to the sauce in the saucepan and reduce the mixture to about 1 cup. Strain the sauce

through a fine screen, such as that of a china cap, swirl in the remaining tablespoon of butter and, while very hot, spoon the sauce over the fish. Serve with Glazed Scallions.

YIELD: 8 servings.   CALORIES PER SERVING: 351.

PRESENTATION: Place the salmon in the center of the plate with the Glazed Scallions (see recipe page 228) radiating out from the fish, evenly spaced around it. Distribute the sauce only over the salmon, so it does not diminish the white-and-green duotone of the scallions.

Shad roe, which is so often served plain, actually blends well with any number of embellishments. Here, I have added the classic combination of flavors offered by tomatoes and garlic to the roe.

SHAD ROE PROVENÇALE

4 pair shad roe (½ pound each)
½ teaspoon salt
Freshly ground black pepper (8 turns of the pepper mill)
2 tablespoons olive oil
2 teaspoons chopped garlic
2 ripe tomatoes, peeled, seeded, and diced (about 1 cup)
¼ cup chopped fresh parsley leaves

1. Sprinkle the roe with salt and pepper.
2. Heat the oil in a nonstick frying pan. Add the roe, cover, and cook over medium heat for 2 minutes. Turn the roe and cook for another 3 minutes.
3. Transfer the roe to a serving platter and keep it warm. Add the garlic to the pan and cook briefly without browning it. Add the tomatoes and chopped parsley. Cook for 1 minute. Spoon the tomatoes and garlic over the roe.

YIELD: 4 servings.   CALORIES PER SERVING: 371.

PRESENTATION: The shad roe pair will naturally look like a pair of wings on the plate. They are attractive with the tomatoes spooned in a wide line straight down the middle, and falling into the gaps between the wings. Parsleyed Potatoes (see recipe page 212) go well with the dish; place one at each end of the roe. On each side of the roe, place 2 spears of steamed asparagus.

Shad roe is most often simply broiled or sautéed with a bit of lemon juice and, perhaps, a slice of bacon. The main difficulty it poses is that it dries out very quickly. This recipe protects against dryness in two ways: Poaching is inherently a moist approach and the lemon sauce keeps the roe moist as well as adding an attractive flavor.

POACHED SHAD ROE WITH LEMON SAUCE

4 tablespoons butter
¼ cup dry white wine
4 pair shad roe (½ pound each)
½ teaspoon salt
4 whole black peppercorns
Juice of 1 lemon
¼ cup chopped scallions
4 tablespoons chopped fresh parsley leaves

1. Heat 2 tablespoons of the butter in a frying pan and add the wine, shad roe, salt, peppercorns, lemon juice, and scallions. Cover tighty and cook for 5 minutes.

2. Transfer the roe to a platter or individual dishes. Swirl the remaining 2 tablespoons of the butter and the parsley into the liquid in the pan. Spoon the liquid over the roe.

YIELD: 4 servings.   CALORIES PER SERVING: 405.

PRESENTATION: Place 1 pair of roe in the center of the plate, with a Parsleyed Potato (see recipe page 212) at the top and another at the bottom. Along the side of the roe arrange a bright vegetable. Especially appealing would be a Melange of Vegetables (see recipe page 234). When you spoon the sauce over the roe, be careful to confine it to the roe so that the colors on the plate remain distinct.

I've presented three roe recipes consecutively here and I prepared them at just about the same time, too. The reason, of course, is that it was the roe season, about three months starting late in the winter and extending into the spring when the shad are heading to the rivers to spawn and they are ripe with eggs. The bordelaise sauce suggested by this recipe is a gentle one. What you need to be very wary of is the possibility of overcooking the roe. It should be fully cooked, that is, no longer pink, but it must retain its moisture. Also, be certain to cook the roe over medium—not high—heat. When cooked too violently, roe tends to break apart.

SHAD ROE BORDELAISE

1 tablespoon olive oil
4 pair shad roe (½ pound each)
½ teaspoon salt
Freshly ground black pepper (8 turns of the pepper mill)
3 tablespoons butter
2 tablespoons fresh bread crumbs
½ teaspoon finely chopped garlic
½ teaspoon finely chopped shallot
2 tablespoons red wine vinegar
¼ cup chopped fresh parsley leaves

1. Heat the olive oil in a nonstick frying pan. Sprinkle the roe with salt and pepper and put it in the pan. Cover the pan and cook the roe over medium heat for 2 minutes. Then turn the roe and cook on the other side for 3 minutes.

2. Remove the roe from the pan and place it on a warm serving platter. In the pan, combine the butter, bread crumbs, garlic, and shallot. Cook, stirring, until the bread crumbs are lightly browned. Add the vinegar and chopped parsley and spoon the mixture over the roe.

YIELD: 4 main-course servings, or 8 as an appetizer　CALORIES PER SERVING: 408 or 204.

PRESENTATION: Spoon the sauce over the roe and serve as in the recipe above, or, as an interesting variation, serve it with Curried Fresh Corn and Tomatoes (see recipe page 224).

A striking combination of flavors is that of dill and fennel. The dill has a slightly bitter taste; the fennel with its redolence of licorice has a slightly sweet flavor. When they merge gently, as they do in this dish, the result is a subtle, truly refined, sweet-and-sour effect.

BROILED FISH FILLETS WITH FENNEL AND DILL SAUCE

2 small fennel bulbs
1 tablespoon butter
4 tablespoons chopped scallions
2 tablespoons dry white wine
1 teaspoon salt
Freshly ground black pepper (12 turns of the pepper mill)
2 pounds white-fleshed fish fillets, such as striped bass,
red snapper, sea trout, cod, or tilefish, cut into 4 pieces of
½ pound each
3 tablespoons olive oil
2 tablespoons fresh lemon juice
2 tablespoons chopped fresh dill
4 sprigs fresh dill

1. Trim away the fennel leaves and cut the fennel bulb into slices about ⅛ inch thick. (You should have about 2 cups.)

2. Melt the butter in a saucepan and add the fennel and scallions. Sauté briefly, stirring. Add the wine, ½ teaspoon of the salt, and the pepper. Cover and cook for about 6 minutes. Set aside and keep warm.

3. Preheat the broiler.

4. Brush the fish with 1 tablespoon of the oil and sprinkle it with salt and pepper. Place it on a broiler pan close to the source of the heat. Broil for 5 to 7 minutes, depending on the thickness of the fish.

5. Heat the remaining 2 tablespoons of the olive oil in a small saucepan and add the lemon juice and chopped dill. Blend it well and keep warm.

YIELD: 4 servings.   CALORIES PER SERVING: 372.

PRESENTATION: Position the fish in the center of each plate, with the fennel in a ring around it. Spoon the warm dill sauce over the fish and place a sprig of dill over each fillet.

This fish has an extraordinarily natural flavor, the result of its cooking primarily in its own liquid and that of the mussels. It is very light, very fast and elegant, too, with a whole variety of textures, topped by the crunch of the bread crumbs. The bread crumbs will not crunch, by the way, unless the oven is very hot. So be sure the oven has reached the necessary 475 degrees.

BAKED FISH FILLETS WITH MUSSELS

32 mussels
½ bay leaf
½ teaspoon dried thyme
¼ cup dry white wine
3 tablespoons butter
4 fish fillets, such as sole, fluke, striped bass, or red snapper, about ½ pound each
½ teaspoon salt
Freshly ground black pepper (8 turns of the pepper mill)
½ cup fresh bread crumbs
4 tablespoons chopped shallots
¼ cup chopped fresh coriander or fresh parsley leaves

1. Preheat the oven to 475 degrees.

2. Scrub the mussels clean. Put the mussels, bay leaf, thyme, and wine in a saucepan and cover it. Bring the liquid to a boil and steam for 3 minutes. Remove the mussels from their shells. Strain and save the cooking liquid. There should be about ½ cup.

3. Brush the bottom of a large baking dish with 1 tablespoon of the butter. Place the fish fillets in the pan and scatter the mussels around them. Add the reserved cooking liquid. Sprinkle the fish with salt and pepper.

4. In a mixing bowl, blend the bread crumbs, shallots, and coriander. Sprinkle this mixture over the fish and mussels. Dot the top with the remaining butter.

5. Place the baking dish in the oven and bake from 6 to 10 minutes, depending on the thickness of the fillets.

YIELD: 4 servings.   CALORIES PER SERVING: 345.

PRESENTATION: Place a fish fillet toward the top of each plate. Beneath the fish, in a crescent, arrange a row of Glazed Scallions (see recipe page 228), with a small Parsleyed Potato (see recipe page 212) at each end of the crescent.

Often, when poaching fish, the vegetables are there just for the perfume. In a court bouillon, you will generally discard the vegetables. By the time they are discarded, all their essence is cooked out of them anyway. Here, I offer poached bass that revels in its vegetables. They are intended to be tender-crisp so that they add texture as well as beauty to the dish. The ginger gives the whole thing a vaguely Oriental air.

POACHED STRIPED BASS WITH GINGER AND VEGETABLES

2 medium-sized carrots, trimmed and scraped
2 small zucchini, ends trimmed
1 leek, cleaned
4 tablespoons butter
2 tablespoons finely chopped shallot
2 tablespoons finely chopped fresh ginger
½ cup dry white wine
¾ cup fumet de poisson (fish stock, see recipe page 29)
2 pounds skinless and boneless striped bass fillets, cut
into 4 steaks about ½ pound each
½ teaspoon salt
Freshly ground black pepper (8 turns of the pepper mill)
½ cup peeled ripe tomatoes cut into ¼-inch cubes
2 tablespoons chopped fresh dill for garnish

1. Slice the carrots to resemble thick matchsticks (close to ¼ inch thick), 1½ inches in length. There should be about 1 cup. Do the same with the zucchini and leek to get about 1 cup each.

2. Melt 1 tablespoon of the butter in a frying pan and add the shallots, carrots, and ginger. Sauté, stirring, for 1 minute. Do not brown. Add the wine and fish stock. Cover and cook for 4 minutes.

3. Place the fish in the pan, along with the salt, pepper, zucchini, leek, and tomatoes. Cover and cook for 5 minutes longer.

4. Transfer the fish to a platter. Cover with foil. Continue to cook the vegetables. Uncover the sauce and reduce the liquid over high heat for about 2 minutes. Add any liquid to the pan that has accumulated around the fish. Swirl in the 3 remaining tablespoons of butter. Serve the fish with the sauce and dill.

YIELD: 4 servings.   CALORIES PER SERVING: 409.

PRESENTATION: Cover each serving plate with a layer of vegetables. Place a fillet over the vegetables and spoon the sauce over the fish. Spinkle the dill over the sauce.

Bouillabaisse is a soup-like dish containing a variety of fish (the fish often served separate from the broth). Among its most important characteristics is the traditional combination of flavors in its broth, the saffron, garlic, tomato, and hot pepper. Here, those flavors are applied to a single fish, striped bass. It is an elegant and simple dish with the flavoring of a bouillabaisse but leaving an entirely different impression. The bass is quickly poached by itself and then sauced.

FILLETS OF STRIPED BASS IN BOUILLABAISSE SAUCE

1 tablespoon olive oil
1 teaspoon finely chopped garlic
½ cup finely chopped onion
½ cup chopped leek
½ cup finely chopped sweet yellow or red pepper
½ teaspoon saffron stems
½ cup peeled and finely chopped ripe tomatoes
½ cup dry white wine
1 bay leaf
⅛ teaspoon hot red pepper flakes
1½ pounds skinless and boneless striped bass,
cut into 4 chunks
½ teaspoon salt
Freshly ground black pepper (8 turns of the pepper mill)

1. Heat the oil in a saucepan and add the garlic, onion, leek, peppers, and saffron and sauté for 3 minutes. Do not brown. Add the tomatoes, wine, bay leaf, and hot pepper flakes, and cook for 5 minutes more.

2. Place the fish fillets in an au gratin pan and sprinkle with salt and pepper. Pour the sauce evenly over the fish. Cover with aluminum foil and simmer on top of the stove for 5 minutes.

YIELD: 4 servings.   CALORIES PER SERVING: 245.

PRESENTATION: Place a fish fillet in the center of each plate. At either end of the fillet, place a single Parsleyed Potato (see recipe page 212). Spoon the sauce over the fish and onto the plate along the side of the fillet, but not over the potato.

Striped bass, which is becoming something of an endangered species, is the finest eating fish the earth has ever produced. Sometimes when I think of fish in general I am really thinking of striped bass in particular, the quintessential fish. The important thing is to treat it well, which this recipe does.

STRIPED BASS WITH VEGETABLES

*2 skinless and boneless striped bass fillets
(about 4 pounds total weight)
3 medium-sized carrots
6 tablespoons butter
½ cup chopped shallots
1½ cups thinly sliced celery
¼ pound mushrooms, thinly sliced
1¼ cups dry white wine
2 teaspoons salt
Freshly ground black pepper (8 turns of the pepper mill)
Juice of ½ lemon
½ cup half-and-half
⅓ cup chopped parsley leaves*

1. Cut the fillets on a slight bias to make 8 steaks.

2. Trim and scrape the carrots, and slice them into thin rounds.

3. To a skillet large enough to hold all the pieces of fish in 1 layer, add 2 tablespoons of the butter. When the butter is hot, add the carrots, shallots, celery, and mushrooms. And ⅔ cup of the wine. Cook until all the wine has evaporated. The vegetables should still be firm.

4. Sprinkle the fish pieces with salt and pepper and arrange them in 1 layer over the vegetables. Pour the remaining wine and the lemon juice over the fish and bring to a boil. Cover and simmer for about 5 minutes.

5. Transfer the fish to a warm serving dish large enough to hold all the pieces and cover the dish with foil.

6. Add the half-and-half to the skillet and bring to a boil over high heat, shaking the vegetables. Reduce to about half its volume and add the remaining 4 tablespoons of butter, bit by bit, while shaking the pan. Serve the fish with the sauce, garnished with parsley.

YIELD: 8 servings.   CALORIES PER SERVING: 373.

PRESENTATION: Place a single steak in the center of a warm serving plate. Spoon some of the sauce over it but do not cover the fish entirely. Arrange a ring of Parsleyed Cucumbers (see recipe page 225) around the fish.

When I coat fish for sautéing, I always strive for lightness, usually with a thin batter. In this instance, the lightness is almost ethereal, provided by a simple coating of nothing more than sesame seeds. In preparing the dish, be sure that the sesame seeds brown only slightly. If the seeds become too dark, they will be bitter. Rather then moistening the fish with butter, as I so frequently do, I've devised a low-calorie tomato sauce for the purpose.

SAUTÉED FISH FILLETS WITH SESAME SEEDS

2 tablespoons olive oil
1 teaspoon finely chopped garlic
2 ripe tomatoes (¾ pound), cored, peeled, and
cut into small cubes
2 tablespoons chopped fresh basil leaves
¾ teaspoon salt
Freshly ground black pepper (8 turns of the pepper mill)
4 tablespoons sesame seeds
4 fish fillets, such as striped bass, sea bass, fluke, lemon
sole, or flounder (1¼ pounds total weight)
Lemon or lime wedges

1. Heat 1 tablespoon of the olive oil in a small saucepan. Add the garlic and cook briefly. Do not brown. Add the tomatoes, basil, ¼ teaspoon of the salt, and 4 turns of the pepper mill and cook for 5 minutes. Keep warm.

2. Spread out the seasame seeds in a large platter. Place the fillets, one side then the other, into the seeds to coat them lightly. Sprinkle with the remaining ½ teaspoon salt and 4 turns of the pepper mill.

3. Heat the remaining tablespoon of olive oil in a large nonstick frying pan and place the fish in it. Cook over high heat until the fish is brown on both sides. (The time will vary depending on the thickness of the fish—striped bass, for instance, will be much thicker than flounder.)

4. Transfer the fish to warm plates and serve with the sauce and lemon or lime wedges.

YIELD: 4 servings.   CALORIES PER SERVING: 279.

PRESENTATION: Place 2 fish fillets next to each other in the center of a plate. In the V formed at either end, place the tomato sauce. Alongside each fillet, place asparagus and mushrooms (see recipe page 219). Place a wedge of lemon at the periphery of the plate.

In a way, the search for attractive, relatively low-calorie approaches to preparing food has been a blessing, pushing me into worthwhile innovations. This dish is an especially successful case in point. I wanted to bake the fish at a high temperature to allow the good-looking pattern of zucchini and summer squash to brown lightly. But I didn't want the fish to dry out. To ensure moistness, I created a blanket of cooked onions to go over the fish and under the zucchini. The flavors do what they're supposed to do: They bind together into a single presence.

BAKED FISH WITH SUMMER SQUASH AND ZUCCHINI

*2 tablespoons vegetable oil
2 cups thinly sliced onions
½ teaspoon salt
Freshly ground black pepper (8 turns of the pepper mill)
2 pounds firm, white-fleshed fish fillets, such as striped
bass, weakfish, red snapper, or sea bass, cut into 4 pieces
1 small yellow squash, ¼ pound and 1 inch in diameter
or as slender as possible, thinly sliced
1 small zucchini, ¼ pound and 1 inch in diameter
or as slender as possible, thinly sliced
Juice of 1 lemon
1 tablespoon olive oil
2 tablespoons chopped shallots
2 small plum tomatoes (½ pound), cut into small cubes
1 tablespoon butter, melted*

1. Preheat the oven to 475 degrees.

2. Heat 1 tablespoon of the vegetable oil in a saucepan and add the onions. Cook them slowly for 15 minutes, stirring frequently, to brown lightly and remove much of the moisture.

3. Spread the remaining tablespoon of the vegetable oil in an au gratin pan. Sprinkle the bottom of the pan with ¼ teaspoon of the salt and 4 turns of the pepper mill. Lay the fish fillets in the pan.

4. Distribute a quarter of the onions evenly over each fillet.

5. Put the sliced squash and zucchini in a mixing bowl. Add the lemon juice and the tablespoon of olive oil, ¼ teaspoon of salt, and 4 turns of the pepper mill. Toss gently.

6. Arrange the squash and zucchini over the onion in 1 layer in an overlapping attractive pattern, taking advantage of the colors. Each fillet will require about 6 to 8 slices of both the squash and zucchini. Pour the lemon juice and oil mixture remaining in the bowl over the top of the fish.

7. Mix the shallots and tomatoes together in a bowl and distribute the mixture around the fish, not over it.

8. Place the fish in the oven and bake for 15 to 20 minutes for thick fillets and less for others.

9. When the vegetables and fish are lightly browned, remove the fish from the oven. Brush the zucchini very lightly with melted butter to impart a thin glaze.

YIELD: 4 servings.   CALORIES PER SERVING: 415.

PRESENTATION: Prepare Broiled Tomatoes Provençale (see recipe page 232) in the oven at the same time as the fish and place 2 halves on each plate, on opposite sides of the fish.

There is very little in the realm of cooking that is as light and, at the same time, as satisfying as poached fish. The term "à la nage" refers to swimming in French and, as it is used in recipe titles, suggests poaching, at the same time that it nicely evokes the sea, the lakes, and the streams. The fish in this recipe is poached in wine and water. I have added 3 tablespoons of butter to the sauce, or ½ tablespoon per serving. That amount of butter in the sauce, to my taste, is absolutely necessary. If you try it this way and think some of it can be sacrificed, be my guest.

FILLETS OF FISH À LA NAGE

4 tablespoons butter
4 tablespoons chopped shallots
¼ pound mushrooms, sliced (2 cups)
1 carrot, cut into julienne strips (1 cup)
1 celery stalk, cut into julienne strips (½ cup)
2 leeks (white part only) cut into julienne strips
of 1½ inches (about 1 cup)
1½ cups dry white wine
½ bay leaf
6 fillets (about ⅓ pound each) boneless, skinless,
white-fleshed fish, such as fluke, striped bass, sea
bass, or red snapper
½ teaspoon salt
Freshly ground black pepper (8 turns of the pepper mill)
1 teaspoon ground coriander
½ cup water
1 ripe tomato, peeled, seeded, and cut into small cubes
(about ¾ cup)
½ cup chopped scallions
½ teaspoon chopped garlic

1. In a saucepan, melt 1 tablespoon of the butter. Add the shallots, mushrooms, carrot, celery, and leeks. Cook, stirring, over low heat for 5 minutes. Add 1 cup of the wine and the bay leaf and reduce the liquid over high heat until there is about ¼ cup. (This will take about 20 minutes.)

2. Sprinkle the fish fillets with salt, pepper, and coriander and place in a large, shallow saucepan. Add the remaining ½ cup of wine and the water. Cover tightly and bring to a boil. Then simmer, still tightly covered, for 5 to 7 minutes. Do not overcook. Drain all the liquid and keep covered.

3. Add the tomatoes, scallions, and garlic to the saucepan with the vegetables. Bring the mixture to a boil. Add any liquid that has accumulated around the fish. Swirl in the remaining 3 tablespoons of butter. Serve the fish with the sauce.

YIELD: 6 servings.   CALORIES PER SERVING: 281.

PRESENTATION: Place the fish in the center of each plate, with
                sauce spooned over and around it. Around the fish
                and sauce create a wall-like effect with 4 spears of
                steamed or Buttered Asparagus (see recipe page
                219).

*If you buy a steamer for no other reason than the preparation of fish it
will prove worth whatever you pay for it. Steaming is a fast method
of cooking fish because the steam penetrates the flesh thoroughly and
almost at once. It imparts no calories of its own to the fish, of course, so
this very lean food remains fat-free. And fish, like virtually nothing else,
benefits from the most natural of preparations by retaining its own
flavor. Steaming accomplishes that.*

STEAMED FISH FILLETS WITH TOMATO AND MUSHROOM SAUCE

2 tablespoons butter
2 tablespoons chopped shallots
¼ pound fresh mushrooms, sliced
¼ cup dry white wine
½ cup **fumet de poisson** *(fish stock, see recipe page 29)*
2 cups diced, peeled and seeded ripe tomatoes
¼ cup chopped scallions
½ teaspoon salt
Freshly ground black pepper (8 turns of the pepper mill)
*4 skinless, firm, white-fleshed fish fillets, such as striped
bass, red snapper, weakfish, or tilefish*

1. Melt 1 tablespoon of the butter in a saucepan and add the shallots. Cook briefly without browning. Add the mushrooms, wine, and fish stock and bring the mixture to the boil. Reduce the liquid to ¼ cup. Then add the tomatoes. Cook for 3 minutes. Add the scallions, remaining butter, salt, and pepper. Keep the sauce warm.

2. Pour water into the steamer. Place the fish fillets on the steamer's rack and cover the steamer. When the water has begun to boil, steam the fish for 5 minutes. Do not overcook. Serve the fish with the sauce.

YIELD: 4 servings.   CALORIES PER SERVING: 273.

PRESENTATION: Spoon the sauce over each serving plate. Place the
                fish over the sauce in the center of each plate.
                Around the periphery of the plate, place four small
                Parsleyed Potatoes or chunks of Parsleyed Cucum-
                bers (see recipes pages 212 and 225). Between
                them, place sprigs of fresh parsley or dill.

Now, here's an interesting approach to the broiling of fish, adding a lot of flavor and very few calories. The fish is marinated in a tangy combination of, among other ingredients, grapefruit juice and mustard and coriander. Then it is given unusual allure with the addition of grapefruit sections. I go into considerable detail on how to make the grapefruit sections appear as unblemished and intact as possible. But there is more to this process than just the looks of the grapefruit: By slicing the fruit in this fashion, one removes almost all of the bitter, chewy membrane.

BROILED BONELESS FISH STEAKS WITH GRAPEFRUIT

2 large ripe grapefruit
2 tablespoons olive oil
1 teaspoon ground ginger
1 teaspoon dry hot mustard
1 teaspoon ground coriander
½ teaspoon salt
Freshly ground black pepper (8 turns of the pepper mill)
4 skinless and boneless fish steaks, such as tilefish, cod, haddock, striped bass, grouper, or red snapper (about ½ pound each)
4 tablespoons chopped scallions

1. Using a knife, remove the skin of the grapefruit. This should be done much the way one skins an apple, starting at the top and cutting in a circular fashion to try to remove the skin in one spiraling piece. You don't want any white membrane to remain on the surface of the grapefruit.

2. Then use the knife to pluck out each of the 24 sections by slicing down alongside each extension of membrane radiating out from the center of the fruit. When the sections are removed, squeeze what remains of the grapefruit (I do this by clasping the fruit in my hands, but cheesecloth or a strainer would be neater) to extract the juice, about ¾ cup. Place the sections in a baking dish and put aside.

3. Using a wire whisk, blend the juice, oil, ginger, mustard, coriander, salt, and pepper.

4. Pour the grapefruit juice mixture into a shallow baking dish and put the fish into the dish with it. Baste the fish with the liquid. Cover with plastic wrap and marinate for ½ hour.

5. Preheat the broiler. Place the fish in a pan 3 or 4 inches from the source of heat. At the same time, place the baking dish with the grapefruit on the floor of the oven.

6. Broil the fish for about 4 minutes, or until the pieces are cooked through and lightly browned. It is not necessary to turn the fish. Sprinkle the fish with chopped scallions. Remove the grapefruit from the oven and garnish the fish with it.

YIELD: 4 servings.   CALORIES PER SERVING: 300.

PRESENTATION: Serve with Braised Endives (see recipe page 225). Place the fish steak toward the top of the plate. Place a single endive beneath it. Arrange the grapefruit sections very neatly in the area between the fish and the endive.

In broiling fish, as with steaming, one has to realize that the fish is really virtually perfect to start with; a cook just has to heat it and not ruin it along the way. I make sure that the fish is very fresh, of course, with no strong fishy odors. I also always preheat the broiler so that it is very hot and will unfailingly impart a broiled taste to the fish. Then, I make certain not to overcook the fish. In fact, it is overdone when it starts to flake. If I broil the fish in an oven, I see no need to turn it. Actually, it is baking through and through while it is broiling. If I broil it over a flame, however, I do turn it because the fish is not heating through in the same fashion. I suggest using a beurre blanc with this swordfish. But a simple touch of butter, lime juice, and parsley or chives or coriander would make it marvelous, too.

BROILED SWORDFISH

2 swordfish steaks (about 3 pounds total weight)
2 tablespoons olive oil
½ teaspoon salt
Freshly ground black pepper (8 turns of the pepper mill)

1. Preheat the broiler.
2. Place the steaks in a baking pan and rub both sides with oil. Sprinkle both sides with salt and pepper.
3. Place the baking pan in the broiler about 4 inches from the flame. Broil for about 5 minutes. Remove the fish from the broiler and place the steaks on a warm platter. Serve with Beurre Blanc (see recipe page 237).

YIELD: 8 servings.   CALORIES PER SERVING: 225.

PRESENTATION: Cut the fish into equal portions and place a portion on a serving plate in the center of the plate, with half a baked tomato with rosemary and garlic (see recipe page 232) at the top and bottom. On each side place a portion of Parsleyed Cucumbers (see recipe page 225). Spoon just a little Beurre Blanc over each piece of fish.

The influence of the Japanese on the French nouvelle cuisine *has been very strong. Raw fish in a variety of guises is one result. The dish I offer here is reminiscent of one I had on the island of Guadeloupe. Only then it was shark instead of tuna. This is intended as an appetizer. If you are able to slice the lime garnish so that it is paper-thin, try eating the tuna and the lime slice in the same bite.*

RAW TUNA WITH LIME AND HOT PEPPER

*1 pound center-cut tuna, in one piece,
with all dark areas removed
4 tablespoons fresh lime juice
4 teaspoons olive oil
Freshly ground black pepper (12 turns of the pepper mill)
½ teaspoon sea salt
1 jalapeño pepper, finely chopped
2 limes, sliced very thin*

1. Chill 4 serving plates.

2. With a good slicing knife, slice the tuna very thinly. Place ¼ pound of tuna on each serving plate. Do not alow the tuna slices to overlap.

3. Spoon a teaspoon of lime juice over each serving. Spoon a teaspoon of oil over each serving. Sprinkle each serving with 3 turns of the pepper mill, and salt. Sprinkle the fish with jalapeño pepper. Garnish with slices of lime, arranged around the edge of the plate.

4. Refrigerate for at least ½ hour, covered with plastic wrap.

YIELD: 4 servings.   CALORIES PER SERVING: 221.

Whiting used to be thought of as trash fish but, increasingly now, the lightness of its white flesh is appreciated. There is plenty of it available and it is inexpensive. The sauce is a beurre noir, which requires that the butter be dark but not burned, and calls for vinegar and frequently capers and parsley as well.

WHITING AUX CAPERS BEURRE NOIR

2 pounds whiting fillets (about 8)
2 tablespoons milk
1 teaspoon salt
Freshly ground black pepper (8 turns of the pepper mill)
4 tablespoons all-purpose flour
2 tablespoons peanut or corn oil
4 tablespoons butter
¼ cup drained capers
2 tablespoons chopped shallots
2 tablespoons red wine vinegar
2 tablespoons chopped fresh parsley leaves

1. Put the fillets in a dish large enough to hold them in 1 layer. Pour the milk over the fish and sprinkle them with salt and pepper. Turn the fish in the milk so the fillets are coated on all sides.

2. Scatter the flour over a large pan or dish. Coat the fish lightly on both sides.

3. Heat the oil in a nonstick frying pan. When it is quite hot, but not smoking, add the fillets. It may be necessary to do this in 2 batches. Brown on one side, about 2 minutes. Turn and brown on the other side. As the fillets are cooked, transfer them to a warm serving platter.

4. Wipe out the pan and melt the butter, shaking the pan until the butter turns brown. Add the capers and cook briefly. Add the shallots, vinegar, and parsley, and pour evenly over each fillet.

YIELD: 4 servings.   CALORIES PER SERVING: 355.

PRESENTATION: Place 2 fillets side by side in the center of each plate. At each end of the fillets, place a Parsleyed Potato (see recipe page 212), wedged into the V formed by the fish. Branching out from the sides, place 2 or 3 spears of Steamed Broccoli (see recipe page 220). Spoon the sauce over the fish, allowing it to drip down the sides of the fish, but avoid getting too much over the broccoli.

..*6*..

Shellfish and Crustaceans

The nutritional dogma about shellfish has been changing lately. It used to be that even though shellfish were extraordinarily low in calories, they were shunned because they were high in cholesterol. Cholesterol isn't a major consideration in this book (low fat usually brings low cholesterol along with it, in any event). But, interestingly, shellfish have been reexamined and are now well on their way to losing their evil reputation among the nutrition gurus. It turns out that most shellfish are not so high in cholesterol as was previously thought. Lobster has no more than chicken. Only shrimp is still deemed too high to be eaten comfortably by those who are cholesterol-conscious.

For my part, I would no sooner relinquish shrimp than I would butter. I admire it for its sublime flavor and texture and for its lack of fat. My preference with shrimp, as with butter, is to eat it in moderation. If you are especially concerned about cholesterol, however, there are a number of other shellfish possibilities here that may please you: Baked Oysters with Fennel Sauce, a Seviche of Scallops, and Steamed Mussels with Green Sauce, among them.

My favorite way of steaming lobster is to use sea water, perhaps with some seaweed thrown in. And that's all. The lobster emerges from that procedure with all the naturalness of the open ocean. If seawater is not available, I create a court bouillon (as in this recipe), which is a traditional way of giving the water some character. Steaming a lobster in this fashion rather than boiling it has an important advantage: It actually cooks the lobster faster, killing it sooner, and resulting in more tender flesh. It is important to use a wide, large kettle so that the lobsters aren't piled on top of each other.

STEAMED LOBSTER

1 quart water
10 whole black peppercorns
1 bay leaf
1 sprig fresh thyme, or ½ teaspoon dried thyme
1 jalapeño pepper, or ¼ teaspoon hot red pepper flakes
4 lobsters (1½ pounds each)

1. Select a wide kettle large enough to hold the lobsters, with the water rising 2 or 3 inches from the bottom. Add the water with all the ingredients, except the lobsters. Bring the water to a rolling boil. Add the lobsters and cover. When the water returns to the boil, cook for 10 minutes more over high heat.

2. Remove the lobsters and let them drain.

3. Split the lobsters lengthwise. Remove the sac near the eyes; this is the lobster's stomach and is usually full of gravel.

4. Serve with melted butter and lemon juice. Or serve cold with mayonnaise or Vinaigrette (see recipe page 243).

YIELD: 4 servings.   CALORIES PER SERVING: 166.

Lobster is either done very simply or very richly. With the exception of lobster américaine, most lobster sauces are involved concoctions almost always heavy with cream. I offer here a recipe for a simple approach that manages to have an unusual, markedly contemporary twist: the addition of ginger.

BAKED LOBSTER WITH GINGER

4 1½-pound lobsters
2 tablespoons olive oil
½ teaspoon salt
Freshly ground black pepper (8 turns of the pepper mill)
4 tablespoons butter
2 tablespoons finely chopped shallots
1 tablespoon grated fresh ginger

1. Preheat the oven to 475 degrees.
2. Turn each lobster on its back and split it lengthwise. Remove and discard the small sac near the eyes.
3. Arrange the lobster halves, split side up, in a baking dish and brush them with oil. Sprinkle them with salt and pepper.
4. Bake the lobsters for 10 to 15 minutes and remove them from the oven. Transfer the lobsters to serving plates.
5. Melt the butter in a saucepan and add the shallots and ginger. Sauté briefly and pour over the lobsters.

YIELD: 4 servings.   CALORIES PER SERVING: 332.

PRESENTATION: Mostly, lobster presents itself. There is nothing that I can think of that you would want to put on the plate with a lobster. I like to serve the lobster alone, with French bread. If there is a vegetable, such as Asparagus with Mushrooms and Coriander (see recipe page 219), I prefer to serve it as a separate course after the lobster, instead of a salad.

I invented the sauce in this recipe. What I wanted was a sauce that was creamy and light at the same time. Mushrooms, rather than some variant of starch, are used in combination with the fennel to bind the sauce. The blender helps in achieving the fluffiness by incorporating some air into the mixture. As for the flavor, I was, of course, familiar with how well the licorice flavor goes with oysters because Pernod is prominent in oysters Rockefeller. For these oysters, that flavor is magnified by the use of fennel as well as a touch of Pernod.

BAKED OYSTERS WITH FENNEL SAUCE

*1 fennel bulb (¾ pound), trimmed and chopped
finely (2 cups)
¼ pound mushrooms, sliced (1½ cups)
¼ cup dry white wine
⅓ cup water
Freshly ground black pepper (4 turns of pepper mill)
24 oysters
¼ cup coarsely chopped fresh dill
4 tablespoons butter
1 tablespoon Pernod*

1. Preheat the oven to 500 degrees.

2. Prepare the sauce by combining the fennel, mushrooms, wine, water, and pepper in a saucepan. Cover tightly and bring to a boil. Simmer for 8 minutes.

3. Pour the mixture, including all the liquid, into a blender. Blend until smooth.

4. Scrub the oyster shells and place them in one layer, bottom down, on a rimmed baking sheet. Bake the oysters for about 7 or 8 minutes. They should pop open just slightly on their own, but be careful not to toughen them by overcooking. Hold the extremely hot oysters in a towel and remove the top shell with the aid of an oyster knife. (This will be much easier if you begin by piercing the pointed back end of the oyster with the point of the knife.)

5. Pour the juice of a few of the oysters into the sauce. The sauce should gain from the flavor but not become too runny. Place the oyster halves on 2 large serving platters or gratin dishes.

6. Blend the sauce to incorporate the oyster juice. Add the dill, butter, and Pernod and blend again.

7. Return the oysters to the oven to warm them. Place the sauce in a saucepan and bring to a boil. Remove immediately and taste to check for seasoning.

8. Remove the oysters from the oven and spoon the sauce over each of the oysters. Serve hot.

YIELD: 6 servings, as an appetizer.

CALORIES PER SERVING: 177.

PRESENTATION: This dish is so unusual, startling, really, in its greenness that it doesn't require much to present it interestingly. Just arranging the oysters on a plate is show enough. But for a bit more finish, you may want to place a small piece of dill on top of each oyster.

Because I like steamed mussels so much, I am constantly experimenting. In this recipe, everything is as it usually is with two changes. Ordinarily, one would see some cream in a recipe like this, and, of course, I have omitted it. There probably would be more butter, too. Where I tried for a slightly different touch is in combining the vinegar and the wine, rather than having one or the other stand alone. The result, I think, has an appealingly pungent acidity.

STEAMED MUSSELS WITH WINE

3 pounds mussels
1 tablespoon butter
3 tablespoons finely chopped shallots
2 tablespoons finely chopped onion
4 tablespoons finely chopped fresh parsley leaves
Freshly ground black pepper (8 turns of the pepper mill)
¼ cup dry white wine
2 tablespoons red wine vinegar

1. Remove the beards and any barnacles from each mussel. Then place the mussels in a large mixing bowl with fresh cold water and swirl them around vigorously so that they rub against each other in a rapid cleaning action. Drain.

2. Melt the butter in a kettle and add the shallots and onion. Cook until wilted. Place the mussels in the pot, along with half the parsley, the pepper, wine, and vinegar. Cover the pot tightly and cook for about 5 minutes, or until the mussels open.

YIELD: 4 servings.　　　　　CALORIES PER SERVING: 146.

PRESENTATION. The mussels can simply be served in a soup plate, the sauce spooned over them and sprinkled with the remaining parsley. Rounds of French bread should be alongside each bowl. More elaborately, the mussels can be served on the half shell, arrayed in a circle around the periphery of the plate and with a second circle inside the larger one. The sauce is spooned over the mussels. A sprig of fresh parsley should then be placed in the center.

A boon for cocktail parties or picnic lunches is a dish that doesn't need to be hot and doesn't need to be cold, but rather is at its peak when it is around room temperature. Such is this mussels dish, which is just right when it is cool or lukewarm. The sauce here is essentially a vinaigrette, with extra mustard to give it some tang.

MUSSELS À LA MOUTARDE

4 pounds mussels
4 sprigs fresh parsley
6 cloves
1 bay leaf
6 whole black peppercorns
2 cups chopped red onions
½ cup coarsley chopped fresh parsley leaves
3 tablespoons Dijon mustard
½ cup red wine vinegar
½ cup vegetable oil
Freshly ground black pepper (6 turns of the pepper mill)

1. Clean and drain the mussels (see step 1 of the recipe for Steamed Mussels with Wine). Place them in a kettle and add the parsley, cloves, bay leaf, and peppercorns. Cover and steam for about 5 minutes, or until the mussels open.

2. Place the warm mussels in a large serving dish, along with the onions and parsley.

3. In a bowl, blend the mustard, vinegar, oil, and pepper and spoon the mixture over the mussels. Toss well. Serve hot or cold.

YIELD: 10 servings.   CALORIES PER SERVING: 175.

PRESENTATION: Serve the mussels simply in a bowl with rounds of French bread. The mussels can be an appetizer, a snack, or the main course for a lunch that might also include a salad, wine (a chilled beaujolais comes to mind), and cheese.

The green sauce in this recipe is green indeed, with all that parsley and the scallions. It is a sauce that evokes the garden. And it gives you yet another way to use inexpensive, low-caloric, nutritious, and, most important—intensely flavorful—mussels. This type of green sauce with mussels is well known in Spanish restaurants in the United States (less well known in Spain, but never mind, it's a terrific dish).

STEAMED MUSSELS WITH GREEN SAUCE

4 pounds mussels
2 tablespoons olive oil
1 tablespoon chopped garlic
½ cup chopped scallions
¾ cup chopped fresh parsley leaves
1 cup dry white wine
⅛ teaspoon hot red pepper flakes
Freshly ground black pepper (10 turns of the pepper mill)

1. Clean and drain the mussels (see step 1 of the recipe for Steamed Mussels with Wine).

2. Heat the oil in a large frying pan or kettle and add the garlic and scallions. Cook them briefly, stirring, without allowing them to brown. Add the parsley, white wine, hot pepper flakes, and ground pepper. Bring the mixture to a boil and simmer for about 5 minutes. Add the mussels and cover. Cook over high heat for 4 to 6 minutes, or until the mussels open.

YIELD: 6 servings.   CALORIES PER SERVING: 152.

PRESENTATION: There are two approaches. One is to simply serve the mussels in a large soup plate, along with crusty rounds of French bread. The other is to remove the top of each mussel and arrange the mussels on the half shell in a neat spiral pattern on each serving plate. Then spoon the sauce over the mussels and serve with rounds of bread.

Squid, like chicken, is one of those nutritious inexpensive foods that can be prepared in countless ways. The recipe offered here uses traditional combinations of flavorings, joined together, in proportions to suit my own taste. I have intentionally cooked the zucchini and the rice only very lightly. I wanted crunchy, not soggy, zucchini. I wanted the rice to resemble a risotto, which is rice prepared meticulously to still offer some resistance when you bite into it.

BAKED SQUID WITH RICE

1 tablespoon olive oil
1 cup finely chopped onions
1 tablespoon chopped garlic
2 red sweet peppers, cut into ½-inch cubes (1½ cups)
10 small squid (about 2½ pounds), cleaned and
cut into cubes (about 3 cups)
½ teaspoon ground cumin
½ teaspoon dried oregano
1 teaspoon salt
Freshly ground black pepper (8 turns of the pepper mill)
¼ teaspoon hot red pepper flakes
1 bay leaf
¾ cup converted rice
2 tablespoons red wine vinegar
½ cup dry white wine
1 cup water
¼ cup chopped fresh parsley leaves
1 tablespoon tomato paste
1 zucchini (½ pound), cut into ¾-inch cubes

1. Heat the olive oil in a saucepan, add the onions, garlic, and sweet red pepper and sauté, stirring, for about 3 minutes. Do not brown.

2. Add the squid, cumin, oregano, salt, pepper, hot pepper flakes, bay leaf, rice, vinegar, wine, water, parsley, and tomato paste, bring to a boil, and cover the pan. Stir and simmer for 14 minutes.

3. Add the zucchini, stir, and cook, covered, for 5 minutes more.

YIELD: 4 servings.   CALORIES PER SERVING: 404.

PRESENTATION: Place each serving of the squid in a mold of about 2 cups in capacity. A deep soup plate might serve as the mold. Place each serving in the center of a plate with parsley sprigs or whole basil leaves positioned around it. Serve with a green salad on the side.

For a long time now, my summers have all been linked to the sunlight in East Hampton. On warm, clear days I venture out into Gardiners Bay to fish or to find shellfish for the evening meal. In recent years—although I never would have imagined it was possible—the summers have been even better than before, as my children bring their grandchildren to visit for days and weeks on end. This dish is named for one of those children, Larissa, born February 24, 1978, the first of my grandchildren. She loves bright colors, and Bay Scallops Larissa could win her appreciation for its looks alone.

BAY SCALLOPS LARISSA

3 ripe tomatoes (¾ pound)
24 snow pea pods (¼ pound)
2 tablespoons butter
4 tablespoons olive oil
2 teaspoons finely chopped garlic
⅓ cup finely chopped shallots
½ teaspoon salt
Freshly ground black pepper (6 turns of the pepper mill)
2 pounds bay scallops or sea scallops,
cut into halves or quarters
3 tablespoons chopped fresh coriander leaves

1. Drop the tomatoes in boiling water for 12 seconds to loosen the skin. Peel them and cut them in half. Squeeze the halves gently to extract the seeds. Chop the tomatoes. There should be about 1½ cups.

2. Trim off the ends of the pea pods. Drop them into boiling water to blanch them for 3 minutes. Drain them and coat them with 1 tablespoon of the butter. Set the pods aside.

3. Heat 3 tablespoons of the olive oil and the remaining tablespoon of the butter in a small saucepan. Add the garlic, shallots, tomatoes, salt, and 3 turns of the pepper mill. Cook for about 3 minutes.

4. Heat the remaining tablespoon of olive oil in a nonstick frying pan and add the scallops along with 3 turns of the pepper mill. Cook for about 2 minutes, stirring.

5. Transfer to individual dishes or a serving platter. Arrange the pea pods around the scallops. Pour the sauce over them. Sprinkle with coriander.

YIELD: 6 servings.   CALORIES PER SERVING: 268.

PRESENTATION: Mold Creole Rice (see recipe page 213) in a cup, such as a timbale or a demitasse cup, and place it in the middle of the plate. Place the scallops around it. Distribute the tomato sauce over the scallops (but not the rice). Place the coriander on top of the tomato sauce. Create another ring on the plate, by arranging the pea pods around the periphery of the dish, radiating out from the scallops.

This is another ecumenical sort of dish, Chinese with a French touch. The flavor of the soy sauce is softened and bound by the butter. The taste is rich and satisfying, although the amount of butter used to accomplish that richness is not excessive in my view.

BAY SCALLOPS WITH CORIANDER

3 tablespoons butter
½ pound large mushrooms
¼ cup chopped scallions
2 tablespoons dry sherry
1 pound bay scallops or sea scallops,
cut into halves or quarters
1 tablespoon grated fresh ginger
2 teaspoons dark soy sauce
2 tablespoons chopped fresh coriander leaves

1. Melt 1 tablespoon of the butter in a nonstick frying pan and sauté the mushrooms over high heat for about 2 minutes. Add the scallions and sauté briefly. Add the sherry, scallops, ginger, and soy sauce and cook briefly, about 1½ minutes.

2. Use a slotted spoon to remove the mushrooms and scallops. Swirl the remaining 2 tablespoons of butter into the pan juices.

3. Pour the pan juices over the scallops and sprinkle with the coriander. Serve with rice.

YIELD: 6 servings.   CALORIES PER SERVING: 129.

PRESENTATION: Serve with molded Creole Rice (see recipe page 213). Place the rice at the periphery of the plate and distribute the scallops around it. The dish can be accompanied by a salad.

Seviche, a cool and tangy preparation of raw seafood and vegetables, has gained enormously in popularity in recent years. As easy as the dish is to make, one finds badly done seviche with startling frequency. Some seviches, in fact, are most memorable for their lack of flavor. The trick is to get a good dose of lime juice into it to ensure the acidic flavor. And the olive oil needs to be added in just the right proportion so that the dish is not dry and has an appealing glaze to it. Perhaps most important, the correct fish should be chosen. It needs to be a firm fish that is at the height of its freshness. Sea bass, red snapper, lemon sole, black fish, salmon, or fluke will do well. It is possible to use one of these or a combination. What I've used in this instance is a delightful component of seviche, bay scallops, which turn out to provide the dish with a desirable resistance that can almost be described as crispiness.

SEVICHE OF BAY SCALLOPS

1 pound fresh bay scallops or sea scallops,
cut into halves or quarters
¼ cup fresh lime juice
¼ cup finely chopped red onion
½ teaspoon finely chopped garlic
1 or 2 teaspoons chopped hot or green pepper, to taste
½ cup peeled and seeded chopped ripe tomato
¼ teaspoon salt
Freshly ground black pepper (6 turns of the pepper mill)
¼ teaspoon ground cumin
1 tablespoon olive oil
¼ cup chopped fresh coriander and romaine leaves or
parsley leaves
4 leaves romaine lettuce

1. Place all ingredients, except for the coriander and romaine, in a bowl. Cover with plastic wrap and refrigerate for 6 hours.

2. When ready to serve, add the coriander and stir well. Serve on crisp romaine lettuce leaves.

YIELD: 4 servings.   CALORIES PER SERVING: 139.

PRESENTATION: Line medium-sized bowls with the lettuce leaves and spoon in the seviche. Tortillas make a nice accompaniment.

The term navarin suggests a stew, usually containing small pieces of veal and lamb surrounded by vegetables. It requires a lighter sauce than, say, a ragout. With the coming of nouvelle cuisine, the term has now extended to other delicate concoctions, including lobster or, as offered here, scallops.

NAVARIN DE COQUILLE ST. JACQUES

3 medium-sized carrots
2 large white turnips
2 small zucchini
2 tablespoons olive oil
¾ cup leek, cut into ¾-inch lengths
12 small white onions
1 teaspoon chopped garlic
2 ripe tomatoes (¾ pound), peeled, seeded,
and diced (1 cup)
2 tablespoons tomato paste
¼ cup dry white wine
1½ cups **fumet de poisson** *(fish stock, see recipe page 29)*
1 bay leaf
½ teaspoon dried thyme
3 tablespoons Pernod
½ teaspoon salt
Freshly ground black pepper (8 turns of the pepper mill)
2 pounds bay scallops or sea scallops,
cut into halves or quarters
4 tablespoons chopped fresh parsley leaves

1. Scrape the carrots and cut them into quarters. Then cut them into 1½-inch lengths. To give this dish a little more finesse, take a paring knife and round off each carrot piece so it looks like an olive or a football with squat ends. There should be ¾ cup. Do the same thing with the turnips and zucchini.

2. Heat 2 tablespoons of the olive oil in a frying pan. Add the leek, onions, garlic, carrots, and turnips. Cook over medium heat, stirring, until the onions and leek are wilted, about 2 minutes. Add the tomatoes, tomato paste, wine, fish stock, bay leaf, thyme, 1 tablespoon of the Pernod, salt, and pepper. Bring to a boil, cover, and simmer for about 15 minutes.

3. Add the zucchini and scallops and stir. Cover and cook for about 4 minutes more. Add the parsley and remaining Pernod. Serve with Croutons (see recipe page 264).

YIELD: 6 servings.   CALORIES PER SERVING: 286.

PRESENTATION: The dish requires no special arrangement, other than to be sure that the all the components of the navarin are distributed to each dish. It will be extremely attractive just as it falls. A sprinkling of fresh parsley makes a good last-minute addition. Serve the croutons on a side dish.

As much as I like virtually unadorned scallops and shrimp, if you asked me what most pleased me about this concoction, I would have to say it was the sauce. The mushrooms and red peppers, when put through a food processor, become the binding ingredients. The result, in this instance, is brilliant and deceptively rich looking.

RAGOUT OF SEA SCALLOPS AND SHRIMP WITH SAFFRON

2 tablespoons olive oil
¼ cup chopped shallots
½ pound mushrooms, washed and sliced (3 cups)
1 cup dry white wine
3 sweet red peppers (½ pound), seeded and cut in half
1 bay leaf
¼ teaspoon dried thyme
½ teaspoon salt
Freshly ground black pepper (8 turns of the pepper mill)
½ teaspoon saffron stems
1 tablespoon chopped garlic
1½ pounds sea scallops (cut in half if very large;
bay scallops can be substituted)
1 pound shrimp, peeled and deveined (30 to the pound)
¾ cup chopped scallions
½ teaspoon fennel seeds

1. Heat 1 tablespoon of the olive oil in a frying pan and add the shallots. Cook briefly. Add the mushrooms and cook for about 5 minutes over medium heat. Add the wine. Cook, reducing it to about 1½ cups.

2. Put the sweet peppers in a saucepan and cover them with water. Bring to a boil and simmer for 8 to 10 minutes, or until the peppers are tender. Drain.

3. Put the mushrooms and sweet peppers in a blender or food processor and blend to a fine purée. Transfer the purée to a saucepan. Add the bay leaf, thyme, ¼ teaspoon of salt, 4 turns of the pepper mill, and the saffron. Bring to a boil and simmer for 5 minutes.

4. Heat the remaining tablespoon of olive oil in a large nonstick frying pan. Add the garlic and cook briefly, stirring. Do not brown. Add the scallops and shrimp, ¼ teaspoon of the salt, and 4 turns of the pepper mill. Continue to cook over high heat, stirring, for about 2 minutes. Add the scallions, fennel seed, and mushroom and sweet pepper sauce. Cook for 3 to 4 minutes. Serve immediately.

YIELD: 6 servings.   CALORIES PER SERVING: 242.

PRESENTATION: Shape Creole Rice (see recipe page 213) in a mold and unmold it into the center of a plate. Surround the rice with the scallops and shrimp. At the edge of the plate, place small Parsleyed Cucumbers (see recipe page 225).

This is a basic recipe for cooking shrimp, and you will be asked to return to it from time to time in other recipes in this book when cooked shrimp is required.

POACHED SHRIMP FOR SALAD OR COCKTAIL

1½ pounds shrimp (about 30)
1 bay leaf
8 whole allspice
2 whole cloves
8 whole black peppercorns
¼ teaspoon hot red pepper flakes
1 celery stalk
4 sprigs fresh parsley

1. Combine all the ingredients in a saucepan and cover with water.
2. Bring the water to a boil and then turn off the heat. Let the shrimp cool in the liquid.
3. Peel and devein the shrimp. Strain the liquid and hold the shrimp in it, if necessary, until ready to serve.

YIELD: 6 servings.   CALORIES PER SERVING: 84.

This dish combines some traditional and new approaches. The oil and vinegar suggests a standard vinaigrette, but the sweetness added by the ginger is one of those additions frequently sought these days. And the marvelous avocado was virtually unknown in my childhood but is now a vital part of the cuisine.

SHRIMP AND AVOCADO WITH GINGER

1 medium-sized sweet red pepper
½ cup olive oil
½ cup red wine vinegar
1¼ pounds shrimp, peeled and deveined
½ cup chopped red onion
1 teaspoon salt
Freshly ground black pepper (10 turns of the pepper mill)
1 tablespoon chopped candied ginger
1 avocado (about 1 pound), peeled and sliced (1½ cups)
2 tablespoons chopped fresh dill

1. Cut the pepper in half and remove the seeds. Blanch it in boiling water for 2 minutes. Cool the pepper and slice it, crosswise, into strips.

2. Heat the olive oil and vinegar in a nonstick frying pan. Add the shrimp, onion, salt, ground pepper, and ginger. Cook the mixture, stirring, for 1 minute. Add the avocado and red pepper strips. Mix the ingredients well and transfer to individual plates. Sprinkle with dill. Serve immediately.

YIELD: 6 servings.   CALORIES PER SERVING: 329.

PRESENTATION: Place the shrimp in the center and arrange some of the avocado wedges so that they radiate out from the shrimp.

I remember how, at the Hôtel de Paris in Monte Carlo, an Indian chef was employed with a simple mission: to prepare the curried dishes on the menu. There was a lamb curry, of course, and a chicken curry. The French have admired curried dishes for centuries. The shrimp curry offered here is especially hot and will appeal to people who have been increasing their threshold of pain through practice on Szechuan food and the like.

SHRIMP INDIAN STYLE

1½ pounds fresh shrimp (24 to the pound)
1 tablespoon olive oil
¾ cup onions
1 tablespoon chopped garlic
2 tablespoons Oriental Curry Powder
(see recipe page 265)
½ teaspoon salt
¼ cup fresh lime juice
½ cup sour cream
1 cup plain yogurt
⅓ cup chopped fresh coriander leaves

1. Peel and devein the shrimp. Rinse well.

2. Heat the oil in a nonstick frying pan and add the onion. Cook briefly and add the garlic, shrimp, curry powder, and salt. Cook, stirring often, for about 3 minutes. Add the lime juice, sour cream, and yogurt. Gently bring the mixture to a boil, stirring. Sprinkle with the coriander.

YIELD: 6 servings.   CALORIES PER SERVING: 183.

PRESENTATION: Creole Rice (see recipe page 213), a mild dish with just the lightest zing offered by the lemon juice it contains, is the perfect foil for a hot dish such as these shrimp. Mold the rice by pressing it into a coffee cup and place it either in the center of the plate or to one side. The shrimp should radiate out from the rice. Spoon the sauce over the shrimp but not over the rice. The sauce will ultimately mix with the rice, but initially you want the colors to remain distinct. (A sprinkling of coriander over the rice is a good optional touch.)

As much as I like Chinese dishes, I often can't help adding French touches. In the following dish, for instance, the typically Chinese shrimp, ginger, and soy sauce is prepared in butter rather than oil. The calories will be roughly the same, but the butter provides a smoothness that might otherwise require the addition of cornstarch. I couldn't resist trying this combination of ingredients with tomatoes. Not terribly Chinese, of course, but the tomatoes offer some appropriate acidity as well as good color. My last French touch is to opt for dry white wine instead of sherry. All wrong in Chinese cooking, but all right by me.

SAUTÉED SHRIMP WITH BROCCOLI FLOWERETS AND GINGER

1 bunch broccoli
2 small, firm ripe tomatoes, preferably plum tomatoes (¼ pound)
2 tablespoons butter
1¼ pounds medium-sized shrimp, peeled and deveined
2 scallions, coarsely chopped (½ cup)
1 tablespoon chopped garlic
1 tablespoon ginger, sliced very thin and then chopped
Freshly ground black pepper (6 turns of the pepper mill)
⅛ teaspoon hot red pepper flakes
1 tablespoon light soy sauce
4 tablespoons dry white wine

1. Cut the broccoli flowerets (the flower with about an inch of stem) away from the main stem. At the base of each make an incision with a paring knife to ensure that the thicker part of the floweret will cook as quickly as the rest.

2. Drop the tomatoes into boiling water for 12 seconds. Remove the skin with a paring knife. Cut them in half and squeeze out the moisture and seeds. Cut the halves into 6 or 7 strips.

3. Blanch the broccoli in boiling water for 2 minutes. Drain.

4. Melt the butter in a frying pan and add the shrimp, scallions, garlic, ginger, tomatoes, black pepper, hot pepper flakes, and soy sauce. Sauté for about 2 minutes. Add the wine and broccoli and toss everything together. Serve immediately.

YIELD: 4 servings.   CALORIES PER SERVING: 223.

PRESENTATION: The dish looks fine simply transferred from the pan to the plates. To be more elaborate, place the broccoli in the center of the plate with the shrimp arranged around the periphery. If you feel the need for rice, mold it in a buttered coffee cup and place it in the center of the plate with the shrimp and vegetables arranged around it.

This rendition of sautéed shrimp has been influenced by at least three cuisines. The French-Italian influence is in the tomatoes, garlic, and olive oil. The Oriental influence is in the ginger and scallions. It turns out to be a memorable dish for two reasons: because it is so so spicy and so beautiful.

SAUTÉED SHRIMP WITH TOMATO SAUCE

1½ pounds large shrimp, about 15 to the pound
2 tablespoons olive oil
1 teaspoon chopped garlic
1½ cups diced, peeled and seeded ripe tomatoes
½ teaspoon salt
¼ teaspoon hot red pepper flakes
2 tablespoons finely chopped ginger
Freshly ground black pepper (6 turns of the pepper mill)
1 cup chopped scallions

1. Peel and devein the shrimp.
2. Heat 1 tablespoon of the oil in a frying pan and add the garlic. Cook briefly without browning the garlic. Add the tomatoes, salt, hot pepper flakes, and 1 tablespoon of the ginger. Cook, reducing the liquid, for 5 minutes. Set aside and keep warm.
3. Heat the remaining tablespoon of oil in a nonstick frying pan and add the shrimp and ground pepper. Sauté over high heat for 1 minute on each side.
4. Add the remaining ginger and the scallions. Blend well, cooking for 1 minute. Place the shrimp over the tomato mixture and serve.

YIELD: 6 servings.   CALORIES PER SERVING: 151.

PRESENTATION: Spoon the tomato mixture onto each plate. Shape Saffron Rice (see recipe page 216) in a mold and un-mold a serving of the rice in the center of each plate, on top of the sauce. Arrange 6 evenly spaced shrimp around the rice, radiating like spokes out from the center.

Sautéed shrimp show up often in this book because it is so fast and unfailingly good to eat. My aim over the years has been to keep finding new and appealing ways to prepare the shrimp. Only in recent years have I been adding one of the mainstays of French classic cuisine, capers. The Pernod in this recipe enhances the smoothness and the complexity of the dish's flavor. Just now, I think this must be my favorite approach to sautéed shrimp.

SAUTÉED SHRIMP WITH GARLIC AND CAPERS

2 tablespoons olive oil
1½ pounds shrimp, peeled and deveined
1 small dried hot pepper
½ teaspoon salt
Freshly ground black pepper (8 turns of the pepper mill)
2 tablespoons finely chopped garlic
¼ cup drained capers
¼ cup fresh lemon juice
1 tablespoon Pernod or Ricard
¼ cup finely chopped fresh parsley leaves

1. Heat the olive oil in a nonstick frying pan. Add the shrimp, hot pepper, salt, and pepper. Cook briefly without browning and add the garlic, capers, and lemon juice. Cook, stirring with a wooden spatula, for 2 minutes. Add the Pernod and parsley. Sauté for 1 minute more, being careful not to overcook the shrimp.

2. Remove to a serving platter or individual dishes and serve with rice.

YIELD: 8 servings.　　　CALORIES PER SERVING: 120.

PRESENTATION: Saffron Rice (see recipe page 216) goes well with this dish. It can be shaped in a mold and unmolded onto the center of an individual serving plate. Arrange the shrimp around the rice in a circle forming a neat, single row, with all the shrimp positioned in the same direction. If this is a main dish rather than an appetizer I would serve it with vegetables, such as sautéed yellow or red peppers, as a side dish.

The conventional Provençale dish weds tomato and garlic. The unusual element here is the addition of dill, which combines with the garlic in a delightful fashion, allowing a new, lighter flavor to emerge.

SAUTÉED SHRIMP WITH TOMATOES AND DILL

2 ripe tomatoes (about ¾ pound)
1 tablespoon olive oil
1¼ pounds shrimp, peeled and deveined
½ teaspoon salt
Freshly ground black pepper (about 6 turns of the pepper mill)
1 tablespoon chopped garlic
1 tablespoon butter
1 tablespoon chopped fresh dill

1. Peel the tomatoes by dropping them in boiling water for 12 seconds to loosen the skins. Remove the skin with a paring knife. Cut the tomatoes in half and squeeze them to extract the seeds. Chop the tomatoes coarsely.

2. Heat the oil in a nonstick frying pan. Add the shrimp, salt, and pepper and sauté for about 30 seconds on each side. Add the tomatoes, garlic, butter, and dill. Continue to cook, stirring, for 1 minute and serve immediately, perhaps with Curried Rice (see recipe page 214).

YIELD: 4 servings.   CALORIES PER SERVING: 182.

PRESENTATION: Unmold the Curried Rice in the center of each plate and surround it with the shrimp.

7

Poultry

In a sense, poultry is the heart of this book. Poultry provides the cook with every opportunity to display his or her skills. It is almost endlessly variable; it is as at home in haute cuisine as it is in peasant cuisine, and yet it is naturally very low in calories. My job in this chapter was to give poultry its rightful stage in a low-calorie approach. Thus in this flourish of recipes you will find chicken, turkey, duck, and Cornish game hen (but mostly chicken) prepared in ways intended to display all of poultry's virtues.

The traditional approaches in this chapter offer poultry in wine or vinegar sauces, for instance. And I have included an old family recipe for stuffing a chicken with what is in essence a sandwich of parsley and chopped liver. In another recipe, I have taken the justly renowned creamy Chicken Vernonique and made it pleasingly light so that the characteristic flavor of the grapes and vermouth is still there but the cream is not. I have rolled and stuffed chicken as if it were veal and offered sliced turkey breast that looks like veal.

Skinless chicken breasts are often used in this chapter because they offer so many possibilities for embellishment, with virtually no fat. Other recipes use chicken that has its skin still intact. My feeling is that the skin often aids in flavoring the chicken and in keeping it moist. Once it is cooked, however, feel free to remove the skin—and with it a great many calories. For that matter, if you are especially weight conscious, many of these dishes can be cooked without the skin and the calorie counts for the recipes illustrate how many calories can be saved when the skin plays no part in the cooking process.

Many cooks, hurriedly attempting to prepare something satisfying for guests or the family, will roast a chicken but, for lack of time, neglect to stuff it. I describe here a roast chicken with perhaps the fastest stuffing on earth. I take no credit for its invention: The stuffing was a favorite of my mother's. It involves making what is in essence a French bread sandwich of parsley and chopped liver and thrusting it into the cavity of the chicken.

ROAST CHICKEN WITH PARSLEYED FRENCH BREAD

1 3-pound chicken
1 end of a French bread loaf, about 5 inches long and 2 inches in diameter
1 garlic clove, peeled
4 tablespoons chopped fresh parsley leaves
1 chicken liver, finely chopped
Freshly ground black pepper (8 turns of the pepper mill)
½ teaspoon salt
1 tablespoon vegetable oil
1 whole onion, peeled
1 tablespoon butter, in pieces
½ cup water

1. Preheat the oven to 425 degrees.

2. Rub the crust of the bread with the garlic. Slice the bread as for a sandwich.

3. Place the parsley and liver in a mixing bowl along with half the pepper and salt. Mix it well and place half of the mixture in the center of the bread, like a sandwich. Smear as much of the mixture on the outside of the bread as possible. Push the bread all the way into the cavity of the chicken along with the remaining liver mixture. Truss the chicken.

4. Sprinkle the chicken with the remaining salt and pepper. Rub it with 1 tablespoon of vegetable oil. Place the chicken on one side in a small roasting pan, with the onion, neck, and gizzard alongside it.

5. Place the chicken in the oven to roast for 20 minutes. Turn on the other side and roast for another 20 minutes. Place the chicken on its back, baste it, and roast it for 10 minutes, basting occasionally.

6. Take the chicken out of the oven. Pour off all the fat in the roasting pan and add the butter and water and scrape the bottom of the pan to dissolve adhering solid particles. Return the chicken to

the oven to roast for 10 minutes longer. Baste, moistening the stuffing in the cavity at the same time.

7. Remove the chicken from the oven, discard the trussing string, and cover the chicken loosely with foil. Let it rest for 10 minutes before carving and serving with the stuffing and pan gravy. To diminish the calories considerably, remove the chicken skin before serving.

YIELD: 4 servings.

CALORIES PER SERVING:
529 cooked and served with the skin.

PRESENTATION: Slice the breast and the dark meat thinly. Place a portion of stuffing in the center of each plate and a slice of light and of dark meat on top of the stuffing. Spoon the pan gravy over and around the meat. Serve the chicken with several string beans radiating away from the slices and half a broiled tomato toward the periphery of the plate.

People are much more adventurous these days, thank goodness. This baked chicken is unusual and contemporary, in the sense that it requires some daring to give it a try.

BAKED CHICKEN WITH GREEN OLIVES AND CORIANDER MOROCCAN STYLE

1 tablespoon olive oil
1 3½-pound chicken, cut into 4 pieces
½ teaspoon salt
Freshly ground black pepper (8 turns of the pepper mill)
1 tablespoon grated fresh ginger
¼ teaspoon saffron stems
¼ teaspoon ground tumeric
1 teaspoon ground cumin
½ teaspoon paprika
½ cup grated onion
1 tablespoon chopped garlic
½ cup chopped fresh coriander leaves
½ cup chopped fresh parsley leaves
1 cup chopped pitted green olives
¼ cup fresh lemon juice

1. Heat the olive oil in a large skillet with a cover. Sprinkle the chicken with salt and pepper. Put the pieces in the skillet to brown lightly on both sides, a total of about 10 minutes.

2. Pour 2 cups of water into the skillet and add all the ingredients except the olives and lemon juice. Cover and simmer for 30 minutes.

3. Meanwhile, place the olives in a saucepan and cover them with water. Bring to a boil and cook for 5 minutes, then drain.

4. Add the olives and lemon juice to the pan with the chicken and continue to cook for about 15 minutes more, or until the chicken is very tender. Reduce the liquid over high heat until it is a thick gravy.

YIELD: 4 servings.   CALORIES PER SERVING:
                               503 cooked with the skin;
                               338 cooked without the skin.

PRESENTATION: Shape a portion of Saffron Rice (see recipe page 216) in a mold and place toward the top of the plate. Place a piece of chicken directly below it, touching the rice. In the bare areas, between the chicken and rice, place 2 small portions of String Beans with Garlic (see recipe page 231).

If ordinary broiled chicken has begun to lose its allure for you, this dish might just bring broiled chicken back to your table. It is a marinated chicken that uses lemon, oil, and vinegar to permeate it with tanginess.

BROILED CHICKEN WITH LEMON

1 3½-pound chicken, split in half for broiling
½ teaspoon salt
Freshly ground black pepper (6 turns of the pepper mill)
½ teaspoon dried thyme, or 2 sprigs fresh thyme
1 cup sliced white onions
½ cup thinly sliced carrots
1 bay leaf cut in half
2 lemons
2 tablespoons olive oil
2 tablespoons red wine vinegar

1. Between sheets of plastic wrap, pound the chicken skin side up to flatten it slightly without crushing it. Sprinkle both sides with salt, pepper, and thyme.

2. Scatter the onions onto the bottom of a shallow roasting dish. Do the same with the carrots. Rest the chicken on the bed of onions and carrots, skin side up. Place half a bay leaf under each piece.

3. Slice one of the lemons very thinly and arrange the slices over the chicken. Mix the oil and vinegar and brush the mixture over the lemon and chicken. Cover with foil and marinate for 3 to 4 hours in the refrigerator.

4. Preheat the oven to 450 degrees. Preheat the broiler.

5. Remove the lemon slices from the chicken but do not discard them. Place the chicken in a separate roasting pan. Baste it with the marinade and place it under the broiler to brown. Turn the chicken and brown it on the other side, basting with the accumulated marinade and juices. Allow 10 minutes for each side.

6. Return the chicken with any marinade in the pan to the original shallow baking dish, skin side up. Place the lemon slices back on the chicken and baste it. Turn off the broiler and bake the chicken in the oven for 25 to 30 minutes. After it has been baking for 10 minutes, sprinkle the chicken with the juice of the remaining lemon.

YIELD: 4 servings.   CALORIES PER SERVING:
                                504 cooked with the skin;
                                338 cooked without the skin.

PRESENTATION: Cut the chicken into 4 pieces. Position each piece on a serving plate over a bed of onions and carrots. On either side of the chicken place a Parsleyed Potato (see recipe page 212).

Although to some people poached chicken is boring, I find them misguided. Prepared properly and displayed beautifully, it bursts with identifiable flavors of the ingredients and it looks fine, too. The wrinkle here is the addition of the small shaped pasta known as orzo.

POACHED CHICKEN WITH VEGETABLES AND ORZO

3 parsnips
3 medium-sized turnips
2 medium-sized carrots
1 whole leek
2 celery stalks
1 3-pound chicken
3 cups water
3 cups chicken stock (see recipe page 30)
1 teaspoon salt
Freshly ground black pepper (6 turns of the pepper mill)
¼ cup orzo

1. Scrape and clean the parsnips, turnips, and carrots. Wash the leek and celery. Cut each of the vegetables into quarters lengthwise. Then cut those pieces into 1½-inch lengths. (More time-consuming, but more elegant, too, is to shape the vegetables with a paring knife so that they are oblong, like footballs.)

2. Truss the chicken and put it in a medium-sized kettle. Cover the chicken with water and bring the water to a boil. Remove the chicken from the kettle. Pour off the water.

3. Return the chicken to the kettle and add the stock, salt, and pepper. Simmer for 20 minutes. Add the vegetables and simmer for 10 minutes. Add the orzo and cook until the chicken is tender, about 10 more minutes. Skim away the fat from the surface.

4. Remove the chicken and untruss it. Cut it into serving pieces.

YIELD: 4 servings.

CALORIES PER SERVING:
575 cooked with the skin;
416 cooked without the skin.

PRESENTATION: There are two options. One is to serve the broth alone as a first course, followed by the chicken, which is placed in the center of a plate and surrounded by the vegetables. The second option is to serve the chicken with its broth and the vegetables all together in a deep soup plate. The key to making this simple dish look beautiful is a gorgeous soup plate. It is a complete meal.

Here is one more use of skinless chicken. But what a distinctive blast of flavor it has! The lemon sauce, so typical in Greece, has been thickened by egg and lemon juice.

POACHED CHICKEN WITH LEMON SAUCE

1 3-pound chicken, skinned and trussed
½ teaspoon salt
4 whole black peppercorns
4 cups chicken stock (see recipe page 30)
1 bay leaf
½ teaspoon dried thyme, or 1 sprig fresh thyme
½ cup coarsely chopped carrot
½ cup coarsely chopped onion
1 celery stalk
2 sprigs fresh parsley
2 teaspoons cornstarch
1 tablespoon water
2 eggs
¼ cup fresh lemon juice
2 tablespoons chopped fresh parsley leaves

1. Place the chicken in a tightly covered kettle or saucepan along with the salt, peppercorns, stock, bay leaf, thyme, carrot, onion, celery, and parsley. Bring to a boil and simmer for 35 minutes, turning the chicken in the kettle 3 times.

2. Remove the chicken. Strain the broth into a saucepan and skim away the fat. Return the chicken to the kettle and cover to keep it warm.

3. Reduce the broth to 1½ cups. Blend the cornstarch in the tablespoon of water. Add the mixture to the broth and mix well.

4. Beat the eggs in a bowl until they are a lemon color. Add the lemon juice, while whipping. Turn off the heat under the saucepan and add the egg mixture to the sauce, stirring constantly with a whisk.

5. Untruss the chicken. Remove its skin, except for that around the wings. Garnish with parsley.

YIELD: 4 servings.　　　　CALORIES PER SERVING: 311.

PRESENTATION:　Serve the chicken with buttered and parsleyed orzo and Glazed Carrots (see recipe page 223). Place 2 pieces of chicken, one light and one dark, toward the top of the plate. Beneath it in the center place a portion of orzo flanked by a portion of carrots on either side.

One of the better dishes at the Pavillon when I was that deceased restaurant's executive chef was simply chicken stew, unlikely as it may seem. This stew is essentially chicken poached in a vegetable broth, with the vegetables puréed later to become a thickening agent for the sauce. Because the vegetables are used in this fashion, the recipe is in keeping with current thinking, which shuns flour-based sauces and frequently employs vegetables in sauces in just this way. The result is a very thick, nutritious sauce for the chicken. The dish, perhaps surprisingly, will ultimately resemble an Irish stew.

CHICKEN STEW

1 3-pound chicken, cut into 10 serving pieces
3 cups chopped endives or cabbage
1 cup parsnips cut into ½-inch cubes
1 cup carrots cut into ½-inch cubes
1 cup rutabaga cut into ½-inch cubes
1 cup coarsely chopped onions
1 tablespoon chopped garlic
1 bay leaf
½ teaspoon dried thyme
1½ cups chicken stock (see recipe page 30)
½ cup dry white wine
¼ cup chopped fresh parsley leaves or coriander leaves, or
1 tablespoon chopped fresh tarragon
½ teaspoon salt
Freshly ground black pepper (6 turns of the pepper mill)

1. Put the chicken pieces in a large, heavy saucepan. Add the endives, parsnips, carrots, rutabaga, onions, garlic, bay leaf, thyme, chicken stock, wine, salt, and pepper.

2. Bring the mixture to a boil, cover, and simmer for 25 minutes. Remove fat from the surface occasionally.

3. Remove the chicken from the pan and pour the vegetable mixture into a food mill or food processor. Purée the vegetables coarsely so the mixture retains its variations in color.

4. Return the sauce to the pan, along with the chicken. Bring it back to a boil, and simmer the chicken for 15 minutes. Add the parsley and serve.

YIELD: 4 servings.   CALORIES PER SERVING:
                              486 cooked with the skin;
                              327 cooked without the skin.

NOTE: If desired, the skin can be removed after cooking in this and many other chicken dishes.

PRESENTATION: Place the chicken, mixing white and dark, in the center of a dish. Spoon the sauce amply over it. This is handsome enough and satisfying enough all by itself. But, if you like, add 2 or 3 small boiled potatoes to the plate. Serve the chicken with Worcestershire sauce on the side.

Very often, creative cooking involves the addition of a single unusual ingredient that turns a familiar dish into something attractively new. In this instance, a chicken au pot is transformed by the simple addition of fresh coriander. The chicken is cooked with the skin, so there will be some fat in the dish; be sure to skim it away. To diminish the calories still further remove the chicken's skin before serving. A variation on this recipe is to add ¼ cup of converted rice along with the vegetables. This will add about 42 calories to each serving.

NAVARIN OF CHICKEN WITH CORIANDER

1 tablespoon butter
1 3½-pound chicken, cut into 10 serving pieces
½ teaspoon salt
Freshly ground black pepper (8 turns of the pepper mill)
2 teaspoons ground coriander
1 cup chopped onions
1 tablespoon chopped garlic
½ cup dry white wine
½ cup chicken stock (see recipe page 30) or water
4 carrots (¾ pound), scraped and cut into ½-inch cubes (about 1½ cups)
3 white turnips (¾ pound), trimmed and cut into ½-inch cubes (1½ cups)
1 dried hot pepper
1 bay leaf
½ teaspoon dried thyme
4 leeks, most of the green part removed, cut into ½-inch cubes (about 1½ cups)
¼ cup chopped fresh coriander leaves

1. Melt the butter in a large saucepan or skillet over low heat. Sprinkle the chicken with salt and pepper and put it in the pot. Add the ground coriander, onions, and garlic. Stir often, cooking for 10 minutes. Do not allow to brown.

2. Add the wine, chicken stock, carrots, turnips, hot pepper, bay leaf, and thyme. Bring to a boil and simmer, tightly covered.

3. After 20 minutes, add the leeks. Simmer, uncovered, for 10 minutes more. Skim off any fat that appears on top. Serve hot, garnished with the chopped coriander.

YIELD: 4 servings.

CALORIES PER SERVING:
552 cooked with the skin;
386 cooked without the skin.

PRESENTATION: Place 2 or 3 chicken pieces in the center of each plate, mixing light and dark meat. Spoon the vegetables around the chicken and sprinkle with fresh chopped coriander.

The key to the success of this dish is in the unusual measure of cooking it in two stages. You broil the chicken first to crisp the skin and burn off most of its fat. Then you bake it briefly with the mustard and bread crumbs. If you put those ingredients on the chicken any earlier than this recipe suggests, they will burn.

GRILLED CHICKEN WITH MUSTARD

1 3-pound chicken, split for broiling
Freshly ground black pepper (8 turns of the pepper mill)
½ teaspoon dried thyme
1 tablespoon vegetable oil
3 tablespoons Dijon mustard
1 tablespoon red wine vinegar
4 tablespoons fresh bread crumbs

1. Preheat the broiler.

2. Sprinkle the chicken with pepper and thyme and brush it all over with oil.

3. Place the chicken skin side up in a broiling pan, 4 to 5 inches from the source of the broiler's heat for 4 or 5 minutes, or until it is golden brown. Turn the chicken and continuing broiling for the same length of time.

4. Blend the mustard with the vinegar. Brush both sides of the chicken and sprinkle it evenly with the bread crumbs.

5. Turn the oven temperature to 400 degrees and place the chicken on the bottom shelf of the oven to bake for 15 to 20 minutes.

YIELD: 4 servings.

CALORIES PER SERVING:
403 cooked with the skin;
261 cooked without the skin.

PRESENTATION: Serve the chicken with Zucchini Bordelaise (see recipe page 233). Place a piece of white meat and a piece of dark meat toward the top of the plate. In the center, below the chicken, place a serving of zucchini.

In line with my current inclinations, I prepared this chicken curry without cream, which I almost always used in the past as a binder for curry sauces. Here, I've added mango to the recipe to give the sauce a firmer texture. It is a very hot curry indeed, and you may want to use a little less curry powder.

FRICASSEE OF CURRIED CHICKEN

1 3-pound chicken, cut into 10 serving pieces
1 teaspoon butter
½ teaspoon salt
2 tablespoons Oriental Curry Powder
(see recipe page 265)
1 cup chopped onions
1 teaspoon chopped garlic
½ cup finely chopped celery
1 bay leaf
1½ cups peeled and diced tart green apple
1 small banana, diced
½ cup chopped mango (the fruit should be firm,
not overripe)
1 tablespoon tomato paste
1 cup chicken stock (see recipe page 30)
12 fresh mint leaves for garnish

1. Remove all the excess fat from the chicken.

2. Melt the butter in a large nonstick frying pan and add the chicken. Sprinkle the chicken with salt and curry powder. Sauté, stirring, for about 3 minutes. Add the onions, garlic, celery, and bay leaf. Cook, stirring, for another 3 minutes.

3. Add the apple, banana, mango, tomato paste, and chicken stock. Cover and cook for about 20 minutes. Uncover and cook for 15 minutes more. Skim off all fat. Serve with rice.

YIELD: 4 servings.   CALORIES PER SERVING:
                                  461 cooked with the skin;
                                  319 cooked without the skin.

PRESENTATION: Shape Creole Rice (see recipe page 213) in a mold and unmold it in the center of a plate. Mixing dark and light pieces, place the chicken pieces around the rice toward the edge of the plate. Spoon the sauce over the chicken. Place 3 mint leaves between the pieces of chicken, radiating out from the rice like spokes.

Sometimes, to feel that they have exercised their cooking skills sufficiently, people seem to want more complexity of a dish than the dish truly needs. The virtue of simplicity is demonstrated by this fast and extremely flavorful chicken recipe. A combination of garlic and lemon juice works beautifully to give it a spark. The sauce, a reduction of wine, stock, lemon juice, and natural juices, is meant only to cover the chicken, not to submerge it.

FRICASSEE OF CHICKEN IN WHITE WINE WITH MUSHROOMS

2 tablespoons olive oil
1 3-pound chicken, cut into 10 serving pieces
½ teaspoon salt
Freshly ground black pepper (6 turns of the pepper mill)
½ pound small button mushrooms
1 tablespoon finely chopped garlic
½ cup dry white wine
¼ cup chicken stock (see recipe page 30)
Juice of 1 lemon
4 tablespoons finely chopped fresh Italian parsley leaves

1. Heat the oil in a heavy skillet. Sprinkle the chicken with salt and pepper. Put the chicken in the skillet in one layer and skin down. Cook, uncovered, until brown, about 10 minutes. Add the mushrooms.

2. Turn the chicken pieces and cook for another 5 minutes.

3. Remove all the fat from the skillet. With the chicken in the skillet, add the garlic and stir. Add the wine and stock. Bring to a boil, scraping the bottom of the pan with a wooden spatula to dissolve the solid particles. Add the lemon juice. Sprinkle the chicken with parsley. Cover and cook for 5 minutes. You want about ½ cup of liquid. If there is more than that in the pan, reduce it over high heat.

YIELD: 4 servings.   CALORIES PER SERVING:
                             441 cooked with the skin;
                             298 cooked without the skin.

PRESENTATION: Serve with Steamed Broccoli (see recipe page 220). Place 2 or 3 pieces of chicken toward the top of each plate. Below the chicken, arrange the broccoli in a fan.

Almost always in fine cooking, dry wine is better than sweet. It enhances the flavor of a dish immeasurably without dominating it. There are some exceptions, of course. I've chosen to use a Sauternes here to give a desired sweetness, without using any sugar. Sweetness is a welcome characteristic, after all, in poultry such as duck and in game birds. The ricotta is a surrogate for cream. It binds, colors, and enriches the sauce while adding very little in calories.

SAUTÉED CHICKEN IN SAUTERNES

1 3-pound chicken, cut into 10 servings pieces
½ teaspoon salt
Freshly ground black pepper (6 turns of the pepper mill)
1 tablespoon butter
1 cup finely chopped onions
½ teaspoon chopped garlic
½ pound mushrooms, sliced
¾ cup wine, Sauternes or Graves
1 bay leaf
½ teaspoon dried thyme
¼ cup ricotta

1. Sprinkle the chicken with salt and pepper.

2. Melt the butter in a heavy skillet and add the chicken pieces skin side down. Add the onions and garlic. Lightly brown the chicken over moderate heat for about 5 minutes. Stir while cooking. Turn the pieces, add the mushrooms, and cook for 5 minutes more, while stirring. Pour off all fat.

3. Add the wine, bay leaf, and thyme. Cover and simmer for 25 minutes. Remove the fat.

4. Transfer the chicken to another skillet. Remove the bay leaf and add the ricotta to the sauce. Then purée the mixture in a blender or food processor. Pour the sauce over the chicken. Heat the sauce and chicken through.

YIELD: 4 servings.

CALORIES PER SERVING:
438 cooked with the skin;
296 cooked without the skin.

PRESENTATION: In the center of the plate, place a small mound of Noodles with Zucchini and Basil (see recipe page 209) and arrange 2 or 3 chicken pieces around the noodles. Spoon the sauce generously over the chicken but not over the noodles.

The term Provençale will show up several times in this book. The reason, beyond the fact that I like this traditional combination of flavors from Provence enormously, is that a dish done in this fashion never needs to be heavy. Provençale requires tomatoes and garlic. After that, it is open to some creativity.

SAUTÉED CHICKEN PROVENÇALE

1 3-pound chicken, cut into 10 serving pieces
1 teaspoon salt
Freshly ground black pepper (6 turns of the pepper mill)
2 tablespoons olive oil
1 tablespoon chopped garlic
¼ cup chopped onion
1 teaspoon dried rosemary
½ teaspoon dried thyme
½ pound small mushrooms
1 cup diced, peeled and seeded ripe tomatoes
¼ cup dry white wine
¼ cup chicken stock (see recipe page 30)
4 tablespoons chopped fresh parsley leaves or basil leaves

1. Sprinkle the chicken with salt and pepper.

2. Heat the oil in a heavy skillet and add the chicken skin side down. Cook for 8 to 10 minutes, or until it is golden brown. Turn the pieces. Add the garlic, onion, rosemary, thyme, and mushrooms. Cook, stirring, for 5 minutes.

3. Pour off the fat in the pan and add the tomatoes, wine, and chicken stock. Scrape the bottom of the pan with a wooden spatula to dissolve the solids. Simmer, uncovered, for 10 minutes. Thicken the sauce by reducing it over high heat briefly. Add the parsley or basil and serve.

YIELD: 4 servings.

CALORIES PER SERVING:
453 cooked with the skin;
311 cooked without the skin.

PRESENTATION: This dish is especially attractive served with artichoke bottoms filled with Watercress Purée (see recipe page 233). Place 2 or 3 chicken pieces in the center of a dish, with 2 artichoke bottoms, one above the chicken and one below it.

Normally, this recipe, like the chicken au vinaigre, calls for a great deal more butter, four times as much butter, as a matter of fact. I found that cutting down on the butter creates a distinctly different dish, certainly less rich, but still extraordinarily flavorful. It is fast and simple.

CHICKEN SAUTÉED WITH MUSHROOMS

1 3-pound chicken, cut into 10 serving pieces
1 teaspoon salt
Freshly ground black pepper (about 8 turns of the pepper mill)
1 tablespoon olive oil
2 tablespoons butter
¼ cup finely chopped onion
1 tablespoon chopped garlic
1 tablespoon dried rosemary
2 tablespoons chopped shallots
¾ pound mushrooms, cut in half
¼ cup dry vermouth
2 tablespoons fresh lemon juice
4 tablespoons chopped fresh parsley leaves

1. Sprinkle the chicken with salt and pepper.

2. Heat the oil in a nonstick skillet. Add the chicken pieces, turning them frequently, and cook until golden brown, about 10 minutes. Remove the chicken and discard the oil.

3. Melt 1 tablespoon of the butter in the skillet. Return the chicken to it and add the onion, garlic, rosemary, shallots, and mushrooms. Cook, stirring, for 5 minutes.

4. Add the vermouth and lemon juice and cook for 5 minutes, stirring to dissolve particles adhering to the pan. Add the remaining butter and parsley. Stir to blend and serve.

YIELD: 4 servings.

CALORIES PER SERVING:
487 cooked with the skin;
345 cooked without the skin.

PRESENTATION: Serve with molded rice; any of the rice preparations suggested in this book will do. Among the suggested vegetables: Glazed Carrots or Melange of Vegetables (see recipes pages 223 and 234). On the plate, the chicken pieces, about 2 per serving, should be arranged in the center with the rice at the bottom of the plate and the vegetables arranged along the periphery of the plate above the chicken. The sauce, no more than 2 tablespoons per serving, should be spooned over the chicken.

Poulet au vinaigre has been around in Burgundy forever. Usually, it is a good deal richer than this. Here, however, the addition of only a single tablespoon of butter to soften the quick vinegar-based sauce provides sufficient smoothness to suit modern tastes. The tangy vinegar sauce is one you'll want to master for other dishes, too (lean pork chops come to mind), because it adds so much in zest and so little in calories.

CHICKEN SAUTÉ AU VINAIGRE

2 tablespoons butter
1 sprig fresh thyme
1 bay leaf
1 3-pound chicken, cut into 10 serving pieces
1 teaspoon salt
Freshly ground black pepper (8 turns of the pepper mill)
4 whole garlic cloves, peeled
½ cup wine red vinegar
½ cup chicken stock (see recipe page 30)
2 tablespoons tomato paste
¼ cup chopped fresh parsley leaves

1. Melt 1 tablespoon of the butter in a heavy-bottomed skillet. Add the thyme, bay leaf, and then the chicken, skin side down. Add the salt, pepper, and garlic. Sauté the chicken, turning the pieces often, for about 10 minutes.

2. Pour off the fat. Add the vinegar, stirring to dissolve the brown particles adhering to the bottom of the skillet. Add the stock and tomato paste. Bring to a boil, reduce the heat, cover, and cook for 10 minutes. Add the remaining butter and the parsley. Stir to make sure the pieces are well coated. Serve.

YIELD: 4 servings.

CALORIES PER SERVING:
411 cooked with the skin;
269 cooked without the skin.

PRESENTATION: Serve with molded rice at the bottom of the plate and the chicken pieces fanning out from the rice, with a brightly colored vegetable, such as pea pods or a broiled tomato, arranged around the periphery.

In my restaurant days I used to make a paupiette de veau, a veal bird, in which the veal was stuffed with mushrooms and spinach. These days the cost of veal has me thinking about chicken breasts instead. Chicken breasts are low in calories and as adaptable as veal. And poor veal will ruin this dish, but chicken breasts are almost foolproof.

ROLLATINE OF CHICKEN

¾ pound fresh spinach
¼ pound mushrooms
3 tablespoons butter
1 cup chopped onions
2 teaspoons chopped garlic
2 teaspoons salt
Freshly ground black pepper (8 turns of the pepper mill)
3 whole skinless and boneless chicken breasts
(about 1¾ pounds total weight)
½ cup finely chopped carrots
½ cup finely chopped celery
½ cup dry white wine
½ cup chicken stock (see recipe page 30)
½ cup whole, peeled and cored tomatoes (fresh or canned)
1 bay leaf
1½ teaspoons dried thyme

1. Pick over the spinach and discard any tough stems. Wash and rinse.

2. Slice the mushrooms and coarsely chop them. Set aside. There should be about 1¾ cups.

3. Melt 1 tablespoon of the butter in a skillet. Add ½ cup of the onions, 1 teaspoon of the garlic, and ½ cup of the chopped mushrooms. Cook for 2 minutes and add the spinach, ½ teaspoon of the salt, and 3 turns of the pepper mill. Cook over high heat while stirring for about 5 minutes, by which time all the moisture should have evaporated. Set aside and cool.

4. Split each chicken breast into halves. Trim away and discard any fat or membranes. Pound lightly with a meat pounder or cleaver on a flat surface. Spoon an equal amount of the filling down the center of each breast half.

5. Bring up the edges of the breast, folding the edges over to enclose the filling and make a package. Tie each bundle in two places with string.

6. Melt the remaining butter in a skillet large enough to hold all the chicken and brown them all over, about 8 minutes.

7. Remove the chicken and add the remaining onions, mushrooms, and garlic. Cook briefly and add the carrots and celery. Stirring, cook for 3 to 4 minutes. Return the chicken rolls to the pan. Add the wine, stock, tomatoes, bay leaf, thyme, and remaining salt and pepper. Bring to a boil, cover, and cook for 15 minutes, or until the chicken is tender.

8. Remove the chicken rolls and reduce the sauce by half. Discard the strings. Spoon the sauce over the chicken and serve hot, perhaps with rice.

YIELD: 6 servings.   CALORIES PER SERVING: 251.

PRESENTATION: Place a single rollatine of chicken in the center of the plate, then create a pattern of vegetables around it. It is attractive, for instance, to alternate asparagus tips radiating out of the chicken with Glazed Carrots (see recipe page 223). The sauce, about 2 or 3 tablespoons per serving, should go over the chicken only, but it will tend to merge with the vegetables.

When chicken is cooked without its skin, it has a tendency to dry out. This tendency is countered in a number of ways. One of them, of course, is to use a lot of sauce. By steaming stuffed breasts of chicken, you manage to keep the meat moist from the start. This dish is one of those especially suited to advance preparation. Prepare the chicken but do not steam it. Prepare the sauce until the last 5-minute stage of cooking and put it aside. Then when you are just about ready to serve the dish, add the tomatoes and lemon juice to the saucepan with the sauce in it. Start the water boiling under the chicken. Cook both for 5 minutes, and you're set.

STEAMED CHICKEN BREASTS DUXELLE

2 whole skinless and boneless chicken breasts, split
(1¼ pounds total weight)
Freshly ground black pepper (8 turns of the pepper mill)
2 tablespoons butter
½ cup chopped onion
1½ teaspoons chopped garlic
½ pound mushrooms, finely chopped (2 cups)
½ teaspoon salt
Juice of 1 lemon
3 tablespoons chopped fresh parsley leaves
⅓ cup chopped scallions
¼ cup chicken stock (see recipe page 30)
2 cups plum tomatoes cut into ¼-inch cubes

1. Pound the breasts between layers of a plastic wrap until they are very thin. Sprinkle with the pepper on both sides, 6 turns of the mill in all.

2. Melt 1 tablespoon of the butter in a saucepan and sauté the onion and ½ teaspoon of the garlic briefly. Do not brown. Add the mushrooms, ¼ teaspoon of the salt, 2 turns of the pepper mill, and half the lemon juice. Cook, stirring, until all the moisture has evaporated. Transfer the mixture to a plate and let it cool. Blend in 1 tablespoon of the parsley.

3. Place the stuffing in even amounts onto the center of each breast. Fold the ends up over the stuffing and then the sides so that it is sealed in like a box.

4. Melt 1 tablespoon of the butter in a saucepan and add the remaining garlic and the scallions. Sauté briefly without browning. Add the chicken stock. Reduce until most of the liquid has evaporated and just the butter is bubbling. Add the tomatoes and ¼ tea-

spoon of the salt and the remaining lemon juice. Stir lightly so as not to break the tomato chunks. After 5 minutes, remove the sauce from the heat and add 1 tablespoon of the chopped parsley.

5. Place the chicken in a steamer. When the water begins to boil, cover and steam for 5 minutes. Serve with the sauce and the remaining parsley as a garnish.

YIELD: 4 servings.   CALORIES PER SERVING: 270.

PRESENTATION: Spoon the sauce on two sides of the chicken. Place buttered fine noodles on the two remaining sides. On top of each piece of chicken, place a small mound of chopped parsley. This is a bright dish that looks remarkably good in the sunlight of an outdoor luncheon.

Often a breast of chicken that has been boned has also been skinned. Generally, that's fine with me. In this recipe, however, the skin must be left on the boneless breast. The reason is that it helps to hold the package for stuffing together and it keeps the chicken moist. After the breasts are cooked, if you like, you can remove the skin. Liver chopped into the stuffing is used here instead of the fattier sausage meat I would ordinarily be inclined to use.

CHICKEN BREASTS STUFFED WITH MUSHROOMS AND CHICKEN LIVERS

*4 boneless chicken breast halves, with skin
(about 6 ounces each)
Freshly ground black pepper (10 turns of the pepper mill)
2 tablespoons butter
½ cup chopped onion
1 cup coarsely chopped mushrooms
2 chicken livers, coarsely chopped (about ¼ cup)
½ teaspoon salt
1 slice white bread, cut into small cubes (¾ cup)
¼ cup water
2 tablespoons chopped fresh parsley leaves
2 tablespoons chopped fresh basil leaves (if not fresh use none)
1 tablespoon olive oil
1 teaspoon chopped garlic
1 large ripe tomato, cut into ¼-inch cubes
1 small zucchini, cut into ¼-inch cubes
¼ teaspoon dried thyme
¼ cup dry white wine
¼ cup chicken stock (see recipe page 30)
Fresh basil leaves sliced broadly or chopped
parsley leaves for garnish*

1. Remove the flap of meat in the center of each breast called the fillet. Butterfly the breast by slicing on the bias for about ¾ of an inch and open the breast up, like the pages of a book. Pound each breast slightly to flatten it further. Pound each fillet lightly. Pepper each piece of chicken, about 2 turns of the pepper mill altogether.

2. Melt 1 tablespoon of the butter in a saucepan and sauté ¼ cup of the onion briefly. Add ½ cup of the mushrooms and continue sautéing, stirring, until the vegetables are wilted but not yet brown. Add the chicken livers, ¼ teaspoon of salt, and 4 turns of the pepper mill. Sauté for another couple of minutes. Stir in the bread cubes. Add the water and blend. Add the chopped parsley and basil and mix well.

3. Place a quarter of the stuffing in the center of each breast. Pat it

down lightly. Place the fillet over each mound of stuffing. Fold the skin at the head of the breast toward the center. Fold each side of the breast toward the center to complete the envelope. (Don't bring the bottom end up toward the center; roll it over on itself to give a tapered look.) The result is a club-shaped envelope.

4. Heat the oil in a heavy, shallow saucepan. Sauté briefly and add the garlic and the remaining onion and mushrooms. Add the tomato, zucchini, thyme, the remaining ¼ teaspoon of salt, and 4 turns of the pepper mill. Push the vegetables toward the edge of the pan and place the chicken packages seam side down in the middle of the pan. Add the wine and stock and cover. Cook over medium heat for about 10 minutes.

5. Remove the chicken to a platter and keep it warm. Reduce the liquid in the pan over high heat until it is one-half its original volume. Swirl in the remaining tablespoon of butter. Spoon the sauce over and around the chicken and serve garnished with the cut basil.

YIELD: 4 servings.   CALORIES PER SERVING: 347.

PRESENTATION: Place a breast in the center of each plate over a bed of rice or noodles and surround it with the vegetables. In addition to the cut basil as a garnish, you might want to place a single whole basil leaf at the periphery of each plate.

The boneless and skinless chicken breasts used so widely in this book because they are light and lean are employed here in a relatively simple, very flavorful preparation that can be made quickly. The dish will get its flair from the artichoke bottoms, and the sauce will be bound splendidly by the addition of some of the pepper purée from the artichoke recipe. The artichokes, by the way, can be prepared a day ahead of time and warmed before serving, making this dish an expeditious one for entertaining. The calorie count may seem a bit high, but notice that the dish includes pasta and a vegetable.

CHICKEN BREASTS WITH MUSHROOMS AND ARTICHOKES

3 whole skinless and boneless chicken breasts (about 2½ pounds total weight)
2 teaspoons salt
Freshly ground black pepper (8 turns of the pepper mill)
3 sweet red peppers (about 1 pound)
1 tablespoon olive oil
3 tablespoons butter
½ pound mushrooms, thinly sliced (3 cups)
3 tablespoons chopped shallots
¼ cup dry vermouth
½ cup half-and-half
½ pound medium noodles
3 pints boiling water
6 Buttered Artichoke Bottoms (see recipe page 218)
3 tablespoons chopped fresh parsley leaves

1. Split each chicken breast in half and trim away the cartilage and much of the membrane. Put the chicken between sheets of plastic wrap and lay it skinned side down on a flat surface. Pound the chicken lightly.

2. Sprinkle the breasts with 1 teaspoon of the salt and the black pepper.

3. Remove the core of each red pepper and cut the peppers into quarters. Discard the seeds. Put the peppers in a saucepan with water to cover them. Bring to a boil and simmer for about 8 minutes. Drain the peppers and put them in a blender or food mill to purée. To remove some of its moisture, pour the purée into a small frying pan and cook it for about 5 minutes.

4. Heat the olive oil and 1 tablespoon of the butter in a large skillet. Place the chicken in the skillet. Cook it for about 2 minutes, loosening the pieces to make sure they don't stick. Turn the breasts and scatter the mushrooms over them. Stir and continue cooking for

about 3 minutes. Sprinkle the shallots over the breasts and continue cooking for about another minute.

5. Transfer the chicken to a warm serving dish. Cover it loosely with aluminum foil.

6. Pour the vermouth into the skillet and bring it to a boil. After about 3 minutes, add the half-and-half and continue cooking for another 3 minutes, stirring the mixture occasionally. Notice if liquid has accumulated around the chicken and add it to the mixture in the pan. Also, add 2 tablespoons of the red pepper purée.

7. Put the noodles in a pot of boiling water along with 1 teaspoon of salt and cook them for 5 minutes, or until they are tender. Drain them well and return them to the pot, adding the remaining butter. Stir.

8. Spoon equal amounts of the pepper purée into the center of each artichoke. Serve the chicken, with the mushroom sauce, accompanied by the noodles and artichokes. Garnish with parsley.

YIELD: 6 servings.   CALORIES PER SERVING: 565.

PRESENTATION: Place a mound of noodles in the center of each plate. Over it place a chicken breast, with the mushrooms divided equally for each breast and placed in the middle of the chicken breast. Then distribute the sauce amply over the chicken and around the noodles. Place a single artichoke bottom toward the periphery of the plate.

Sometimes familiar ingredients become remarkable because they are prepared in a surprising fashion. When you read through the recipe, notice that I cut the tomatoes in strips. I also chose to use whole basil leaves, which can, incidentally, be eaten just as if they had been chopped. I almost added no butter fat at all. But it really did need a little something to make it smooth. Hence that single tablespoon of butter.

BREAST OF CHICKEN WITH FRESH VEGETABLES

4 firm ripe tomatoes (¾ pound), preferably Italian
plum tomatoes
2 zucchini (½ pound)
2 tablespoons olive oil
2 skinless and boneless chicken breasts (1½ pounds total
weight), split in half, fat and membranes cut away
⅓ cup chopped onion
1 tablespoon finely chopped garlic
¼ teaspoon dried thyme
½ cup dry white wine
1 tablespoon butter
16 fresh basil leaves

1. Drop the tomatoes into boiling water for 12 seconds and, with a paring knife, remove their skins. Cut them in half lengthwise. Gently squeeze out the moisture. Cut each half into 6 strips. There should be about 2 cups.

2. Cut the zucchini into thirds lengthwise and then slice the strips into pieces ½ inch thick. There should be about 1¾ cups.

3. Heat the oil in a frying pan and lightly brown the chicken, 2 minutes on one side and 4 minutes on the other. Transfer the chicken to another pan or a platter and cover to keep it warm. In the hot pan, brown the onion lightly and then add the garlic and zucchini and stir and cook briefly. Add the thyme. Add the wine and tomatoes. Stir and simmer for 5 minutes.

4. Return the chicken to the pan, along with its juices. Add the butter and simmer for 5 minutes.

5. Remove the chicken and reduce the sauce to thicken it slightly. Serve garnished with the basil leaves.

YIELD: 4 servings.   CALORIES PER SERVING: 326.

PRESENTATION: Place the chicken in the center of the plate. Surround it with the vegetables, being sure to spoon some of the liquid over the breasts. Place 4 basil leaves at equidistant points around the periphery of each plate.

Once you learn the method involved in preparing a good curry sauce, there are an incredible number of possibilities. In this recipe, I have applied it to that lean and light meat, the skinless chicken breast. Try the same approach with shrimp or scallops or a combination of them. Sauté the seafood first and then add the sauce. It's a good twist for steamed or sautéed vegetables, too.

CHICKEN BREAST WITH CURRY SAUCE

2 tablespoons butter
¾ cup finely chopped onions
1 tablespoon finely chopped garlic
1 tablespoon Oriental Curry Powder (see recipe page 265)
1 apple, diced (¾ cup)
1 banana, diced (½ cup)
1½ cups chicken stock (see recipe page 30)
¼ cup ricotta
4 skinless and boneless chicken breasts (2¼ pounds
total weight)
½ teaspoon salt

1. Melt 1 tablespoon of the butter in a saucepan and add the onions, sautéing them until they wilt but do not brown. Add the garlic and sauté it briefly. Add the curry, apple, and banana. Sauté, stirring, for 2 minutes. Add the stock and cook for 10 minutes more. Stir in the ricotta. Transfer the mixture to a food processor or blender and purée it. There should be about 2 cups.

2. Melt the remaining tablespoon of butter in a large nonstick frying pan. Add the chicken and salt. Cook for about 3 minutes on each side over medium heat to brown the chicken only lightly.

3. Add the sauce and bring it to a simmer, stirring. Cook for about a minute. Serve piping hot.

YIELD: 6 servings.   CALORIES PER SERVING: 279.

PRESENTATION: Place a breast of chicken in the center of each plate and spoon the sauce amply over it. Mold Creole Rice (see recipe page 213) in a cup and unmold it on the side of the chicken, but do not spoon the sauce over it.

The classic dish is called Chicken Veronique. The sauce always involves grapes, and usually it is very rich with butter or cream. This variation, which I tried for the first time while writing this book, is not rich: It has no cream and relatively little butter. The result is a fresh-tasting dish in which the grapes are highlighted rather than submerged. The fruity taste is also enhanced by the vermouth.

BONELESS CHICKEN BREASTS
AU VERMOUTH

4 skinless and boneless chicken breasts (about 1¾ pounds total weight)
1 cup fresh seedless grapes
4 tablespoons butter
1 teaspoon salt
Freshly ground black pepper to taste
2 tablespoons finely chopped onion
¼ cup dry vermouth
Juice of ½ lemon
½ cup chicken stock (see recipe page 30)

1. Trim away all traces of fat and white membrane from the breasts. Place the pieces on a flat surface and, using a flat meat mallet, pound them lightly. Cut the breasts into ½-inch strips.

2. Remove the grapes from their stems; rinse and dry the grapes well.

3. Melt 2 tablespoons of the butter in a large frying pan. When it is very hot, add the chicken. Sprinkle with salt and pepper and cook over high heat. Stir constantly so the pieces cook evenly.

4. In 3 or 4 minutes, when the chicken is just barely cooked through and its raw look is gone, use a slotted spoon to transfer the pieces to another pan.

5. To the first pan, add the onion and cook briefly, stirring. Pour in the vermouth and lemon juice and deglaze the pan by dissolving the solids over high heat, stirring and scraping with a wooden spatula. Meanwhile, notice if liquid has accumulated around the chicken breasts in the other pan and add that liquid to the vermouth sauce.

6. When the sauce is reduced by half, add the chicken stock and grapes. Cook and reduce for another 3 to 4 minutes.

7. Transfer the chicken into the sauce and heat through, but be careful not to overcook; the grapes should retain their shape. Swirl in the remaining butter.

YIELD: 6 servings.   CALORIES PER SERVING: 252.

PRESENTATION: Serve with Zucchini Bordelaise (see recipe page 233) and Buttered Artichoke Bottoms (see recipe page 218) filled with Watercress Purée (see recipe page 233).

Chicken Florentine, in its various forms, is a classic and common dish, employing a smooth cream or milk-enriched cheese sauce and spinach. The challenge was to produce a satisfying, smooth version without the cream. So what we did was to prepare the sauce separately, a mushroom-bound sauce that is almost silken, even if light. The cheese is placed inside the stuffed breast, along with the spinach and, when it melts, it creates its own sauce from the interior of the meat. The combination turns out to be extremely pleasing and I am indebted to this book project for leading me toward it.

STUFFED STEAMED BREAST OF CHICKEN FLORENTINE

4 skinless and boneless chicken breasts (½ pound each)
Freshly ground black pepper (18 turns of the pepper mill)
10 ounces fresh spinach leaves
3 tablespoons plus 1 teaspoon butter
2 tablespoons chopped shallots
2 teaspoons salt
¹⁄₁₆ teaspoon grated nutmeg
2 ounces Gruyère cheese, cut into ¼-inch cubes
½ pound mushrooms, sliced
2 tablespoons fresh lemon juice
¼ cup dry white wine
1 cup chicken stock (see recipe page 30)
1 cup diced, peeled and seeded ripe tomatoes
8 fresh basil leaves

1. Pound the chicken breasts lightly between sheets of plastic wrap and sprinkle them with 1 teaspoon of the salt and 8 turns of the pepper mill.

2. Pick over the spinach, pulling away any tough stems and blemished leaves. Rinse and dry the spinach.

3. Heat 1 tablespoon of the butter in a saucepan or skillet and add the shallots. Cook briefly. Add the spinach, ½ teaspoon of salt, 6 turns of the pepper mill, and the nutmeg. Cook, stirring, until the spinach is wilted and most of its moisture has evaporated. Remove the spinach from the pan and allow it to cool.

4. In the center of each chicken breast, place an equal portion of the spinach along with about 2 tablespoons of diced cheese. Fold the sides and then the ends over the stuffing so that a box is formed. Place the chicken in a steamer. When the water boils, cover and steam for 5 minutes.

5. Melt 1 tablespoon of butter in a small saucepan and add the sliced mushrooms, lemon juice, the remaining salt, and 4 turns of

the pepper mill and cook briefly. Add the wine and chicken stock and reduce the liquid by half. Transfer the liquid to a blender, along with the remaining tablespoon of butter, and blend until fine and keep warm.

6. Melt the 1 teaspoon of butter in a saucepan and add the diced tomatoes. Cook for 1 minute. Serve over the breasts of chicken. Garnish with the basil leaves.

YIELD: 4 servings.   CALORIES PER SERVING: 458.

PRESENTATION: Place a breast of chicken in the center of each plate and spoon the mushroom sauce over and around it. Place the diced tomatoes over the sauce and garnish with 2 basil leaves. To one side of the chicken and away from the sauce, place a small portion of Glazed Carrots (see recipe page 223).

When chicken legs are baked at a high temperature, all the fat is rendered out and the skin crackles, like a roast duck's. The crunchiness of it is increased by the use of bread crumbs. This chicken is, of course, like a broiled chicken leg, but it is not as dry. It is a typical dish of the south of France, as the garlic and herbs will testify.

BAKED CHICKEN LEGS WITH FRESH HERBS

6 whole chicken legs (about 1 pound each)
½ teaspoon salt
Freshly ground black pepper (6 turns of the pepper mill)
1 tablespoon butter
1 tablespoon olive oil
½ cup fresh bread crumbs
1 teaspoon finely chopped garlic
1 tablespoon finely chopped shallots
1 tablespoon finely chopped fresh parsley leaves
1 tablespoon finely chopped fresh basil leaves or tarragon
1 teaspoon finely chopped fresh thyme
½ cup dry white wine

1. Preheat the oven to 425 degrees.

2. Sprinkle the chicken with salt and pepper. On the stovetop, melt the butter and add the oil to a baking dish large enough to hold the legs in one layer. Place the legs in the dish and turn them until they are coated with oil and butter. Arrange the pieces skin side down.

3. Place the dish on the bottom of the oven and bake for 25 minutes.

4. Combine the bread crumbs, garlic, shallots, parsley, basil, and thyme.

5. Turn the legs skin side up and sprinkle them with the bread crumb mixture. Bake for another 25 minutes. Pour the wine around the legs and bake for 5 minutes longer before serving.

YIELD: 6 servings. CALORIES PER SERVING:
577 cooked with the skin;
410 cooked without the skin.

PRESENTATION: Place a leg in the center of the plate, with half a Baked Tomato with Garlic and Rosemary (see recipe page 232) at the bottom end and Steamed Broccoli (see recipe page 220) on either side.

I spend so much time outdoors during the summer that I am constantly looking for ways to vary the kinds of things I can do on a charcoal grill. Cornish game hens are common in supermarkets and butcher shops in the United States. When I grill one over coals, it reminds me of the small chickens called poussin *that are often grilled in France. It also is enough like pigeon and quail, two birds that can be difficult to obtain here, to satisfy me. This recipe is not limited to the outdoor grill; try it in a preheated broiler, too.*

GRILLED CORNISH GAME HENS WITH GINGER

*4 Cornish game hens (about 1 pound each), split
in half for broiling
1 teaspoon salt
Freshly ground black pepper (8 turns of the pepper mill)
2 tablespoons finely chopped fresh ginger
2 tablespoons finely chopped garlic
2 tablespoons fresh lemon juice
2 tablespoons red wine vinegar
2 tablespoons olive oil
2 tablespoons chopped fresh coriander leaves or
Italian parsley leaves
2 tablespoons melted butter*

1. Sprinkle the hens with salt and pepper and put them in a baking dish. Blend the ginger, garlic, lemon juice, vinegar, oil, and coriander together. Pour the marinade over the hens. Cover them with plastic wrap and marinate for 3 to 4 hours in the refrigerator.

2. Preheat a charcoal grill

3. Drain the hens and place them skin side down on the grill. When the skin is nicely browned, turn the hens and continue cooking on the other side. Baste the hens. Continue turning and basting every 5 minutes for about 15 minutes, or until the hens are done. Serve with melted butter brushed over the hens, if desired.

YIELD: 4 servings.

CALORIES PER SERVING:
564 cooked with the skin;
375 cooked without the skin.

PRESENTATION: Place 2 hen halves toward the top of each plate. Below the hens, arrange Snow Peas with Sesame Seeds (see recipe page 228) in a crescent.

Capons have a lot going for them. They are larger and more flavorful than chickens, thanks to their advanced age. Because they take longer to cook than chickens they can produce richer broths. Stuffed boiled capon is a wholesome peasant dish that you're not likely to find in a restaurant. The stuffing here, although it is extremely simple—mostly bread crumbs and onions—is surprisingly tasty and light. The sauce, rather than a rich sauce supreme or the like, can be just a bit of broth on top, with mustard on the side. To give it some more bite, try horseradish sauce instead of the mustard.

STUFFED BOILED CAPON

THE STUFFING
Liver and heart from the capon
2½ cups fresh coarse bread crumbs
1½ cups finely chopped onions
¼ cup finely chopped shallots
¼ cup chopped fresh parsley leaves
2 tablespoons chopped fresh tarragon
2 teaspoons chopped garlic
¼ teaspoon dried thyme
1 egg
½ teaspoon salt
Freshly ground black pepper (8 turns of the pepper mill)

THE CAPON
1 7-pound capon
½ teaspoon dried thyme
1 bay leaf
4 whole black peppercorns
1 onion, peeled and studded with a clove
1 tablespoon salt
6 leeks, cleaned and tied together
30 baby carrots (1 pound)
2 celery stalks

1. To make the stuffing, chop the liver and heart coarsely. Place them in a mixing bowl and add all the remaining ingredients for the stuffing. Blend the mixture well. Stuff the capon's cavity and sew it closed. Truss the bird.

2. Place the bird in a large kettle with the thyme, bay leaf, peppercorns, and onion. Pour enough water over it to completely cover the capon. Add the salt and bring the water to a boil. Skim away any foam on the surface. Lower the heat, cover the pot, and simmer for 1 hour. Add the leeks, carrots, and celery. Simmer for another hour.

3. Remove all the skin if desired. Carve the capon: Cut the legs

away first. Separate the thigh from the drumstick. Slice the meat evenly from the drumstick and the thigh. Remove the wings. Slice the breast meat into long thin slices. Remove the stuffing. Serve the capon, combining dark and light meat.

YIELD: 8 servings.   CALORIES PER SERVING: 591.

PRESENTATION: Place a portion of stuffing in the center of the plate. Position 3 or 4 slices of capon on top of the stuffing. Surround the meat with the vegetables it was cooked with. Moisten it with broth from the pot. On a side dish place some mustard and on another put small French pickles. Or, also on a side dish, place some Tomato and Horseradish Sauce (see recipe page 242).

The turkey here is roasted in an ordinary fashion, except that I've chosen to use only the breast. The result is much less fatty than if the whole bird were cooked. There is another advantage: The turkey cooks more evenly. A whole turkey tends to cook at different rates, with some of it almost inevitably too dry. This breast, done correctly, will be pure, moist white meat (when I made it on one occasion, my guests were under the impression, as the sliced turkey approached the table, that it was veal).

ROAST BREAST OF TURKEY BEAUSEJOUR

1 4-pound turkey breast, its bone intact but without wings
½ teaspoon salt
Freshly ground black pepper (8 turns of the mill)
1 tablespoon vegetable oil
½ teaspoon dried thyme or 2 sprigs fresh thyme
2 small whole onions (½ pound)
1 bay leaf
2 garlic cloves
¼ cup dry white wine
½ cup chicken stock (see recipe page 30)

1. Preheat the oven to 400 degrees.
2. Sprinkle the breast with salt and pepper. Brush it with the oil. Rub the inside of the breast with thyme. Place the turkey in a roasting pan skin side up along with the onions, bay leaf, and garlic. Roast for 1 hour, basting often. Pour off the fat in the pan.
3. To the pan, add the white wine and chicken stock and roast for 10 minutes more. Allow the turkey to rest for 10 minutes before slicing.

YIELD: 6 servings.   CALORIES PER SERVING: 433.

PRESENTATION: Place a serving of Fettucine with Goat Cheese and Asparagus (see recipe page 207) in the center of each serving plate. Slice the breast very thinly, and place 4 slices around the edge of the plate. Spoon the gravy over the turkey only.

One of the most pleasing and popular Burgundian dishes is, of course, coq au vin, chicken in wine sauce. It became so popular, lamentably, that it is now a bit of a cliché in the United States. A less well known, but satisfying, variation is this one, using duck—cooked well to remove the fat.

BRAISED DUCK WITH BEAUJOLAIS

2   4½-pound ready-to-cook ducks
1 teaspoon salt
½ teaspoon freshly ground black pepper
1½ cups coarsely chopped onion (½ pound)
1½ cups coarsely chopped celery (4 stalks)
1½ cups coarsely chopped carrots (½ pound)
1 tablespoon chopped garlic
2 bay leaves
½ teaspoon dried thyme
4 fresh parsley sprigs
¼ cup all-purpose flour
¼ cup Cognac
24 ounces beaujolais
2 cups chicken stock (see recipe page 30)
2 whole cloves

1. Separate the leg and thigh pieces and the breast pieces from the ducks. Remove the excess fat and skin, especially from the legs. Season the duck pieces with salt and pepper. Chop the backs, which are largely bone, into manageable pieces.

2. In a very hot, large cast-iron skillet, sauté the breasts and legs skin side down until the fat is mostly cooked out, about 10 minutes. Remove and set aside the duck pieces. Leave the fat in the pan.

3. Brown the chopped backbones in the skillet. Add the vegetables, garlic, bay leaves, thyme, and parsley. Cook for about 2 minutes. Pour the vegetables and bones into a strainer to separate the ingredients from the fat. Discard the fat.

4. Return the bones and vegetables to the skillet. Add the flour and cook briefly, stirring. Add 3 tablespoons of the Cognac, then the wine, stock, and cloves. Cook over low heat for 30 minutes, occasionally scraping the bottom of the skillet with a wooden spatula.

5. Add the breasts and legs. Cover and cook for 45 minutes.

6. Remove the legs and breast pieces to a warm serving platter. Pour the sauce through a fine strainer, such as a *chinois* and add the remaining Cognac to the sauce. There should be about 2 cups of sauce. Ladle it over the duck.

YIELD: 6 servings.   CALORIES PER SERVING: 548.

PRESENTATION: Serve with Rice and Wild Rice and Braised Endives (see recipes pages 215 and 225). Using a small mold, place a portion of rice at the edge of the plate. On either side place a whole endive. In the center, place 2 pieces of duck, spooning the sauce liberally over it.

Guinea hen is similar to game birds, firmer than chicken, darker and more flavorful. It is a lean bird that is very well known in Europe, although quite unfamiliar to Americans. (It seems that some of my long Island neighbors have taken a liking to it, however, and are raising guinea hens themselves; every now and then I swerve my car so as not to be the agent of a premature demise for one of these terrific little animals.) When it is served in restaurants, usually just the breast is brought to the table because the legs have a tendency to be tough. Guinea hen is not available everywhere; some supermarkets will carry the hens frozen but the fresh hen is better and for that you need a good butcher shop or a specialty store. Incidentally, the vinegar used in this stew to supply the acid that wine more commonly provides in stews has its tradition in the hearty fare of Burgundy, where poulet au vinaigre is a beloved dish.

GUINEA HEN AU VINAIGRE

2 tablespoons vegetable oil
1 2¼-pound guinea hen, cut into 10 serving pieces
(chop carcass and bones)
½ teaspoon salt
Freshly ground black pepper (8 turns of the pepper mill)
¾ cup chopped onions
1 teaspoon chopped garlic
1 bay leaf
½ teaspoon dried thyme
3 tablespoons red wine vinegar
1¼ cups chicken stock (see recipe page 30)
2 tablespoons tomato paste
3 sprigs fresh parsley

1. Heat the oil in a skillet. Sprinkle the hen with salt and pepper.
2. Place the hen and its bones in the skillet. Brown the meat on both sides and add the onions, garlic, bay leaf, and thyme. Cook for a few minutes, stirring. When the onion is lightly browned, drain the fat from the pan. Add the vinegar, stirring. Add the chicken stock, tomato paste, and parsley, scraping the bottom of the pan with a wooden spatula.
3. Bring the liquid to a boil and cover. Simmer for 30 minutes.
4. Remove the bones and parsley sprigs. Transfer the hen pieces to a platter. There should be about 1 cup of sauce in the pan. (If desired it can be made smoother by forcing it through a strainer.)

YIELD: 4 servings.

CALORIES PER SERVING:
396 cooked with the skin;
245 cooked without the skin.

PRESENTATION: Prepare Rice with Wild Rice (see recipe page 215) and shape it in a mold; unmold it in the center of each plate and place 2 or 3 pieces of hen around the rice. Garnish each plate with 2 or 3 sprigs of parsley.

This is an absolutely luxurious approach to a somewhat exotic, lean bird, the pheasant. It is time-consuming but not difficult. The time is largely given over to the production of a sauce that requires a great deal of reduction of red wine and Cognac.

BREAST AND THIGH OF PHEASANT IN
RED WINE

2 pheasants (2¼ pounds each)
¾ cup chopped onions
½ cup chopped carrots
½ cup chopped celery
1 garlic clove, coarsely chopped
1 bay leaf
½ teaspoon dried thyme
½ teaspoon dried rosemary
1 bottle plus ½ cup beaujolais or Burgundy
1 whole clove
6 whole black peppercorns
2 cups water
2 sprigs fresh parsley
1 tablespoon olive oil
½ teaspoon salt
3 tablespoons chopped shallots
Freshly ground black pepper (8 turns of the pepper mill)
3 tablespoons Cognac
2 tablespoons butter

1. Remove the breasts and thighs from the birds. Remove the skin. (The butcher can do the cutting, if you like.) Separate the thighs from the drumsticks. Chop the bones of the remaining carcass and the drumsticks into small pieces. Reserve some of the fat from the birds, about 2 tablespoons.

2. Heat the reserved fat in a saucepan. Add the carcass and drumstick bones. Brown for about 7 minutes, stirring often. Add the onions, carrots, celery, garlic, bay leaf, thyme, and rosemary. Stir and brown for 5 minutes more. Drain the fat and add the bottle of wine, along with the clove, peppercorns, water, and parsley. Bring to a boil and simmer, uncovered, for 1½ hours. Strain. There should be about 2 cups of liquid. Remove the fat that accumulates on top.

3. Transfer the mixture to a smaller saucepan and reduce it to ¾ cup over high heat.

4. Heat the olive oil in a skillet. Season the pheasant with salt and pepper and put it in the skillet to cook over low heat for about 5

minutes on each side. The pieces should brown lightly. Do not over-cook.

5. Remove the pheasant and keep them warm under foil.

6. Remove the fat from the skillet and add the shallots. Cook briefly. Add 2 tablespoons of the Cognac and the ½ cup of wine. Reduce the liquid by half, stirring and scraping. Add the ¾ cup of sauce from the saucepan. Bring the mixture to a boil and simmer for 2 minutes. Strain, using a fine-mesh sieve. Return to the skillet to warm. Remove from the heat and swirl in the 2 tablespoons of butter and the remaining tablespoon of Cognac.

YIELD: 6 servings.   CALORIES PER SERVING: 458.

PRESENTATION: Place julienned vegetables in the center of each plate. Slice the breast into thin pieces and distribute it and the thighs around the vegetables. Pour the sauce over it. Spoon the sauce over the meat, not the vegetables. There isn't much sauce so be sure to distribute it evenly.

...8...

Veal

Good veal is the leanest, subtlest meat a cow can produce. But please note I refer only to *good* veal. When you go to the supermarket and buy something labeled scaloppine, for instance, the butcher seems to think that his only requirement is to make the veal slices thin. The meat itself might come from almost anywhere on the animal's body. There's a good chance the meat will be much tougher than it should be. Far better to choose the veal properly in the first place. At its best, veal scaloppine comes from the loin or the round, which is the tender part of the leg. And the best veal is milk-fed. There are two excellent brands I am familiar with: Plume de Veau and Provimi.

If you choose the meat well, the possibilities for lean veal dishes are endless. Here, we have dishes that use scaloppines in several variations. And veal is used in meat loaf, in stew, as a steak, and thinly pounded as a paillard.

To me, the tastiest part of the veal is the breast. It can be stuffed and braised or roasted. Here, the latter option is chosen. Done right, it is crisp, the fat all rendered away.

ROASTED BREAST OF VEAL WITH HERBS AND CARROTS

1 garlic clove, chopped
1 bay leaf
¼ teaspoon dried thyme
¼ teaspoon dried rosemary
¼ teaspoon dried sage
1   4-pound oven-ready breast of milk-fed veal
½ teaspoon salt
Freshly ground black pepper (8 turns of the pepper mill)
2 tablespoons vegetable oil
2 onions (½ pound), cut into ¾-inch cubes (2 cups)
½ cup dry white wine
1½ cups chicken stock (see recipe page 30)
6 carrots (1¼ pounds), trimmed and scraped, cut into 1½-inch lengths (3 cups)

1. Preheat the oven to 400 degrees.

2. Chop very finely and blend together the garlic, bay leaf, thyme, rosemary, and sage.

3. Place the meat in a shallow roasting pan that fits it well. Rub the meat all over with the herb-and-garlic mixture. Sprinkle it with salt and pepper and rub it with the oil.

4. Place the roasting pan in the bottom of the oven and brown the meat on each side, about 10 minutes a side. Pour off all the fat from the roasting pan. Place the onions around the meat. Lower the oven temperature to 375 degrees. Brown the onions for about 5 minutes.

5. Add the wine and chicken stock and cover tightly with foil. Cook for about 30 minutes. Add the carrots. Cover again and bake for 30 minutes more. Skim away the fat and serve the meat with its own sauce and the vegetables.

Yield: 8 servings.   Calories per Serving: 393.

Presentation: The meat should be carved very thinly. Do this by slicing it on the bias over the bone. (This method leaves a lot of good meat between the bones, although I can offer no elegant way of eating it.) An alternative is to cut down between the bone as with ribs. Place slices of the meat in the center of the plate, surrounded by the carrots and sauce. If available, a few whole basil leaves placed around the periphery of the plate add to the color.

What makes a veal paillard good is good veal. It should be very lean and tender. Beyond that, it is supposed to be seared on the outside without being dried out on the inside. This is accomplished by cooking it rapidly in an extremely hot pan. This same approach can be used for well-pounded, skinless chicken breast or for very lean slices of beef.

VEAL PAILLARD

4 thinly sliced veal steaks (½ pound each)
½ teaspoon salt
Freshly ground black pepper (8 turns of the pepper mill)
1 tablespoon vegetable oil
1 tablespoon butter, melted
2 tablespoons chopped parsley leaves or a mixture of
chives, tarragon, coriander, parsley, and chervil or
any other combination that suits you
4 lemon wedges

1. Place the veal between sheets of plastic wrap and pound it with a flat meat mallet until it is no more than ¼ inch thick.

2. Season the meat with salt and pepper and brush both sides with oil.

3. Heat a grill or cast-iron pan until it is very hot and place the meat in it. The cooking should take about 40 seconds on each side. The meat should have a handsome, seared look.

4. Place the meat on a warmed plate and brush it with the melted butter. Sprinkle it with the herbs and serve with the lemon wedges.

YIELD: 4 servings.   CALORIES PER SERVING: 432.

PRESENTATION: Place the paillard in the center of the plate. Along one side, place sections of broiled tomato or some other bright vegetable. On the other side place a lemon wedge.

In French there are a number of useful distinctions when dealing with veal. A scallopine of veal refers to thin strips. A thicker piece of meat, one cut like a modest beefsteak, is called escalope of veal. That distinction doesn't seem to be available in English, so let me simply call this a veal steak dish. At its best the veal steak is a solid piece of meat cut from the leg or the butt. The best veal is milk-fed. Good milk-fed veal, cooked in this way, will be white all the way through when it is done. The use of mustard seed here grows directly out of nouvelle cuisine *as exercised by the brothers Troisgros.*

VEAL STEAK WITH MUSHROOMS AND MUSTARD SEEDS

1 tablespoon olive oil
4 veal steaks, about ¼ inch thick (1½ pounds total weight)
1 teaspoon salt
Freshly ground black pepper (8 turns of the pepper mill)
2 tablespoons mustard seeds
1 tablespoon butter
½ pound mushrooms, sliced (1½ cups)
2 tablespoons chopped shallots
2 tablespoons red wine vinegar
⅓ cup chicken stock (see recipe page 30)
2 tablespoons chopped fresh parsley leaves

1. Heat the olive oil in a large nonstick frying pan.

2. Sprinkle the veal with salt, pepper, and mustard seeds on both sides. Add the veal to the frying pan and sauté over high heat for about 3 minutes on each side. Transfer the meat to a serving platter and keep it warm.

3. Melt the butter in the pan and add the shallots and mushrooms. Sauté, stirring, for about 2 minutes.

4. Pour the vinegar and chicken stock into the pan and stir. Reduce the liquid by half. Spoon the sauce over the veal steaks and sprinkle with parsley.

YIELD: 4 servings.   CALORIES PER SERVING: 386.

PRESENTATION: Place a steak in the center of each plate. On each side of the steak place a serving of Julienned Carrots and Snow Peas (see recipe page 222). Spoon the sauce evenly over each steak, but not over the vegetables.

This is an expensive dish, but to my mind it is worth it, as long as the chops are prepared properly. It is a classic dish, usually made with cream sauce, but here it is presented with a light gravy. The secret in browning the veal chops is to do it slowly—I stipulate medium heat—so they don't dry out. And be careful in preparing the morels. They can be sandy like spinach. The sand will drop out while they soak. When they are swollen from the water, lift them straight out so the sand does not cling to them again.

VEAL CHOPS WITH MORELS

24 dry morels (about 1 cup)
4 veal chops (6 ounces each)
½ teaspoon salt
Freshly ground black pepper (8 turns of the pepper mill)
1 tablespoon butter
½ cup chopped onion
¼ cup dry white wine
¼ cup water
8 fresh basil leaves

1. Soak the dry morels in 4 cups of cold water for 5 minutes. Move them around in the water to free them of any sand. Then let them sit still while they absorb moisture. Remove them from the water carefully so as not to pick up any sand.

2. Sprinkle the veal chops on both sides with salt and pepper. Heat the butter in a nonstick frying pan and add the veal chops.

3. Cook the chops over medium heat until browned on each side, about 10 minutes per side.

4. Put the chopped onion and morels in the pan and cook, stirring, for about 5 minutes. Then add the wine and water. Cover and simmer for about 10 minutes.

5. Remove the cover and reduce the sauce to about ½ cup over high heat. Serve the chops with the sauce and the basil leaves as garnish.

YIELD: 4 servings.   CALORIES PER SERVING: 315.

PRESENTATION: Place a single chop toward the top of each plate with a basil leaf on top of it. Below the chop place a portion of Home-Fried Potatoes (see recipe page 213) flanked by 2 Braised Endives (see recipe page 225).

At the Pavillon, my predecessors as chef invented a term, beausejour, for just about anything that has thyme, bay leaf, and whole garlic cloves—about as traditional a combination of seasonings as you can find. They called these dishes beausejour, or beautiful sojourn, because, I think, this distinctive French flavoring must have had the effect of transporting them back home in their mind's eye. It does that for me sometimes, too, because it is so redolent of the countryside. At the Pavillon, these dishes always had a lot of butter. I have eliminated it here, with no tremendous loss because the veal chop is moist, rich meat. I've also taken the liberty of adding tomato to enliven the color and bind the sauce.

VEAL CHOPS BEAUSEJOUR

1 tablespoon olive oil
4 veal chops (6 ounces each)
½ teaspoon salt
Freshly ground black pepper (8 turns of the pepper mill)
4 garlic cloves
2 bay leaves
½ teaspoon dried thyme, or 2 sprigs fresh thyme
¼ cup dry white wine
¼ cup water
1 cup diced, peeled ripe tomatoes

1. Heat the oil in a frying pan. Sprinkle the chops with salt and pepper. When the oil is hot add the veal and cook it over medium heat for 5 minutes. Turn the chops, and add the garlic, bay leaves, and thyme. Cook for 5 minutes.

2. Pour in the wine, scraping and stirring to dissolve any solid particles clinging to the pan. Add the water and tomatoes. Bring to a boil. Cover and simmer for 30 minutes. Uncover and reduce the liquid by half over high heat. Serve the chops with the sauce.

YIELD: 4 servings.   CALORIES PER SERVING: 293.

PRESENTATION: Place a chop on each dish, toward the rim. Divide the sauce over the chops. There should be enough for about 2 tablespoons of sauce for each serving. Arrange Snow Peas with Sweet Pepper and Poppy Seeds (see recipe page 229) neatly at the edge of each chop.

This dish is another of those that owe something to the chicken beausejour I learned to make in my restaurant days. In that approach, the chicken is combined with garlic, bay leaves, thyme, white wine, and butter. Here, the veal is substituted for the chicken, although a breast of capon, sliced thin would have done as well. Beausejour has always suggested a light dish to me. In this instance, it has a bit more bite thanks to the addition of mustard.

VEAL SCALOPPINE BEAUSEJOUR

1¼ pounds veal scaloppine (about 18 very thin pieces)
2 teaspoons salt
Freshly ground black pepper (8 turns of the pepper mill)
2 tablespoons vegetable oil
2 tablespoons butter
4 garlic cloves
½ teaspoon dried thyme, or 1 sprig fresh thyme
1 bay leaf
2 tablespoons dry white wine
2 tablespoons chicken stock (see recipe page 30)
1 tablespoon Dijon mustard
4 tablespoons chopped fresh parsley leaves

1. Place the meat on a flat surface and pound it lightly with a flat meat mallet. Sprinkle the meat with salt and pepper.

2. Heat the oil in 1 or 2 frying pans and, when it is very hot, add the meat. Cook for 30 seconds on each side. As the pieces brown lightly, transfer them to a warm platter.

3. Remove the fat from the pan and add the butter, garlic, thyme, and bay leaf. Cook briefly. Add the wine, chicken stock, and mustard. Scrape the bottom of the pan with a wooden spoon as the mixture cooks to dissolve solids and to blend well. Add the veal and its accumulated liquid to the pan along with the parsley. Cook for 30 seconds.

YIELD: 6 servings.   CALORIES PER SERVING: 238.

PRESENTATION: This dish can be served with Avocados and Mushrooms and Carrot Custard (see recipes pages 220 and 222). On each plate, arrange 3 overlapping slices of veal below the center of the plate in a crescent. Distribute the mushrooms over the meat. Place a wedge of Carrot Custard above the veal in the center of the plate. On both sides of the Carrot Custard place a wedge of avocado so that the wedges fan out from the carrots.

Throughout this book I have made a strenuous effort to cut down on fats. Making this classic dish in the ordinary fashion, I would have used double the amount of oil as well as some butter. So I cut down on both but eliminated neither for this recipe. I find that the butter is an important addition to lend the dish richness and smoothness—and all that richness can come from as little as 1 tablespoon of the magical stuff, as you will see.

VEAL SCALOPPINE WITH LEMON

8 thin veal scaloppine (about 1 pound)
½ teaspoon salt
Freshly ground black pepper (8 turns of the pepper mill)
2 tablespoons olive oil
1 tablespoon butter
¼ cup dry white wine
¼ cup chicken stock (see recipe page 30)
Juice of 1 lemon
2 tablespoons chopped fresh parsley leaves

1. Pound the veal to flatten it. Sprinkle the meat with salt and pepper.

2. Heat 1 tablespoon of the olive oil in a large nonstick frying pan and, when it is quite hot, add as many pieces of veal as the pan will hold in one layer. Sauté over high heat to brown the meat on one side, about 1 minute. Turn the meat and brown it on the other side. Transfer the veal to a warm platter.

3. Heat the butter and the remaining olive oil in the frying pan. Return the meat to the pan and cook it briefly on both sides. Add any liquid that accumulated on the platter. Add the wine, chicken stock, lemon juice, and parsley. Turn the veal in the pan to cook it evenly. When the sauce has reduced somewhat and bound into a smooth consistency, remove the pan from the heat.

YIELD: 4 servings.   CALORIES PER SERVING: 280.

PRESENTATION: Place 2 strips of veal in the center of each plate. Place 4 broiled tomato halves (see recipe page 232) around the meat. Alternate the tomatoes with small, whole Parsleyed Potatoes (see recipe page 212). Spoon the sauce over the meat.

The most common sauce for veal scaloppine with mustard seed is a cream sauce. But I've decided to diverge from that for the sake of this recipe. Tomato goes well with veal and the Fresh Tomato Sauce suggested here is extremely light. A small variation here, too, is the use of two kinds of mustard to be sure we get some zip into the preparation.

VEAL SCALOPPINE WITH MUSTARD SEED

10 to 12 thin veal scaloppine (about 1 ¼ pounds)
Freshly ground black pepper (8 turns of the pepper mill)
1 tablespoon coarse mustard, such as Meaux
2 tablespoons mustard seeds
2 tablespoons olive oil
½ cup chopped scallions
1 ½ cups Fresh Tomato Sauce (see recipe page 241)

1. Pound the scaloppine lightly. Sprinkle with the pepper.

2. Spread half the mustard on one side of the scaloppine. Sprinkle with half the mustard seeds. Turn the veal and repeat.

3. Heat 1 tablespoon of the olive oil in a nonstick frying pan. Add half of the veal and sauté over high heat to brown the veal lightly on one side. This should take about a minute. Turn and cook for another minute. Set aside and sauté the remaining veal.

4. Heat the remaining olive oil in another nonstick pan and sauté the scallions briefly to serve as a garnish.

5. Serve the veal with the tomato sauce.

YIELD: 4 servings.   CALORIES PER SERVING: 368.

PRESENTATION: Place the sauce on each plate first so it covers the dish. Place 3 strips of scaloppine in the center of each plate. Then spoon some of the scallions on top of each piece of veal. A good addition to this dish would be Buttered Artichoke Bottoms (see recipe page 218). Quarter the artichoke bottoms and arrange them around the edge of the plate.

*In some scaloppine preparations, almost all the cooking wisdom goes
into the acquisition of first-rate ingredients. After that the preparation is
a rapid-fire of simple cooking steps. Quickly sautéed veal with a touch of
vermouth, parsley, and butter leaves little more anyone could want from
a light, gorgeous, quickly prepared dish.*

VEAL SCALOPPINE AU VERMOUTH

12 thin veal scaloppine (about 1½ pounds)
½ teaspoon salt
Freshly ground black pepper (6 turns of the pepper mill)
1 tablespoon olive oil
½ cup dry vermouth
2 tablespoons butter
2 tablespoons chopped fresh parsley leaves

1. On a flat surface, pound the meat lightly between sheets of
plastic wrap. Sprinkle the meat with salt and pepper.

2. Heat the oil in a large nonstick frying pan. When it is hot, place
the meat in it and cook for about 1 minute on each side. This may be
done in two steps: Sauté half the veal and transfer it to a platter,
then cook the other half. All the veal should be placed in the pan,
however, before going on to the next step.

3. Add the vermouth, butter, and parsley and cook for 3 minutes.
Serve at once.

YIELD: 6 servings.   CALORIES PER SERVING: 261.

PRESENTATION: Arrange the veal at the center of the plate so that
the slices radiate away from the center like flower
petals. Place 2 slices of veal on each plate, each
touching at its base and radiating out toward the
edge of the plate. Place a serving of a different vegetable in the spaces between and below the veal
slices. Try Glazed Carrots, String Beans with Garlic, and Baked Tomatoes with Rosemary and Garlic or Broiled Tomatoes Provençale (see recipes
pages 223, 231, and 232).

Mostly, lamb or beef are skewered for charcoal broiling. But if you're looking for a leaner alternative, veal works beautifully well. It is expensive, I know, but delicious. Because I was using veal here, I employed seasonings appropriate to it and not to lamb. That is, I used coriander or tarragon to enhance the veal flavor. Also, veal does well with sherry wine vinegar, which gives it just a touch of sweetness. If you can't find it, red wine vinegar will do.

BROCHETTE OF VEAL FINES HERBES

1½ pounds lean veal from the leg or loin
½ pound button mushrooms
1 tablespoon vegetable oil
½ teaspoon salt
Freshly ground black pepper (8 turns of the pepper mill)
1 tablespoon sherry wine vinegar or red wine vinegar
½ teaspoon chopped fresh thyme, or ¼ teaspoon
dried thyme
1 bay leaf, crushed
1 tablespoon chopped fresh coriander or tarragon leaves
1 tablespoon chopped garlic
2 tablespoons butter, melted

1. Cut the veal into 1-inch cubes and place them in a mixing bowl. Add all the remaining ingredients, cover, and marinate for 1 to 2 hours at room temperature. Stir the mixture occasionally.

2. Arrange the cubed veal and the mushrooms on 6 skewers.

3. Prepare a charcoal fire. Brush the grill lightly with oil. Place the skewered veal on the grill and cook, turning, for 10 to 15 minutes.

YIELD: 6 servings.   CALORIES PER SERVING: 229.

PRESENTATION: Serve with Rice with Zucchini and Sweet Red Peppers (see recipe page 215). Place the rice in the center of each plate. Position a single skewer over the rice.

Stew is such a wonderful wintertime food that I didn't want to deprive anyone of it, even in the context of this book. The important variation here is the omission of any starch, the familiar flour or cornstarch that we all once thought was essential in binding a gravy as the stew cooked. Here the meat is seared as usual to ensure that the gravy will have a rich color. The solids that adhere to the pan after the browning will prove to be important in the gravy-making process, too. The gravy will be thickened—in the absence of starch—in the manner of so many gravies in this book. That is, it will be reduced over high heat after having the opportunity to absorb all the essence of the many vegetables and the meat in this stew. The unusual vegetable additions here are the zucchini and eggplant. To contribute to the lightness of the stew, only lean veal is used, and veal, of course, starts out with fewer calories than beef.

LIGHT VEAL STEW WITH
GARDEN VEGETABLES

2 tablespoons vegetable oil
*4 pounds lean veal shoulder, neck, or breast, cut
into 1½-inch cubes*
1 teaspoon salt
Freshly ground black pepper (10 turns of the pepper mill)
1½ cups chopped onions
2 teaspoons chopped garlic
1½ cups dry white wine
2½ cups chicken stock (see recipe page 30)
*1 pound ripe tomatoes, peeled and cut into ½-inch
cubes (about 2 cups)*
1 bay leaf
4 sprigs fresh thyme, or ½ teaspoon dried thyme
4 sprigs fresh parsley
1 pound carrots, trimmed and scraped
1 pound zucchini, the smallest possible
4 celery stalks (½ pound)
1 eggplant (¾ pound)
¼ cup chopped fresh parsley leaves for garnish

1. Heat the oil in a large cast-iron Dutch oven and brown the veal well on all sides, removing all its moisture. (Depending on the size of the pot, it may be more efficient to brown the meat in two batches.) Add the salt and pepper.

2. Add the onions and brown lightly. Add the garlic and cook briefly, without browning. Add the wine and stir. Add the stock, tomatoes, bay leaf, thyme, and parsley. Simmer for 1 hour.

3. Meanwhile, cut the carrots and zucchini into lengths of 1½

inches and quarter each piece. There should be about 2 cups. Scrape the celery, cut it into lengths of 1½ inches, and then slice those pieces lengthwise into strips about ½ inch wide. There should be about 1¾ cups. Peel the eggplant and cut it into ¾-inch cubes, making about 3 cups.

4. Add the celery and carrots to the pot and cook for 15 minutes. Add the remaining vegetables and stir. Cook for another 15 minutes, uncovered for the last 10 minutes, to reduce the gravy. Skim away any fat on the surface of the stew. Remove the bay leaf and serve. Garnish each serving with parsley.

YIELD: 10 servings.   CALORIES PER SERVING: 415.

PRESENTATION: Spoon the meat first onto each plate so that you know how much each portion comprises. Then distribute the vegetables around the meat.

As stews go, this is a lean, light one. The veal starts out lean; there's very little fat added beyond that, except for a couple of tablespoons of oil, which is ultimately drained. A navarin, by the way, is a word usually used to describe a lamb stew garnished with delicately cut vegetables. But it has been broadened in use to shellfish, chicken, and, in my kitchen, to veal. The dish requires a good deal of cooking, and, if you have the patience for it, the work will result in an extremely tasty stew.

NAVARIN DE VEAU AUX PETITS LEGUMES

*3½ pounds very lean stewing veal, cut
into 1-inch cubes
½ teaspoon salt
Freshly ground black pepper (8 turns of the pepper mill)
2 tablespoons vegetable oil
1¼ cups chopped onions
1 garlic clove, finely chopped
¾ cup dry white wine
1 cup chopped ripe tomatoes
1 cup chicken stock (see recipe page 30)
½ teaspoon dried thyme
1 bay leaf
1 cup carrots quartered lengthwise and cut into
1½-inch lengths
1 cup white turnips cut into 1½-inch strips
¾ cup celery cut into 1½-inch strips
¾ cup fresh or frozen peas (fresh peas need to be cooked in
boiling water for 3 or 4 minutes; frozen ones need only to
be run under warm water and drained)
¼ cup chopped fresh parsley leaves*

1. Sprinkle the veal with salt and pepper.

2. Heat the oil in a large casserole or Dutch oven and add the veal. Cook over high heat until evenly browned. This should take about 15 minutes.

3. Add the onions and garlic and stir, cooking for a few minutes. Add the wine, tomatoes, stock, thyme, and bay leaf. Cover and cook for 30 minutes, or until tender.

4. Meanwhile, drop the carrots, turnips, and celery into boiling water, cover, and cook for about 1 minute. Drain well.

5. Remove the lid of the casserole and add the carrots, turnips, and celery. Cook for about 15 minutes. If there appears to be too much liquid, reduce the sauce by half over high heat. Add the peas and serve with a sprinkling of parsley.

Yield: 8 servings.   Calories per Serving: 424.

PRESENTATION: Place the meat in the center of each plate and arrange the vegetables neatly around it. Around the
edge of each plate, place a few small Parsleyed Potatoes (see recipe page 212).

*For the sake of leanness, I've chosen to use only veal in this dish rather
than combining veal with a fattier meat, such as beef or pork. (This
dish could be done with ground chicken, too.) The variation in texture in
this instance will be supplied by the pistachio nuts. This loaf, by the way,
is superb served cold.*

VEAL LOAF WITH PISTACHIOS

1 tablespoon olive oil
¼ cup chopped scallions
1¼ cups chopped onions
½ teaspoon chopped garlic
2 pounds ground veal
⅓ cup chopped pistachio nuts
½ pound calf's liver
1 cup fresh bread crumbs
4 tablespoons chopped fresh parsley leaves
½ teaspoon salt
Freshly ground black pepper (6 turns of the pepper mill)
Fresh Tomato Sauce (see recipe page 241)

1. Preheat the oven to 375 degrees.
2. Heat the olive oil in a saucepan and add the scallions, onions,
and garlic. Sauté, stirring, for 5 minutes.
3. Place the veal and the onion mixture in a bowl.
4. Chop the liver very finely and add it to the mixture along with
the bread crumbs, parsley, salt, and pepper. Blend well.
5. Spoon the mixture into a 9- by 5- by 3-inch loaf pan. Cover the
pan with foil and place it in the oven. Bake for 1 hour. Remove the
foil and bake 15 minutes longer. Serve with Fresh Tomato Sauce.

YIELD: 6 servings.   CALORIES PER SERVING: 386.

PRESENTATION: Spoon the sauce onto the bare plate. Place a slice of
the veal loaf in the center. Place 1 small scoop of
mashed potatoes on either side of the slice (a fancy
option is to distribute the potatoes in a swirling
row with a pastry bag). Along the other sides of the
slice place a vegetable, such as String Beans with
Shallots and Tarragon (see recipe page 230).

The veal loaf that appears above is similar to this one. But this one happens to be even leaner. The use of chicken breast along with the veal makes it so. And so does the use of mushrooms, which have a great deal of body but no fat. Meat loaf has gotten itself a bad name in the United States—deservedly so, with all the filler and poor meat that's used. With this recipe, the result is more like a good pâté than any of those ersatz meat loaves.

VEAL, CHICKEN, AND MUSHROOM LOAF

1 tablespoon butter
½ pound mushrooms, sliced (about 2 cups)
¼ teaspoon dried thyme
1 bay leaf
½ cup finely chopped onion
1 teaspoon chopped garlic
1 pound ground veal
½ pound skinless and boneless chicken breast, ground
½ teaspoon salt
Freshly ground black pepper (8 turns of the pepper mill)
1 cup fresh bread crumbs
¼ cup chicken stock (see recipe page 30)
4 tablespoons chopped fresh parsley leaves
2 large eggs, lightly beaten

1. Preheat the oven to 375 degrees.
2. Melt the butter in a frying pan. Add the mushrooms, thyme, bay leaf, onion, and garlic. Sauté until the mushrooms have given up most of their liquid. Let cool.
3. Remove the bay leaf. Transfer the mushroom mixture to a bowl and combine with the veal, chicken, salt, pepper, bread crumbs, chicken stock, parsley, and eggs. Work the mixture with the hands until thoroughly blended.
4. Pack the mixture into a 9- by 5- by 3-inch loaf pan. Smooth over the top. Bake uncovered, for 1 hour. Let stand about 15 minutes before serving.

YIELD: 8 servings.   CALORIES PER SERVING: 182.

PRESENTATION: Serve with Fresh Tomato Sauce or Creole Sauce (see recipes pages 241 and 239). Place 2 slices of meat loaf in the center of each plate. Toward the top of the plate and toward the bottom, place a large spoonful of sauce. On either side of the meat, arrange String Beans with Garlic (see recipe page 231), with the beans aligned in one direction.

Actually, meatballs can be made with just about any ground meat, not just beef, although beef seems to be almost always identified with this dish. Since we have been looking for a lighter approach in this book, I offer here an excellent lean meatball dish with veal and chicken as the meat. It could also be done with chicken alone.

VEAL AND CHICKEN MEATBALLS WITH FRESH TOMATO SAUCE

½ *pound skinless and boneless chicken breast, ground*
½ *pound ground veal*
1 teaspoon butter
½ *cup finely chopped onion*
½ *teaspoon chopped garlic*
½ *cup bread crumbs*
½ *cup chicken stock (see recipe page 30)*
1 large egg, lightly beaten
⅛ *teaspoon ground allspice*
½ *teaspoon salt*
Freshly ground black pepper (8 turns of the pepper mill)
1 tablespoon olive oil
2¼ *cups Fresh Tomato Sauce (see recipe page 241)*
¼ *cup finely chopped fresh Italian parsley leaves*

1. Combine the chicken and veal in a mixing bowl.

2. Melt the butter in a small saucepan. Add the onion and garlic and sauté, stirring, until wilted. Combine the bread crumbs with the chicken stock in a bowl.

3. Combine the meat, onions, garlic, the bread crumb mixture, egg, allspice, salt, and pepper and blend well.

4. Shape the meat into 24 or more meatballs.

5. Heat the olive oil in a large frying pan. Add the meatballs and cook over medium heat, turning them carefully so they brown evenly. This should take about 5 minutes. Drain the fat. Add the Fresh Tomato Sauce to the pan. Bring to a simmer and sprinkle with parsley. Serve.

YIELD: 4 servings.   CALORIES PER SERVING: 335.

PRESENTATION: Prepare a bed of Noodles and Zucchini with Basil (see recipe page 209) and arrange 6 meatballs over the top. Spoon the sauce over the meat, allowing it to run down somewhat into the pasta and zucchini.

Calf's liver is more variable than you might think. One approach, of course, is to flour the liver and quickly sauté it to be pink and juicy inside. Another, offered here, is to start with very thin pieces of liver and a very hot pan. There will be no flouring. The idea is to cook the liver fast and crisp (the interior will of necessity not be pink) and serve it with a tangy sauce.

CALF'S LIVER WITH LEMON SAUCE

12 thin slices calf's liver (about 1¾ pounds)
½ teaspoon salt
Freshly ground black pepper (8 turns of the pepper mill)
1 tablespoon vegetable oil
3 tablespoons butter
Juice of 1 lemon
4 tablespoons chopped fresh parsley leaves

1. Sprinkle the liver with salt and pepper.

2. Heat the oil in a nonstick frying pan and sauté as many pieces of liver as will fit in it at one time for about 1½ minutes, or until browned. Turn the liver and sauté for another minute, or until it has reached the desired degree of doneness.

3. Remove the liver to a warm platter and keep it warm.

4. Pour off the fat from the pan. Add the butter and cook it over high heat until it turns a hazelnut color. Add the lemon juice and pour the hot butter over the liver. Sprinkle with the parsley.

YIELD: 6 servings.   CALORIES PER SERVING: 258.

PRESENTATION: Serve with Braised Endives and Parsleyed Potatoes (see recipes pages 225 and 212). Place 2 overlapping slices in the center of each dish. With 2 endives and 2 small potatoes, alternate the vegetables in a circle around the liver.

Calf's liver starts out as a delicate meat. Raspberry vinegar adds a sweet elegance to it.

SAUTÉED CALF'S LIVER WITH SHALLOTS AND RASPBERRY VINEGAR

¼ cup all-purpose flour
½ teaspoon salt
Freshly ground black pepper (8 turns of the pepper mill)
12 slices calf's liver (1¾ pounds)
4 tablespoons butter
4 tablespoons finely chopped shallots
½ cup raspberry vinegar
4 tablespoons finely chopped fresh parsley leaves

1. Blend the flour and salt and pepper together. Dredge the liver slices in the flour mixutre.

2. Melt 1 tablespoon of the butter in a large nonstick frying pan. Sauté the liver on one side for 2 minutes. Turn and sauté the other side for 2 minutes. This will produce a rare liver; if medium is desired, sauté a little longer. Set the liver aside.

3. Add the remaining butter to the pan. Add the shallots and sauté briefly. Pour in the vinegar and swirl it in the pan. Pour the sauce over the liver and sprinkle with the parsley.

YIELD: 6 servings.   CALORIES PER SERVING: 281.

PRESENTATION: Place 2 slices of liver in the center of the plate. Using a pastry bag, make four small, evenly spaced swirls of puréed carrot around the liver. Between each swirl, place a small Parsleyed Potato (see recipe page 212).

I've eaten and enjoyed brains all my life. It used to be that one of the main virtues of brains was that they were so inexpensive. That is less true now. An enduring virtue, however, is that brains are among the meats with the fewest calories. Thus, the calories tend to come from the sauce. If you manage to keep the fat in the sauce to a minimum, as I have in the recipe for brains with capers that follows this one, you can dine with abandon.

CALF'S BRAINS (BASIC PROCEDURE)

2 pair calf's brains
4 cups cold water
½ teaspoon salt
6 whole black peppercorns
3 tablespoons white wine vinegar
1 bay leaf
1 sprig fresh thyme, or ½ teaspoon dried thyme

1. Soak the brains in cold water for several hours in the refrigerator. Drain.

2. Remove and discard all the fiber-like threads and membranes adhering to the brains.

3. Place the brains in a saucepan and add the remaining ingredients. Bring the liquid to a boil and simmer for about 2 minutes. Remove the brains from the heat and let stand. The brains can be served immediately with a Vinaigrette (see recipe page 243) or with capers (see recipe below)

YIELD: 4 servings.   CALORIES PER SERVING: 284.

CALF'S BRAINS WITH CAPERS

2 pair cooked calf's brains (see preceding recipe for
basic procedure)
½ teaspoon salt
Freshly ground black pepper (8 turns of the pepper mill)
2 tablespoons butter
3 tablespoons drained capers
1 tablespoon red wine vinegar
3 tablespoons chopped fresh parsley leaves

1. Butterfly each half brain by slicing it in two lengthwise and spreading it open. Sprinkle the brains with salt and pepper.

2. Melt the butter in a nonstick frying pan and add the brains. Sauté on one side over medium heat until lightly browned, about 5 minutes. Turn the brains and sauté for about 2 minutes. Sprinkle the capers in the pan around the brains. Sauté over high heat for 2 or 3 more minutes. Add the vinegar and chopped parsley and serve immediately.

YIELD: 4 servings.   CALORIES PER SERVING: 337.

PRESENTATION: Brains are traditionally served with Parsleyed Potatoes (see recipe page 212). Place the split half brain in the center of the plate with 2 small potatoes at each end. On the side arrange a portion of bright, firm vegetable such as String Beans with Garlic (see recipe page 231).

The pity is that sweetbreads are expensive in the United States. Here is a meat whose advantage always was that not only was it nutritious and flavorful but it cost next to nothing. So now Americans are finally learning to appreciate it and the cost soars at the same time. Although the recipe offered here is a basic one, it uses almost no fat at all (but for the one little tablespoon of butter).

BRAISED SWEETBREADS

6 sweetbreads, about 2 pounds
1 tablespoon butter
1 carrot, scraped and sliced (½ cup)
1 onion, peeled and cut into ¼-inch slices (about ½ cup)
¼ cup chopped celery
1 garlic clove, chopped
3 sprigs fresh parsley
1 bay leaf
¼ teaspoon dried thyme
½ teaspoon salt
Freshly ground black pepper (6 turns of the pepper mill)
¼ cup dry white wine
1 cup chicken stock (see recipe page 30)
½ cup diced ripe tomatoes

1. Remove and discard any tough membranes from the sweetbreads. Soak them in cold water for several hours. Drain the sweetbreads and place them in a saucepan. Cover with cold water. Bring the water to a boil and simmer for 5 minutes. Drain. Cool the sweetbreads under running water.

2. To improve the sweetbreads' texture and remove the moisture, place them on a wire rack. Then place a baking dish over them and put weights in it. A large can of tomatoes works well. Refrigerate for at least 2 hours.

3. Preheat the oven to 400 degrees.

4. Melt the butter in a saucepan large enough to hold the sweetbreads in one layer. Add the carrot, onion, celery, garlic, parsley, bay leaf, and thyme. Cook, stirring, until the onion is lightly browned. Lay the sweetbreads on top and sprinkle with salt and pepper.

5. Add the wine, chicken stock, and tomatoes. Bring to a boil.

6. Place the saucepan in the oven and bake the sweetbreads for 20 minutes, basting occasionally.

7. Remove from the oven. Pour the liquid through a strainer to prepare a smooth sauce. There should be ¾ cup. Discard the vegetables.

8. Pour the sauce over the top of the sweetbreads and return them to the oven for 10 minutes. Baste once or twice.

YIELD: 6 servings.   CALORIES PER SERVING: 353.

PRESENTATION: Place 1 sweetbread in the center of the plate and serve with Fresh Peas and Tarragon (see recipe page 227) and Glazed Carrots (see recipe page 223). Alternate 2 small servings of peas with 2 small servings of carrots around the sweetbread. Sprinkle the sweetbreads with chopped parsley.

...9...

Lamb

The rich flavor of lamb is often imparted to it by its surrounding fat. But from long experience I know that lamb is still a marvelous, tender, and moist meat even when the fat is completely trimmed away. A number of the recipes here will stipulate that you do just that.

An understanding of lamb is often made difficult by all the terms that are used in describing it. Here's a quick primer for the better cuts: The "rack" of a lamb refers to the ribs, usually seven of them, just below the shoulder (if you go too far, you are into the shoulder and, thus, into a different area of the meat). Cradled by the rack is the "loin," the most tender and satisfying part of the lamb. It is surrounded by fat. This dense round of meat remains one of the jewels in all of cooking, even stripped of its fat. A "medallion" of lamb refers to a slice of the loin.

In this chapter are recipes for all of those expensive cuts of lamb. But we've also got recipes here for leg of lamb—boiled and roasted—for lamb meatballs and for exotic lamb burgers.

Once, if meat tasted "gamy" many people found it deplorable. Now, I think, many of those same people are more daring. It even makes sense these days to inentionally impart a gamy flavor to meat that would not otherwise have it. That is what I've none with this lamb dish. In fact, you will probably find that it tastes a great deal like venison.

BROILED LEG OF LAMB MARINATED IN RED WINE AND HERBS

1 7½-pound leg of lamb
½ teaspoon salt
Freshly ground black pepper (8 turns of the pepper mill)
1 teaspoon ground cumin
1 cup sliced onions
1 cup sliced carrots
1 tablespoon dried rosemary leaves
1 teaspoon dried thyme
1 tablespoon coriander seeds
1 tablespoon finely chopped garlic
1 bay leaf, crushed
1 bottle strong dry red wine
1 tablespoon butter

1. Have the butcher butterfly a leg of lamb for broiling, with all the excess fat and gristle removed.

2. Season both sides of the lamb with salt, pepper, and cumin. Place the lamb in a flat roasting pan and surround it with the onions and carrots. Sprinkle it with the rosemary, thyme, coriander, garlic, and bay leaf. Pour the wine over it and cover it with plastic wrap. Refrigerate for at least 6 hours, turning occasionally.

3. Preheat the broiler. Remove the lamb from the pan and pat it dry. Place the lamb in another pan and put it in the broiler, 6 inches from the source of the heat. Broil for 15 minutes on each side.

4. While the meat is broiling, pour the marinade in the original pan into a saucepan. Reduce it to ½ cup. Swirl in the butter and strain the sauce. Set it aside.

5. Transfer the lamb to a carving platter. Pour the sauce over it and let it rest in a warm place for about 10 minutes before slicing. Slice the lamb on the bias and serve.

YIELD: 8 servings.　　　　CALORIES PER SERVING: 433.

PRESENTATION: Place 3 slices of lamb in the center of each plate. On opposing sides, place two small portions of

Braised Red Cabbage (see recipe page 221). On each of the other opposing sides, place a Parsleyed Potato (see recipe page 212).

BOILED LEG OF LAMB ENGLISH STYLE

1 7-pound leg of lamb, trimmed of fat and
shinbone removed
1 tablespoon salt
4 whole black peppercorns
Water to barely cover, about 3 quarts
1 cup chopped leek, green portion only
1 cup chopped celery
1 cup chopped carrots
1 bay leaf
½ teaspoon dried thyme
1 clove garlic
2 sprigs fresh parsley
1 cup Caper Sauce (see recipe page 238)

1. Put the lamb in a large casserole, such as a Dutch oven. If your largest pot is too small, have the butcher remove the shank of the leg to make it shorter. Add water to cover and all the remaining ingredients. Bring to a boil, cover, and simmer for 1½ hours, turning the meat in the kettle every 15 minutes to ensure even cooking. After 1½ hours the lamb should be pink, with an internal temperature of about 135 degrees. If well-done meat is desired, continue cooking.

2. Let the lamb rest for 10 to 15 minutes in the pot before serving. Slice it very thinly, and serve it with Caper Sauce on the side.

YIELD: 10 servings.   CALORIES PER SERVING: 324.

PRESENTATION: Place 3 or 4 slices of lamb in the center of each plate. Position a small portion of Lentil Purée (see recipe page 226) at the top and at the bottom. On each side place a portion of string beans.

What we have here is a pair of small roasts of lamb, pure, intensely flavored meat with very little fat. Rather than roast meat like this, I've chosen to grill it, as if it were a steak, in very little oil, just enough to prevent sticking, and then to moisten it with a sauce made from deglazing the pan. The browning is the critical step; it needs to sear the meat, actually, to trap the juices inside the meat. This recipe ends up with meat that is rare, which is how I always prefer my rack of lamb. If you prefer lamb that is more thoroughly cooked, obviously you will have to adjust the cooking time.

BONELESS RACK OF LAMB ROSEMARY

**2 fatless, boneless loins of lamb, about 1½ pounds each,
cut from racks of 2 pounds each
2 teaspoons freshly ground rosemary
1 teaspoon salt
Freshly ground black pepper (8 turns of the pepper mill)
2 teaspoons olive oil
1 tablespoon butter
4 tablespoons chopped onion
2 teaspoons chopped garlic
¼ cup dry white wine
1 tablespoon tomato paste
½ cup chicken stock (see recipe page 30)
2 tablespoons chopped fresh parsley leaves**

1. Sprinkle the lamb with rosemary, salt, and pepper.

2. Heat the oil in a black iron skillet and add the lamb. Brown the meat quickly on all sides and continue to cook over medium heat for about 10 minutes more, turning the lamb occasionally.

3. Transfer the lamb to a warm plate. Cover it with foil.

4. Remove all the fat from the pan. Melt the butter in the skillet. Add the chopped onion and garlic, stirring until they are wilted. Pour in the wine and scrape the bottom of the pan with a wooden spatula to dissolve any solids. At high heat reduce the liquid by half. Add the tomato paste, stock, and any juice that has accumulated around the lamb. Reduce the sauce by half.

5. Pour the sauce over the lamb, along with the chopped parsley.

YIELD: 6 servings.   CALORIES PER SERVING: 375.

PRESENTATION: Cover precisely one half of the plate with gravy (leaving the other half for vegetables). Then take 6 very thin slices of lamb, cut on the bias, and place them over the pool of sauce in an overlapping row. On the side of the plate that has no gravy, you might try a Broiled Tomato Provençale (see recipe page 232) flanked by two small servings of a vegetable purée, such as carrot or broccoli or the String Bean Purée (see recipe page 231).

Lamb is moist enough without the layer of fat it is always covered with. This dish takes advantage of that fact, stripping the rack of virtually all its fat, leaving the pure loin intact with a graceful arch of naked bone reaching away from it. The meat is superb unadorned, but what I usually do—and I urge all but the super-calorie-conscious to do it as well—is place a tablespoon of butter on top of the lamb after it is cooked, while it is resting before being sliced. The butter drips down with the natural juices, enriching them. The liquid that accumulates in the carving platter is now a light, fine gravy and just the smallest touch of it will do. Incidentally, my desire to collect natural juices almost always compels me to carve on a platter rather than a board (unless the board has a well to hold the juice).

BROILED LEAN RACK OF LAMB

2 racks of lamb, 2½ pounds total weight after trimming (Have the butcher remove the backbone, leaving the loin exposed.)
½ teaspoon freshly ground black pepper
½ teaspoon ground coriander
½ teaspoon ground cumin
½ teaspoon chopped garlic
2 teaspoons dried rosemary leaves
½ teaspoon salt
1 tablespoon butter, optional

1. Preheat the broiler (if the broiler is heated separately, preheat it to 500 degrees).

2. Using a boning knife, remove all the exposed fat on the surface of the racks (do not dig into the meat to remove any that is marbled through). The loin and ribs arching away from the meat should be almost totally rid of fat.

3. Blend all the spices and the salt, and sprinkle the mixture over the meat. Place the racks in a broiler pan.

4. Place the racks about 3 to 4 inches from the source of the broiler's heat for about 5 minutes, or until they are well browned. Turn them over and broil for another 4 to 5 minutes. (Inadequate broilers will require more time, of course, perhaps 8 to 10 minutes on each side.)

5. Transfer the meat to a warm platter in a warm place. Dot the roast with butter, if a light gravy is desired. Allow the roast to rest for 5 minutes before slicing.

YIELD: 4 servings.   CALORIES PER SERVING: 234.

PRESENTATION: Slice the meat through each division in the ribs into individual chops, each with its own arched tail of bare bone. Place 3 slices of meat in a row toward the top of each plate, and below it place a small portion of Zucchini Bordelaise (see recipe page 233) and one of Sliced Potatoes au Gratin (see recipe page 212). Spoon a touch of gravy, as little as 1 teaspoon, over each portion of meat.

The term "medallion" usually refers to the very best portion of meat that anyone can cut. This recipe is for medallions of lamb, which is to say it is something of an elite dish.

MEDALLIONS OF LAMB WITH TARRAGON SAUCE AND SPINACH

10 ounces spinach leaves
3 tablespoons butter
½ cup thinly sliced onion
1 teaspoon salt
Freshly ground black pepper (10 turns of the pepper mill)
Pinch of grated nutmeg
2 boneless lamb loins, about ¾ pound each, cut in half
(The loins should come from 2 racks of lamb about
1¼ pounds each.)
1 tablespoon vegetable oil
2 tablespoons chopped fresh tarragon
2 tablespoons water

1. Pick over the spinach, pulling away and discarding any tough stems and blemished leaves. Rinse and dry the spinach.

2. Melt 1 tablespoon of butter in a saucepan and add the sliced onion. Cook briefly, stirring, but do not brown. Add the spinach, ½ teaspoon of salt, 5 turns of the pepper mill, and the nutmeg. Cook, stirring, until the spinach is wilted and most of its moisture has evaporated. Set aside and keep warm.

3. Sprinkle the lamb with the remaining salt and pepper.

4. Heat the oil in a frying pan and add the lamb. Brown the meat quickly on all sides over high heat for about 7 minutes and discard all fat. Reduce the heat and add the remaining 2 tablespoons of butter. Continue to cook for 2 minutes longer. Then add the tarragon and water. Remove the lamb from the heat and let it rest for 5 minutes. Slice the lamb in the pan to add juice to the gravy in the pan. Serve with the spinach and gravy.

YIELD: 6 servings.   CALORIES PER SERVING: 256.

PRESENTATION: Place a mound of spinach in the center of a warm plate. Surround the spinach with several ¼-inch slices of lamb. Spoon sauce over the lamb, allowing it to drip onto the periphery of the plate. Do not cover the lamb completely with the sauce; you want to the pink to show through.

The Duchess of Windsor (if I can be forgiven for dropping a name) would come to the Pavillon when I was its chef and practically survive on the simplest and leanest of lamb dishes. The secret is entirely in the preparation rather than the seasonings. The cooking is so rapid that everything else should be prepared ahead of the lamb.

BROILED LAMB CHOPS À LA FRANÇAISE

1 2-pound rack of lamb (Have the butcher remove the backbone so the loin is exposed.)
½ teaspoon salt
Freshly ground black pepper (6 turns of the pepper mill)
2 teaspoons vegetable oil
1 tablespoon butter, melted

1. With a boning knife remove all the fat to expose the loin and the bones of the ribs. The fat will tend to come off as a single large flap. The ribs arching away from the loin should be nearly fatless. Slice the rack into 6 chops about even in size. This will result in some chops with one bone and some with two. So cut away any extra bones by sliding the boning knife down between the 2 bones. At the base of the bones the extra one should slice away easily.

2. Place the chops between plastic wrap and pound them until they are quite thin, not much more than ⅛ inch (the meat should resemble a paillard of veal or beef). Take care not to separate the meat from the bone. The bone should be flattened somewhat along with the meat.

3. Sprinkle the meat with salt and pepper on one side. Brush it with the oil on one side.

4. Heat a cast-iron pan until it is smoking. Place the chops in it oil side down. Turn the lamb 2 or 3 times to be sure it is browned evenly. It will be done after about 2 minutes of cooking. The signal that it is done is the moisture rising through the lamb and bubbling on its surface. Brush the meat with butter.

Yield: 3 servings.   Calories per Serving: 306.

Presentation: The lamb is so simple that you want to accompany it with flavorful vegetgables. Place the lamb toward the top of the dish with the meat overlapping and the bones going in the same direction. Place a broiled tomato on either side with a small portion of Zucchini Bordelaise (see recipe page 233) below it.

I present here a French-style chop with an accompaniment that I have come to like a great deal, braised sweet pepper. The peppers can be red or yellow or, for that matter, a mixture of the two.

BROILED LAMB CHOPS WITH BRAISED SWEET PEPPERS

4 rib lamb chops, each ½ pound and 1½ inches thick (All fat should be trimmed away, leaving a bare bone and a round of meat.)
½ teaspoon salt
Freshly ground black pepper (12 turns of the pepper mill)
½ teaspoon ground cumin seed
1 teaspoon dried rosemary leaves
1 tablespoon olive oil
1 teaspoon finely chopped garlic
2 onions thickly sliced (2 cups)
2 sweet red or yellow ("banana") peppers, sliced (2 cups)
2 tomatoes, cored and cut into ¾-inch cubes (2 cups)
1 teaspoon Oriental Curry Powder (see recipe page 265)
2 tablespoons chopped fresh parsley leaves

1. Sprinkle the chops with half the salt and pepper along with the cumin and rosemary. Set aside.

2. Heat the olive oil in a frying pan. Add the garlic and cook briefly without browning the garlic. Add the onions and peppers and sauté, stirring, for about 5 minutes. Add the tomatoes, curry powder, and the remaining salt and pepper and bring to a boil. Cover and simmer for 20 minutes, stirring occasionally.

3. Preheat the broiler. Place the lamb chops about 4 inches from the source of the heat. Broil for 5 minutes and turn the chops. Broil 5 minutes more. The meat should be pink inside. Sprinkle with the chopped parsley and serve with the sauce.

YIELD: 4 servings.   CALORIES PER SERVING: 294.

PRESENTATION: Place a single lamb chop at the center of the serving plate with a laurel of vegetables around it. A small bunch of watercress adds still more color and is a flavorful garnish.

Good lamb is expensive these days. But an excellent way to use inexpensive cuts of meat, from the leg and the neck, is to ask the butcher to grind it. Be sure to ask him to remove as much fat as possible. The following recipe produces a tasty, slightly exotic dish that is a terrific change of pace. A tip on preparing meatballs: Always moisten the fingertips continuously as you roll the meat.

LAMB MEATBALLS WITH PIGNOLIS

½ cup pignolis
1 teaspoon butter
¾ cup chopped scallions
1 teaspoon chopped garlic
1½ pounds lean ground lamb
½ cup chopped fresh parsley leaves
½ teaspoon ground rosemary
¾ cup coarse fresh bread crumbs
½ cup sharp Cheddar cheese cut into ¼-inch cubes
½ teaspoon salt
Freshly ground black pepper (6 turns of the pepper mill)
1 large egg, lightly beaten
1 teaspoon vegetable oil
2¼ cups Fresh Tomato Sauce (see recipe page 241)

1. Toast the pignolis in a dry nonstick pan, stirring, until golden brown.

2. Melt the butter in a small skillet and add the scallions and garlic, sautéing briefly without browning them. Allow to cool for a moment.

3. Put the ground lamb in a mixing bowl and add the scallions and garlic, the parsley, rosemary, pignolis, bread crumbs, cheese, salt, pepper, and egg. Use your hands to blend the mixture well. Shape the mixture into 36 equal golf-ball-size shapes.

4. Heat the oil in a nonstick frying pan and cook one third of the meatballs at a time, browning them evenly for about 5 minutes.

5. When all the meatballs are browned, return them to the frying pan and add the tomato sauce. Bring it to a boil and simmer for 2 minutes. Serve hot with the sauce.

YIELD: 6 servings.   CALORIES PER SERVING: 361.

PRESENTATION: Shape Creole Rice (see recipe page 213) in a mold and place it in the center of each plate. Place 6 meatballs in a ring around the rice and spoon the sauce over the meatballs, allowing it to run down toward the rice.

When I was still a teenager—that was in the thirties, heaven help me—I spent one exotic winter season working in Morocco, in Marrakesh, where Europeans would flock, then as now, for the steamy heat. A flavor that stays with me from that hot winter is of a North African lamb sausage called merguez. *What I've done here is to design a similar lamb preparation to be served as a burger to lend some spice, literally, to a good old North American barbecue (and add fewer calories to it than beef would).*

LAMB BURGERS WITH GOAT CHEESE

2 pounds very lean chopped lamb
2 tablespoons finely chopped garlic
½ teaspoon ground cumin
½ teasoon hot red pepper flakes
½ teaspoon salt
Freshly ground black pepper (12 turns of the pepper mill)
6 ounces French or California goat cheese, such as
Boucheron or St. André
1½ teaspoons dried rosemary leaves

1. Mix the lamb, garlic, cumin, hot pepper flakes, salt, and black pepper together and prepare 6 patties, 3 inches in diameter and an inch thick.

2. Place the patties over a hot charcoal or gas grill and cook for 4 to 5 minutes. Turn the patties and place a mound of about 1 ounce of cheese on top of each. Sprinkle each burger with ¼ teaspoon of the rosemary.

3. Close the top of the grill and cook the patties for another 4 to 5 minutes. If the grill has no top, create one with strips of aluminum foil. (This last stage can also be done beneath the flame of a broiler.)

YIELD: 6 servings.   CALORIES PER SERVING: 360.

PRESENTATION: This burger is not intended to be served on a bun, which would hide its looks. I like to serve it with a raw salad, such as the Morroccan-style Carrot and Orange Salad (see recipe page 47). Place the burger in the center of a serving plate with a small portion of salad on either side. A possibility is to use one serving of Morroccan salad and another of String Bean and Mushroom Salad (see recipe page 49).

...*10*...

ℒork

When you learn to cook it properly—and are willing to spend the money to buy only the best cuts—pork can be an admirably subtle and lean meat. When it is trimmed of all fat, the loin, or center cut, of pork can be as lean as veal but with its own distinctive flavor. It can, in fact, be prepared as veal would be—for scaloppines. It can be roasted in its own hearty fashion, with garlic and rosemary. For people with a bit of a sweet tooth, pork can be nudged up to the realm of the sublime with raisins soaked in Madeira. And lean pork can be as exotic as you want it to be. For this book I designed a recipe for pork burgers with coriander and ginger. The result is a lovely, lean burger that resembles no hamburger you've ever eaten before.

Sliced thinly with a light gravy—rather than the heavy gravies ordinarily used—this pork roast will seem as delicate as one of veal. I should mention, too, that the seasoning has an unusual wrinkle: The marriage of garlic and rosemary is Italian, the cumin is North African, but when they combine it seems as though they should have always been together.

ROAST PORK WITH GARLIC AND ROSEMARY

3 large garlic cloves
1 6-pound center-cut pork roast, with excess fat removed
2 teaspoons salt
Freshly ground black pepper (8 turns of the pepper mill)
½ teaspoon ground cumin
1 tablespoon dried rosemary
1 medium-sized onion, peeled and halved
¾ cup water

1. Preheat the oven to 400 degrees.

2. Cut each garlic clove into several slivers. With a paring knife, create small pockets for the garlic slivers near the bone end of the meat and in the fat. Insert the slivers.

3. Mix the salt, pepper, cumin, and rosemary together and rub the meat with the mixture. Place the roast fat side down in a roasting pan. Add the onion halves to the pan.

4. Roast for 30 minutes; then turn the roast so that it is fat side up. Remove the melted fat from the pan. Cook for 30 minutes longer.

5. Remove the fat from the pan again and add the water, stirring to disolve the solids adhering to the pan. Return the roast to the oven and reduce the oven temperature to 375 degrees. Continue roasting for 20 minutes, basting occasionally.

YIELD: 8 servings.   CALORIES PER SERVING: 379.

PRESENTATION: Slice the roast very thinly. On each plate place 4 overlapping slices in the center. Place 2 small portions of Lentil Purée (see recipe page 226) on opposite sides of the meat. Drizzle the gravy over the meat, without covering it entirely, and allow the gravy to pool in the uncovered areas of the plate. If vegetables, such as Braised Red Cabbage (see recipe page 221), are desired, place a small serving of the vegetable in the areas between the portions of purée.

Pork is one of those meats that weather well under tl
powerful flavors. In this dish, it still remains delicate,
combination of capers, wine vinegar, and Dijon must

PORK CHOPS WITH CAPER.

4 center-cut pork chops (½ pound each),
trimmed of most fat
½ teaspoon salt
Freshly ground black pepper (8 turns of the pepper mill)
1 teaspoon vegetable oil
⅓ cup drained large capers
¾ cup chopped onions
2 teaspoons chopped garlic
2 tablespoons white wine vinegar
¾ cup chicken stock (see recipe page 30)
½ cup diced ripe tomato
1 tablespoon Dijon mustard
1 tablespoon chopped fresh parsley leaves

1. Sprinkle the chops with salt and pepper. Heat the oil in a non-stick frying pan. When the oil is very hot, put the chops in it and brown them well on each side, about 5 minutes a side. Lower the heat and let the chops cook through, about another 20 minutes. Turn the chops frequently as they cook. Remove the chops to a warm platter and cover them to keep them warm. Discard all the fat in the pan.

2. Add the capers to the pan. Sauté briefly. Add the onion and sauté, shaking the pan. Stir the capers and onions together. Brown slightly. Add the garlic. Sauté briefly without browning it. Add the vinegar and stir to dissolve any meat particles in the pan. Add the stock and tomato and any liquid accumulated around the chops.

3. Allow the sauce to boil vigorously until most of the moisture has evaporated. Stir in the mustard and pour the over the chops immediately. Garnish with the chopped parsley.

YIELD: 4 servings.   CALORIES PER SERVING: 260.

PRESENTATION: Mold Rice Pilaf in a cup (see recipe page 214) and position the rice at the top edge of the plate. Place one chop next to the rice and spoon a little of the sauce over the chop. Garnish the chop with parsley. Arrange a portion of Buttered Asparagus (see recipe page 219) between the pork chop and the rice.

Center-cut pork chops start out with very little fat, and then, when you trim them well, there is no sense of greasiness at all. For this recipe, I've used only 1 tablespoon of butter to aid in the browning and to add an incalculable amount of flavor. Moreover, that sense of leanness is further amplified by the use of cabbage, which takes up the fat, enhancing its own flavor while diminishing the greasiness of the dish as a whole.

PORK CHOPS WITH GREEN CABBAGE

1 2½-pound green cabbage
1 tablespoon butter
4 center-cut pork chops (about ½ pound each)
2 teaspoons salt
Freshly ground black pepper (12 turns of the pepper mill)
1½ cups sliced onions
2 teaspoons chopped garlic
½ cup dry white wine
1 bay leaf
½ teaspoon dried thyme
2 whole cloves
½ cup chicken stock (see recipe page 30)

1. Cut away and discard the core of the cabbage. Cut the cabbage into 8 pieces and then into ¼-inch-thick slices, about 16 loosely packed cups.

2. Melt the butter in a Dutch oven casserole. Sprinkle the chops with 1 teaspoon of the salt and 6 turns of the pepper mill and lay them in the casserole. Cook them over high heat for about 2 minutes on each side, or until they are browned. Scatter the onions and garlic around the chops and cook, stirring, until the onions are wilted. Add the wine and stir it in. Add the cabbage, bay leaf, thyme, cloves, chicken stock, and remaining salt and pepper. Cover and cook for about 45 minutes. If there is much more than 1½ cups of liquid, uncover the pot and reduce the liquid over high heat.

YIELD: 4 servings.   CALORIES PER SERVING: 343.

PRESENTATION: The cabbage should be molded in a cup, such as a demitasse cup or a timbale or a common coffee cup. Do this by pressing the cabbage into the cup tightly. It will unmold easily when the cup is inverted over the plate. Place 1 to 3 mounds of cabbage along one side of a single chop, with the chop

positioned at the top of the plate. On either side of
the chop, it's a nice idea to place a Parsleyed Potato
(see recipe page 212). Spoon a little of the liquid
from the pan over the meat, allowing some to drizzle over everything else, too.

This recipe employs the leanest of pork to prepare scaloppines as fine, in my view, as those you would obtain from veal. But the surprise here is in the use a coarse mustard, so coarse that the seed is recognizable. It is called moutarde de Meaux. (Meaux is a town in France, just as Dijon is.) The result is less refined than it would be with other mustards; a memorable, cruder country feeling is given to the pork.

PORK SCALOPPINE WITH COARSE MUSTARD SAUCE

**12 thin and lean slices (about 3 ounces each)
boneless pork loin
1 teaspoon salt
Freshly ground black pepper (8 turns of the pepper mill)
2 tablespoons vegetable oil
½ cup finely chopped onion
1 teaspoon finely chopped garlic
2 tablespoons red wine vinegar
¼ cup chicken stock (see recipe page 30)
1 tablespoon tomato paste
1 bay leaf
½ teaspoon dried thyme
2 teaspoons ground cumin
2 tablespoons moutarde de Meaux
4 tablespoons chopped fresh parsley leaves**

1. Put the pork slices between sheets of plastic wrap and, on a flat surface, pound them to flatten them without breaking the meat. You want something not quite as thin as a veal scaloppine: a little less than ¼ inch thick. Sprinkle the meat with salt and pepper.

2. Heat the oil in a large frying pan. When the oil is hot, brown the meat in it, about 10 minutes. Transfer the meat to a platter and cover with foil.

3. Remove the fat from the pan. Add the onion and garlic to the pan and cook, stirring, until they are lightly browned. Add the vinegar and cook briefly. Add the stock, scraping the bottom of the pan with a wooden spatula to dissolve any solids adhering to the pan. Add the tomato paste, bay leaf, thyme, cumin, and any juice that has accumulated around the meat. Bring the mixture to a boil and add the mustard, blending it into the liquid. Simmer for about 5 minutes. Reduce the liquid by half over high heat. Spoon the sauce over the meat. Serve garnished with parsley.

YIELD: 6 servings.   CALORIES PER SERVING: 363.

PRESENTATION: Place 2 scaloppines in overlapping fashion toward the top of the plate. Below them, center a serving of Lentil Purée (see recipe page 226), flanked by Steamed Broccoli spears (see recipe page 220). Spoon the sauce over the meat. Sprinkle the meat with parsley.

The leanest part of the pork is the loin. With all the fat removed, it will still be remarkably moist even when grilled—as this brochette is—especially if it has been properly marinated. The marinade has the ability to infuse it with flavor and tenderize it at the same time.

BROCHETTES OF PORK WITH HERBS

1½ pounds boneless lean pork loin, cut into 1-inch cubes
¼ cup fresh lemon juice
1 tablespoon minced garlic
4 sprigs fresh thyme, or 1 teaspoon dried thyme
1 bay leaf, crushed
10 fresh basil leaves, or 1 tablespoon dried basil
2 tablespoons chopped Italian parsley leaves
1 tablespoon grated lemon rind
2 tablespoons red wine vinegar
1 tablespoon olive oil
Freshly ground black pepper (8 turns of the pepper mill)
½ teaspoon salt

1. Combine the meat and all the ingredients in a mixing bowl. Blend well. Cover with plastic wrap and refrigerate to marinate for 4 hours at least (the longer the better).

2. Drain the meat and arrange equal portions on each of 6 skewers.

3. Preheat a charcoal grill or oven broiler and grill for 15 minutes, or until the pork is cooked. Turn the pork often.

YIELD: 6 servings.   CALORIES PER SERVING: 244.

PRESENTATION: Place a serving of Rice with Zucchini and Sweet Red Peppers (see recipe page 215) in the center of each plate, with a skewer of pork over the middle of each. Arrange Snow Peas with Sesame Seeds (see recipe page 228) at the periphery of the plate, pointing away from the skewer.

Sweet and sour sauces go well with pork and duck, and I like them enormously, as long as they aren't sticky from starch. Here, the sauce is anything but heavy, with sweetness from the Madeira and the raisins and sharpness from an abundance of lime. Lime is tart but softer than vinegar, which is more common in such preparations.

PORK CUTLET WITH LIME AND MADEIRA SAUCE

½ cup raisins
½ cup Madeira
2 tablespoons vegetable oil
8 ½-inch-thick pork cutlets, cut from the loin, about 6 ounces each (All fat should be removed and the pork should be pounded slightly to flatten it.)
½ teaspoon salt
Freshly ground black pepper (8 turns of the pepper mill)
½ cup chopped onion
4 plum tomatoes (½ pound), peeled and diced (about 1 cup)
2 tablespoons fresh lime juice
1 cup chicken stock (see recipe page 30)
1 large peeled lime, seeded and cut into small cubes (¼ cup)
½ teaspoon grated lime rind
1 tablespoon butter
2 tablespoons chopped fresh coriander leaves or parsley leaves

1. Soak the raisins in the Madeira for ½ hour.

2. Heat the oil in a large nonstick frying pan. Sprinkle the cutlets with salt and pepper.

3. Lay the cutlets in the pan and cook over medium heat. When they are browned on both sides, cook for another 10 minutes.

4. Remove the cutlets to another frying pan, cover, and keep them warm. Discard all the fat in the first frying pan and add the chopped onion. Stir and brown lightly. Add the tomatoes and pour in the lime juice and then the chicken stock. Add the cubed lime. With a wooden spatula, scrape and stir to dissolve any solids in the pan. Add the raisins and Madeira and the lime rind.

5. Reduce the liquid in the pan to about 1 cup. Swirl in the butter. Pour the sauce over the cutlets. Serve very hot garnished with the chopped coriander.

YIELD: 8 servings.   CALORIES PER SERVING: 409.

PRESENTATION: Place a cutlet toward the top of each plate. Spoon the sauce over and around the meat, taking care to get the raisins to fall onto the meat rather than alongside. Below the meat and bare of sauce, place a serving of Puréed Potatoes (see recipe page 212), shaped more or less as an oblong. To make the potatoes a bit more ornate, dip a serving spoon in warm water, invert it over the potatoes and lightly press down all along the length of the oblong. The result will be a curved ripple effect.

This is a pork hamburger (sounds redundant); it really doesn't resemble the beef version much at all. The flavoring is unusual and the meat starts out much leaner than the meat in a hamburger would be. Beef burgers, after all, will contain as much as 30 percent fat.

PORK BURGERS WITH CORIANDER AND GINGER

1¾ pounds lean ground pork
½ cup chopped scallions
1 teaspoon ground coriander
2 teaspoons grated fresh ginger
1 teaspoon finely chopped garlic
½ cup fresh bread crumbs
1 teaspoon light soy sauce
¼ cup chicken stock (see recipe page 30)
Freshly ground black pepper (8 turns of the pepper mill)
1 tablespoon vegetable oil

1. Put the pork in a mixing bowl and add all the ingredients, except the oil. Blend well.

2. Divide the mixture into 8 equal portions and form them into hamburger shapes, about 1 inch thick.

3. Heat the oil in a frying pan. Put the burgers in the pan and cook for 7 to 8 minutes over medium heat. Grill the other side for 7 to 8 minutes.

YIELD: 4 servings.   CALORIES PER SERVING: 319.

PRESENTATION: Spoon Fresh Tomato Sauce (see recipe page 241) onto half of each serving plate. Place 2 burgers over the sauce on each plate. On the bare half of the plate, place a serving of Steamed Broccoli (see recipe page 220).

...11...

Beef

For a while I wondered whether there should be any beef at all in this book. I decided, ultimately, that even though beef is the most fat-laden of meats, it is possible to come to grips with it in a low-calorie approach. The cuts of meat would have to be chosen with special care, and so would the methods of preparation. (I am not in favor of destroying meat by drying out all of its moisture in an effort to expunge all of its fat.) The results are satisfying, I believe.

For the one steak offered here, I suggest using the New York cut, which has an easily removed strip of fat. I use the cut of beef known as the fillet in another recipe, because it is extraordinarily lean for meat so tender. The Beef Paillard—beef pounded thin and quickly grilled—has the virtue of looking like a lot more meat than it is. And for the hamburger au poivre I urge you to use ground sirloin. The best idea is to grind it yourself in a good food processor (employing the chopping blade). You'll get an excellent texture that way—not the mush one finds in supermarkets—and at the same time you can control how much fat will go into each patty. Stores, after all, actually add fat, in some instances, to their ground beef concoctions.

Of all the cuts of meat one of the leanest and tenderest is the fillet. Americans are very familiar with: fillet mignon, of course. Each of those steaks is a slice of the larger fillet. The whole roast, like the fillet mignon, has little fat and no gristle. It is so good that I particularly like it virtually unadorned, that is, au naturel, with only its own juices as the gravy.

ROAST FILLET OF BEEF AU NATUREL

1 2¼-pound fillet, trimmed of all fat and gristle
½ teaspoon salt
Freshly ground black pepper (8 turns of the pepper mill)
1 tablespoon oil
1 tablespoon butter

1. Preheat the oven to 475 degrees.

2. Place the fillet in a small roasting pan and sprinkle it with salt and pepper. Brush it with oil. Put the pan on the bottom rack. Roast for 10 minutes, basting occasionally. Turn and roast on the other side for 10 minutes. Remove the fat from the pan. Dot the fillet with the butter and roast for another 5 minutes. Remove the meat from the oven and let it rest for 10 minutes in a warm place.

3. To serve, slice the fillet in the pan so the juice from the meat blends with the drippings to form a gravy.

YIELD: 8 servings.   CALORIES PER SERVING: 274.

PRESENTATION: The fillet should be cut on the bias, with slices about ¼ inch thick to produce larger slices. Position 3 slices, overlapping slightly, in the center of each plate. Centered below the meat, place a portion of puréed carrots, flanked by Snow Peas with Sesame Seeds (see recipe page 228). Spoon the gravy over the meat just before serving.

Up until ten years ago, raw beef, with the exception of steak tartare, was very uncommon in this country. But along with the popularity of the raw fish of the Japanese, an Italian entry has begun to gain acceptance. It is called carpaccio, *beef sliced as thinly as smoked salmon and served with a pungent sauce. The use of yogurt in this recipe allows for a good deal less oil than would otherwise be the case. I suggest that your butcher do the slicing of the meat, but, if that is not possible, slice it yourself. To do that, use a chunk of semi-frozen meat and, with a good slicing knife, cut against the grain. Whoever slices the meat, it should not be done more than 2 hours in advance, or it will lose its color.*

CARPACCIO

*1½ pounds raw, lean beef, such as top round,
sliced as thinly as possible
1¼ cups red wine vinegar
¼ cup drained capers
¼ cup chopped fresh parsley leaves
¼ cup fresh basil leaves
¼ cup Dijon mustard
¼ cup coarsely chopped onion
1 garlic clove
¼ cup olive oil
¼ cup lowfat plain yogurt
2 tablespoons water
Freshly ground black pepper (8 turns of the pepper mill)*

1. Trim the meat to remove all possible fat.
2. Arrange the meat in one layer—a fan pattern is attractive—on a cold serving plate.
3. Put all the remaining ingredients into a blender or food processor and blend until smooth. Spoon the sauce over the meat and serve.

YIELD: 6 servings.   CALORIES PER SERVING: 264.

PRESENTATION: The plate should look summery, decorated with fresh sprigs of herbs, such as basil, chervil, or tarragon, perhaps in combination.

Beef stew is a hearty, if a bit ordinary, dish. I put my mind to the job of creating a beef stew that was exotic, literally. To do that I added the Eastern flavorings of ginger and cumin, which work beautifully together, and the tumeric, which gives the stew an unusual golden color, evocative of curry. The stew is like a curry, in fact, but it is mild rather than hot. The sauce, in keeping with the approach of this book, is light, with no flour. The binding is done by the vegetables themselves.

ORIENTAL BEEF STEW

1 tablespoon grated fresh ginger
1 tablespoon ground tumeric
1 teaspoon ground cumin
½ teaspoon salt
Freshly ground black pepper (8 turns of the pepper mill)
4 pounds top round, fat removed, cut into 1-inch cubes
1 tablespoon vegetable oil
½ cup chopped onion
1 teaspoon chopped garlic
1 cup carrots cut into ¾-inch cubes
1 cup celery cut into ¾-inch cubes
1 cup peeled and diced ripe tomatoes
¾ cup beef stock (see recipe page 31)
½ teaspoon dried thyme
1 bay leaf

1. Combine the ginger, tumeric, cumin, salt, and pepper and dredge the meat in the mixture.

2. Heat the oil in a heavy casserole and add the meat, browning it evenly over high heat for 10 minutes. Discard the fat.

3. Add the onion, garlic, carrots, and celery and cook for 5 minutes. Add the tomatoes, beef stock, thyme, and bay leaf. Bring the stew to a boil. Simmer for 1 hour and 45 minutes, or until the meat is tender. Uncover the casserole and continue cooking for 15 minutes, stirring gently, to reduce the gravy.

YIELD: 8 servings.   CALORIES PER SERVING: 315.

PRESENTATION: Mold Rice Pilaf (see recipe page 214) in a cup and position the mound of rice in the center of each plate, surrounded by the stew.

Steak benefits from a sharp sauce. For the sake of being slightly unusual, I've chosen here to create a sauce with the coarse mustard known as Meaux. The cut of meat suggested here is meant to be lean to diminish its heaviness and also because it goes especially well with the sauce. The cut suggested is known around much of the country as a New York cut, which is simply a boneless strip of sirloin. It can be made very lean by slicing away the strip of fat on the rim.

STEAK À LA MOUTARDE DE MEAUX

4 New York-cut boneless sirloin steaks, without fat, about
½ pound each (A fillet mignon will do nicely, too.)
½ teaspoon salt
Freshly ground black pepper (8 turns of the pepper mill)
2 tablespoons butter
2 tablespoons finely chopped shallots
2 tablespoons Cognac
¼ cup chicken stock (see recipe page 30)
3 tablespoons moutarde de Meaux or Dijon mustard
2 tablespoons chopped fresh parsley leaves

1. Heat a 10-inch black iron skillet (a pan that is too large will have bare spots that cause the liquid to evaporate too quickly). Sprinkle the steaks with salt and pepper. When the pan is very hot, place the steaks in it and sear the meat for 4 minutes. Turn the steaks and cook for 4 or 5 minutes longer, or until they reach the desired degree of doneness.

2. Remove the steaks to a serving platter and keep them warm. Pour off all the fat in the pan. Melt the butter in the pan. Add the shallots and stir. Add the Cognac (it may ignite, which is fine).

3. Add the stock. Over high heat, add the mustard. Pour in any liquid that has accumulated around the steaks. With a whisk, blend the sauce well and spoon it over the steaks. Garnish with parsley.

YIELD: 4 servings.   CALORIES PER SERVING: 415.

PRESENTATION: Serve with Macedoine of Vegetables and Sliced Potatoes au Gratin (see recipes pages 234 and 212). Place the steak in the center of the plate, with the potatoes arranged on one side and the vegetables on the other.

The first of the paillard dishes—lean meat, pounded flat and cooked fast—was beef. Only later were the leaner veal and chicken employed. The story is that the method was named long ago after a Parisian restaurateur, Monsieur Paillard. It remains a magnificent approach to beef. As usual with simple preparations such as these paillard dishes, the secret is in the quality of the ingredients. Buy the best sirloin you can. Make sure the grill, pan, or broiler is very hot. Then sear the pounded meat rapidly.

BEEF PAILLARD

4 New York-cut sirloin steaks, ½ pound each,
all the fat removed
½ teaspoon salt
Freshly ground black pepper (8 turns of the pepper mill)
1 tablespoon oil for brushing
1 tablespoon butter, melted
2 tablespoons chopped fresh parsley leaves

1. Place the steak between sheets of plastic wrap and pound it with a flat meat pounder until it is ¼ inch thick or a little less.

2. Season the meat with salt and pepper and brush it lightly with the oil.

3. Make a cast-iron skillet or a stove-top grill very hot and cook the meat for 30 seconds on each side. It should sear rapidly.

4. Place the meat on a hot plate and rub with the butter. Sprinkle with parsley.

YIELD: 4 servings.   CALORIES PER SERVING: 381.

PRESENTATION: Position the steak in the center of a hot plate. Below it place a serving of Home-Fried Potatoes (see recipe page 213). Above it should go a small bunch of watercress.

Boiled meats are often scorned because they are inherently bland. But they are wholesome indeed, and when their flavor is given a boost by some sharp addition they are among my favorite foods. Customarily, a boiled beef shank might be presented with sea salt, mustard, and cornichons to give it that boost. Here, a horseradish sauce that is somewhat lower in calories than other such sauces serves the purpose well.

BOILED SHANK OF BEEF WITH VEGETABLES

1 sprig fresh thyme, or ½ teaspoon dried thyme
1 bay leaf
6 sprigs fresh parsley
6 slices beef shank or shin with bone,
about 1¼ inch thick and 1 pound each
4 quarts water
1 tablespoon salt
2 whole cloves
1 onion
1 garlic clove
5 whole black peppercorns
6 small leeks
8 medium-sized carrots (about ¾ pound), peeled
8 small white turnips (about ¾ pound), peeled
1 2¼-pound cabbage, halved
Tomato and Horseradish Sauce (see recipe page 242)

1. Prepare a bouquet garni of the thyme, bay leaf, and parsley by simply tying the fresh herbs together. If using dried thyme, place the herbs in a piece of cheesecloth and tie it closed.

2. Place the beef in a large kettle and add the cold water and salt. Bring to a boil and, using a skimmer or slotted spoon, skim off any foam that comes to the surface. Add the bouquet garni. Stick a clove into each end of the onion and drop the onion into the pot. Add the garlic and peppercorns.

3. Lower the heat and simmer, uncovered, for 2½ hours.

4. Clean the leeks by splitting the green parts lengthwise twice with a paring knife and then running the vegetable under cool water. Tie the leeks into 2 bundles of 3 each.

5. Add the leeks and other vegetables to the kettle and simmer for 30 minutes more. Serve with Horseradish Sauce.

YIELD: 6 servings.   CALORIES PER SERVING: 534.

PRESENTATION: One option is to serve a bowl of the bouillon with Croutons (see recipe page 264) and a sprinkling of parsley as a first course. (If the bouillon is not used, refrigerate or freeze it for soup or sauce later.) To serve the meat, place a single shank in the center of each plate. Place a tablespoon of Horseradish Sauce on each side of the shank. Then, keeping each of the vegetables separate from the others, alternate them in a pattern around the meat.

The cooking avant guarde has fallen in love with goat cheese. And I'm delighted. I had nearly forgotten about it—nearly forgotten how as a boy I would pop little rounds of the cheese (called crottins*) into my mouth as if they were wedges of candy. Now, I am devouring goat cheese again. It is especially good with almost any broiled meat. It makes for a cheeseburger that is like no other.*

HAMBURGERS WITH GOAT CHEESE

2 pounds freshly chopped lean round steak
½ teaspoon ground coriander
½ teaspoon coarse black pepper
½ teaspoon salt
¼ pound goat cheese, crumbled
2 tablespoons chopped fresh chives or tarragon
or a combination of the two

1. Form 6 hamburgers of 3 inches in diameter and ¾ inch thick. Do not handle the meat more than necessary or the texture will be ruined.

2. Blend the coriander, black pepper, and salt together. Sprinkle the mixture over each side of the hamburgers.

3. Heat an outdoor grill or preheat a kitchen broiler. Place the hamburgers 3 inches from the source of the heat.

4. Broil the meat for 3 minutes, then turn and broil for 2 minutes longer. Place 1 ounce of cheese on the center of each burger and broil for 2 minutes. Transfer to serving plates and garnish with herbs.

YIELD: 6 servings.   CALORIES PER SERVING: 293.

PRESENTATION: Do not serve this dish with rolls. Instead, place each burger in the center of a plate surrounded by Snow Peas with Sesame Seeds (see recipe page 228) and a broiled tomato.

The virtues of white pepper are underappreciated. I use it in sauces, when I don't want black specks to disturb their looks. I also use it when I'm looking for something subtler than the power of black pepper. For instance, as the recipe here will demonstrate, it contributes to a hamburger au poivre that is very peppery but at the same time much smoother than a similar recipe prepared with black pepper. In this instance, I have stipulated that the burgers be thick so that they are like chopped steak and to accommodate that steak idea I've also added Cognac, which is a typical flavoring in steak au poivre.

HAMBURGERS AU POIVRE BLANC

2 pounds lean ground sirloin
½ teaspoon salt
2 tablespoons crushed white peppercorns (They can be
crushed with the bottom of a heavy pan.)
2 tablespoons chopped shallots
2 tablespoons Cognac
¼ cup dry red wine
¼ cup chicken or beef stock (see recipes pages 30 and 31)
1 tablespoon butter

1. Shape the meat into 6 hamburgers, about 3 inches in diameter and ¾ inch thick. Sprinkle the burgers with salt and press the crushed peppercorns onto the meat. Press down on the meat to help the pepper adhere.

2. Heat a black iron skillet. Place the hamburgers in the skillet and grill for 3 to 4 minutes on one side. Grill for 4 to 5 minutes on the other side.

3. Transfer the burgers to a warm platter. Discard all the fat from the skillet and add the shallots. Cook briefly. The shallots should not brown. Add the Cognac and red wine. Reduce the liquid by half and add the chicken stock. Reduce to about 6 tablespoons. Swirl in the butter and pour the sauce over the hamburgers.

YIELD: 6 servings.   CALORIES PER SERVING: 258.

PRESENTATION: Place the hamburger in the center of the plate with Home-Fried Potatoes (see recipe page 213) above and below it and Sautéed Sweet Red or Yellow Peppers on each side (see recipe page 227).

...*12*...

Pasta

Pasta's reputation has been changing rapidly in the last few years. It used to be thought of as a tasty road to obesity. Now it is seen as almost a health food—thanks to the passion for it displayed by joggers and the like. Moreover, it really doesn't have to be a heavy dish anymore, as long as the sauces are light, even sprightly, as is the case with the fast-cooking clam sauce offered here. The savoire-faire demonstrated in this dish comes about because the spaghetti is cooked in two stages. The spaghetti initially needs a lot of water, even when it's fresh rather than dried, which is the ingredient used here. But after it is largely but not completely cooked you need to let it cook for a while with the other ingredients, absorbing their flavors. That way the dish is a harmonious whole rather than a matter of covering pasta with an alien sauce. Incidentally, there is a bit of a debate over whether it is appropriate to use Parmesan cheese with seafood-pasta dishes. Purists say it shouldn't be used, and I haven't here. But the truth is that cheese and just about any pasta, seafood or no, suits my taste just fine.

SPAGHETTI WITH CLAM SAUCE

24 cherrystone clams
2 quarts water
1 pound spaghetti
4 tablespoons olive oil
1 tablespoon chopped garlic
2 pounds ripe tomatoes, cut into ½-inch cubes (4 cups)
¼ teaspoon hot red pepper flakes
Freshly ground black pepper (12 turns of the pepper mill)
1 cup coarsely chopped fresh basil leaves

1. Open and drain the clams, reserving the juice. Chop them coarsely. There should be about 1½ cups of clams and 2 cups of juice.

2. Bring the water to the boil in a kettle. Add the spaghetti and cook for about 7 minutes. Drain.

3. While the spaghetti is cooking, heat the oil in a large heavy frying pan and sauté the garlic briefly without browning it. Add the tomatoes, hot pepper, clam juice, and ground pepper and bring the mixture to a boil. Add the partially cooked spaghetti and continue cooking it until it is *al dente.* Add the clams and cook for 1 minute more, stirring. Add the basil and serve immediately.

YIELD: 8 servings.   CALORIES PER SERVING: 346.

PRESENTATION: In placing the spaghetti on the plate, I like to try to give it some form, shaping it into a mound resembling a beehive or an inverted whirlpool. That can be done with a fork, but my preference is to serve the pasta with a metal tonged pasta spoon, called by some a spoon-fork, which makes swirling it onto the plate a simple matter.

This recipe uses tubular, ridged pasta to which the melted cheese clings in an admirably chewy fashion.

PENNE RIGATE WITH CHEESE

4 cups water
¼ teaspoon salt
¼ pound penne rigate (an Italian tube pasta)
1 tablespoon butter
Pinch of grated nutmeg
Freshly ground black pepper (4 turns of the pepper mill)
2 ounces grated Parmesan or Gruyère cheese

1. Bring the water to a boil in a saucepan. Add the salt and penne. Bring to a boil again, stirring. Cook for about 12 minutes, or until the pasta is *al dente.* Drain.

2. Transfer the pasta to a saucepan. Add the butter, nutmeg, pepper, and cheese. Mix well and transfer to a serving platter.

YIELD: 4 servings.   CALORIES PER SERVING: 195.

What we have here is something akin to a primavera, that pasta dish with vegetables and cream. But it is, of course, a lot lighter while still having that sense of spring freshness about it. To make it moist—rather than adding copious amounts of butter, as one is tempted to do—I use an old trick of mine, which is to return some of the water from the pot at the very end.

FETTUCCINE WITH GOAT CHEESE AND ASPARAGUS

1½ pounds fresh asparagus
½ teaspoon salt
1 pound fettuccine
¼ pound goat cheese
2 tablespoons butter
2 tablespoons chopped fresh chives
Freshly ground black pepper (8 turns of the pepper mill)

1. Scrape and trim the asparagus. Slice the spears on the bias, creating lengths of ¼ inch. There should be about 3 cups.

2. In a kettle, bring 3 to 4 quarts of water to a boil. Add the salt and the fettuccine, boiling vigorously for 9 to 12 minutes. Do not overcook: The pasta should be *al dente.* Reserve ¼ cup of the cooking water and drain the pasta.

3. Melt the butter in the kettle and add the asparagus. Sauté for about 1 minute and add the fettuccine, goat cheese, chives, and the pepper. Pour in the reserved water. Toss well and serve.

YIELD: 8 servings.   CALORIES PER SERVING: 335.

This is a colorful, fresh cold salad, with a vinaigrette dressing. It is prepared in a large batch here, because it is meant as part of a buffet. If it is to be a main course or a lunch, you might try adding 2 cups of cooked white chicken meat in chunks or 2 cups of boiled shrimp.

PASTA WITH MANGO AND VEGETABLES

½ pound macaroni twists
1 tablespoon plus 1 teaspoon salt
1 bunch broccoli
2 small zucchini (½ pound), halved and sliced (3 cups)
2 ripe tomatoes (¾ pound), cut into ½-inch cubes (2 cups)
¼ pound mushrooms, cut into ¼-inch-thick slices (2 cups)
1 cup chopped scallions
1 mango, in ¼-inch slices, cut into lengths of 1 or 2 inches
(½ cup)
1 cup Vinaigrette (see recipe page 243)

1. Boil the pasta with 1 teaspoon of the salt for 10 minutes, or until it is *al dente.* Drain the pasta and allow it to cool.

2. Cut the flowerets away from the thick stems of the broccoli. If they are large, make 2 slices in the floweret's stem or cut it in half to ensure even cooking. Blanch the broccoli in boiling water for 3 minutes. Drain and cool.

3. Blanch the zucchini in boiling water for 2 minutes. Drain and cool.

4. Combine the vegetables, mango, and pasta in a large mixing bowl. Toss gently. Add the Vinaigrette dressing and toss again.

YIELD: 8 servings.   CALORIES PER SERVING: 320.

BUTTERED FINE NOODLES WITH
SESAME SEEDS

½ pound fine noodles
2 tablespoons butter
2 tablespoons sesame seeds
¼ teaspoon salt
Freshly ground black pepper to taste

1. Boil the noodles in a large quantity of water for 2 or 3 minutes, or until they are just tender (do not overcook). Drain.

2. Melt the butter in a frying pan. Add the sesame seeds and sauté

them briefly. Add the noodles, tossing them with the butter. Add the salt and pepper. Serve hot.

YIELD: 6 servings.   CALORIES PER SERVING: 196.

BUTTERED FINE NOODLES
WITH PARMESAN

½ teaspoon salt
¾ pound fine noodles
1 tablespoon butter
1 tablespoon grated Parmesan cheese
Freshly ground black pepper (8 turns of the pepper mill)

1. Bring 2 quarts of water to a boil in a kettle. Add the salt and noodles. Stir well and bring the water back to the boil. Cook for about 3 minutes, or until the noodles are just tender.
2. Reserve 2 tablespoons of the cooking liquid. Then drain the noodles. Return the noodles to the kettle and add the reserved water, butter, cheese, and pepper. Blend well and serve hot.

YIELD: 6 servings.   CALORIES PER SERVING: 241.

NOODLES AND ZUCCHINI WITH BASIL

¾ pound small zucchini, washed and trimmed
2 quarts water
⅓ pound fine egg noodles
2 tablespoons olive oil
½ teaspoon salt
Freshly ground black pepper (8 turns of the pepper mill)
1 teaspoon chopped garlic
2 tablespoons chopped fresh basil leaves

1. Slice the zucchini into long julienne strips.
2. Bring 2 quarts of water to a boil in a kettle and cook the noodles until tender. Drain and reserve ¼ cup of the cooking liquid.
3. Heat the oil and add the zucchini and sprinkle it with salt and pepper. Sauté briefly, just to heat the zucchini through. Add the garlic and basil. Add the noodles and reserved cooking liquid. Cook, stirring gently, until the mixture is hot. Serve with grated Parmesan cheese if desired.

YIELD: 6 servings.   CALORIES PER SERVING: 148.

...*13*...

Potatoes and Rice

There is nothing inherently fattening about potatoes and rice. But they are inherently nourishing, having sustained whole civilizations by themselves. The trick in preparing them is in keeping the fat used in the process down to a minimum, as I have attempted to do throughout this section.

A note on molding rice: When rice accompanies a dish in this book, I generally specify that the rice should be molded. This can be done in a great variety of containers; a good one is a small coffee cup. If there is ample butter in the rice already you will not have to butter the mold, but if the rice has little or no butter you will have to grease the mold. Then pack the rice into the mold tightly. It should unmold easily and hold its shape.

SLICED POTATOES AU GRATIN

2 pounds potatoes, peeled and sliced very thin,
washed and dried with paper towels
2 cups very thinly sliced onions
1 tablespoon finely chopped garlic
½ teaspoon salt
Pinch of grated nutmeg
Freshly ground black pepper (8 turns of the pepper mill)
2½ cups scalded milk

1. Preheat oven to 400 degrees.

2. In a mixing bowl, combine the potatoes, onions, garlic, salt, nutmeg, and pepper. Blend well and transfer to a 6-cup au gratin dish. Add the milk.

3. Bring the mixture to a boil on top of the stove. Place the dish on the bottom shelf of the oven and bake for 1 hour. The top should be well browned.

YIELD: 8 servings.   CALORIES PER SERVING: 134.

PARSLEYED OR DILLED POTATOES

12 small red new potatoes (about 2 pounds)
½ teaspoon salt
2 tablespoons butter
Freshly ground black pepper (4 turns of the pepper mill)
¼ cup finely chopped parsley or ¼ cup finely chopped
fresh dill

1. For an attractive touch, use a paring knife to remove a thin band of skin around the middle of each potato. Leave the rest of the skin intact.

2. Wash the potatoes and put them in a saucepan with water to cover. Add the salt. Bring to a boil and simmer for about 20 minutes.

3. Drain the potatoes and add the butter, pepper, and parsley. Toss well, and serve hot.

YIELD: 4 servings.   CALORIES PER SERVING: 225.

PURÉED POTATOES

2 pounds potatoes
½ teaspoon salt
1 cup milk
1 tablespoon butter
Freshly ground pepper, preferably white pepper
(6 turns of the pepper mill)

1. Peel the potatoes and cut them into 2-inch cubes.

2. Put the potatoes in a saucepan and cover them with water. Add the salt. Bring to a boil; simmer for 20 minutes, or until tender.

3. Drain the potatoes and force them through a food mill. Return the purée to the saucepan.

4. Bring the milk to the boil.

5. Stir the butter and pepper into the potatoes with a wooden spoon. Add the milk while beating with the spoon.

YIELD: 6 servings.   CALORIES PER SERVING: 135.

HOME-FRIED POTATOES

1 pound small red potatoes, peeled and sliced
¼ inch thick (about 3 cups)
1 tablespoon vegetable oil
½ teaspoon salt
1 teaspoon butter
1 teaspoon chopped garlic
Freshly ground black pepper (4 turns of the pepper mill)
2 tablespoons chopped fresh parsley leaves

1. Put the potatoes in a saucepan, cover them with water, and bring to a boil. Drain.

2. Heat the oil in a nonstick frying pan. Add the potatoes and salt. When the potatoes are lightly browned and almost ready, melt in the butter. Sprinkle the potatoes with the garlic and pepper. Sauté briefly but do not brown the garlic. Add the parsley at the last minute and serve.

YIELD: 6 servings.   CALORIES PER SERVING: 76.

CREOLE RICE

4 cups water
1½ cups long grain rice
1 tablespoon butter
½ teaspoon salt
Freshly ground black pepper (4 turns of the pepper mill)
2 teaspoons fresh lemon juice

1. Bring the water to a boil in a saucepan and add the rice. Boil for 15 minutes, stirring occasionally.

2. Drain the rice in a collander and run hot water over it.

3. Add the butter, salt, and pepper. Sprinkle the rice with lemon juice and toss.

YIELD: 6 servings.   CALORIES PER SERVING: 192.

CURRIED RICE

1 tablespoon butter
¼ cup finely chopped onion
1 cup converted rice
2 tablespoons black or golden raisins
1 tablespoon curry powder
(see recipe for Oriental Curry Powder page 265)
1½ cups water
Freshly ground black pepper (8 turns of the pepper mill)
½ teaspoon salt
1 bay leaf

1. Melt the butter in a saucepan. Add the onion and sauté until the onion is wilted. Add the remaining ingredients and bring to a boil, stirring. Tightly cover the pot and simmer for 17 minutes.

2. Remove the bay leaf. Cover the rice and set it aside in a warm place until you are ready to serve it.

YIELD: 6 servings.   CALORIES PER SERVING: 146.

RICE PILAF

2 tablespoons butter
¼ cup chopped onion
½ teaspoon chopped garlic
1 cup converted rice
3 sprigs fresh parsley
2 sprigs fresh thyme, or ¼ teaspoon dried thyme
4 drops Tabasco sauce
1 bay leaf
1½ cups water
½ teaspoon salt
Freshly ground black pepper (6 turns of the pepper mill)

1. Melt 1 tablespoon of the butter in a saucepan and add the onion and garlic. Cook, stirring, until the onion is wilted. Add the rice, parsley, thyme, Tabasco, bay leaf, water, salt, and pepper. Bring it to a boil, stirring. Cover the pan tightly and simmer for 17 minutes.

2. Discard the parsley, thyme, and bay leaf. With a fork, distribute the remaining butter through the rice. Keep the rice covered in a warm place until you are ready to serve it.

YIELD: 8 servings.   CALORIES PER SERVING: 113.

RICE AND WILD RICE

6 cups water
1 cup wild rice
1 cup converted rice
1 tablespoon butter
1 teaspoon salt
Freshly ground black pepper (8 turns of the pepper mill)

1. Bring half the water to a boil in a saucepan and add the wild rice. Cook for about 45 minutes. Drain the rice.

2. In another saucepan, after about 25 minutes, bring the rest of the water to a boil. Add the converted rice and cook for 17 minutes. Drain the rice.

3. In a single saucepan, combine the rices, butter, salt, and pepper. Mix well and serve hot.

YIELD: 8 servings.   CALORIES PER SERVING: 169.

RICE WITH ZUCCHINI AND
SWEET RED PEPPERS

2 small zucchini (about ½ pound)
1 tablespoon butter
½ cup finely chopped onion
1 teaspoon chopped garlic
½ teaspoon salt
Freshly ground black pepper (6 turns of the pepper mill)
1 teaspoon ground tumeric
1 cup converted rice
¼ pound sweet red peppers, diced (½ cup)
1 bay leaf
½ teaspoon dried thyme, or 2 sprigs fresh thyme
4 drops Tabasco sauce
1¼ cups water

1. Trim and wash the zucchini. Cut them into ½-inch cubes. You should have 2 cups.

2. Melt the butter in a saucepan and add the onion and garlic. Sauté, stirring, until the onion is wilted. Add the remaining ingredients and bring to a boil. Cover and simmer for 17 minutes.

YIELD: 6 servings.   CALORIES PER SERVING: 149.

SAFFRON RICE

2 tablespoons butter
¼ cup chopped onion
½ teaspoon chopped garlic
1 cup converted rice
¼ cup pignolis
½ teaspoon saffron stems
3 sprigs fresh parsley
2 sprigs fresh thyme, or ¼ teaspoon dried thyme
4 drops Tabasco sauce
1 bay leaf
1½ cups water
½ teaspoon salt
Freshly ground black pepper (6 turns of the pepper mill)

1. Melt 1 tablespoon of the butter in a saucepan and add the onion and garlic. Cook, stirring, until the onion is wilted. Add the rice, pignolis, saffron, parsley, thyme, Tabasco, bay leaf, water, salt, and pepper. Bring it to a boil, stirring. Cover the pot tightly and simmer for 17 minutes.

2. Discard the parsley, thyme, and bay leaf. With a fork, distribute the remaining butter through the rice. Keep the rice covered in a warm place until it is served.

YIELD: 6 servings.   CALORIES PER SERVING: 185.

...*14*...

Vegetables

I offer recipes for vegetables here that are, for the most part, so uncomplicated that they require no individual discussion. Suffice it to say that my intention throughout was to make the vegetables produce the flavors they were born with rather than to mask those flavors. My tendency has been to strive for vegetables that are generally tender-crisp (a useful term, although a bit silly to the ear) and colorful.

BUTTERED ARTICHOKE BOTTOMS

1 tablespoon all-purpose flour
2 cups water
Juice of 1 lemon
½ teaspoon salt
6 small artichokes (about ½ pound each)
1 tablespoon butter

1. Put the flour in a small sieve and pass it through to a small saucepan. Pour the water over the flour, stirring to dissolve it. Add the lemon juice and salt.

2. Turn the artichokes on their sides on a flat surface and cut away the stem and all the leaves, top and bottom. A clean, leafless base should be left. Trim each base carefully to remove all the green portions. Each artichoke bottom should be about 1 inch thick.

3. Place the artichokes in the saucepan with the flour-water mixture and bring the liquid to a boil. Let the artichokes simmer for 20 minutes, when they should be tender but not mushy. Allow the bottoms to cool in the cooking liquid.

4. When cool enough to handle, remove the fuzzy choke in the center of each artichoke bottom. This can be done with your fingers or a spoon.

5. Melt the butter in a small saucepan and place the artichoke bottoms in the pan. Cook them for 2 minutes, lightly browning them all over.

YIELD: 6 servings.   CALORIES PER SERVING: 62.

PRESENTATION: The artichoke bottoms can be served plain, brushed with butter, perhaps sliced on the bias and spread out like a fan. As an appetizer, a vinaigrette sauce is a nice touch. For lunch, a poached egg can be placed on the whole artichoke bottom and topped, perhaps with a hollandaise or béarnaise sauce. But as a vegetable accompaniment for meat, the presentation I like best is to stuff the artichoke with some kind of vegetable purée, such as a purée of red peppers. It can also be stuffed with purées of string beans (see recipe page 231), broccoli, carrots, or anything that strikes your fancy.

BUTTERED ASPARAGUS

24 fresh asparagus
½ teaspoon salt
Freshly ground black pepper (6 turns of the pepper mill)
1 tablespoon butter, melted

1. Cut off the white ends of the asparagus, about 3 inches from the bottom. Use a vegetable peeler to scrape the spears.

2. Put the asparagus, salt, and enough water to cover the asparagus in a saucepan. Bring to a boil, and cook the asparagus for 2 to 5 minutes, depending on the size of the spears. They should be tender but still crisp.

3. Drain the asparagus quickly, sprinkle with pepper, and brush with melted butter.

YIELD: 6 servings.   CALORIES PER SERVING: 43.

ASPARAGUS AND MUSHROOMS WITH
FRESH CORIANDER

1 pound fresh asparagus
2 tablespoons butter
½ pound mushrooms, sliced (2 cups)
2 tablespoons chopped shallots
½ teaspoon salt
Freshly ground black pepper (4 turns of the pepper mill)
4 tablespoons chopped fresh coriander leaves

1. Trim off the tough part of the asparagus stalk about 2 or 3 inches from the bottom. Use a vegetable peeler to scrape the asparagus to about 1 inch from the top. Cut the asparagus on the diagonal into 1-inch pieces.

2. Melt the butter in a nonstick frying pan. Add the mushrooms and cook over high heat, tossing and shaking, until the mushrooms are lightly browned. Add the asparagus. Cook, stirring and tossing, for about 1 minute. Add the shallot, salt, and pepper. Sprinkle with the coriander. Cook for 30 seconds.

YIELD: 6 servings.   CALORIES PER SERVING: 68.

AVOCADOS AND MUSHROOMS

1 unripe avocado (about 1¼ pounds)
2 tablespoons butter
½ pound mushrooms, washed, drained, and sliced
(2 cups)
1 teaspoon salt
Freshly ground black pepper (4 turns of the pepper mill)
3 tablespoons chopped shallots
1 tablespoon red wine vinegar

1. Peel and cut the avocado lengthwise into 8 pieces. Cut the pieces into ¼-inch-thick slices.

2. Bring 2 cups of water to a boil in a saucepan. Add the avocado pieces and blanch them for 3 minutes and drain. (They should remain firm or *al dente*.)

3. Melt the butter in a nonstick frying pan and sauté the mushrooms until they brown lightly. Add the avocado slices, salt, pepper, and shallots. Cook for 2 minutes while tossing and stirring. Add the vinegar and toss. Serve.

YIELD: 6 servings.   CALORIES PER SERVING: 163.

STEAMED BROCCOLI

1 bunch broccoli
2 tablespoons olive oil
2 teaspoons chopped garlic
Juice of 1 lemon
½ teaspoon salt
Freshly ground black pepper (4 turns of the pepper mill)

1. Using a paring knife, cut off and discard the tough bottoms of the stalks. Cut and trim the broccoli into flowerets.

2. Put the broccoli into a steamer and steam for 3 to 4 minutes.

3. Heat the oil in a frying pan. Add the garlic, lemon juice, broccoli, salt, and pepper. Sauté for 2 to 3 minutes.

YIELD: 4 servings.   CALORIES PER SERVING: 101.

BRAISED RED CABBAGE

1 red cabbage (about 1¼ pounds)
1 golden Delicious apple
1 tablespoon butter
1 large onion (about ¼ pound), chopped
½ teaspoon salt
Freshly ground black pepper (6 turns of the pepper mill)
1 tablespoon dark brown sugar
1 cup water
1 tablespoon red wine vinegar

1. Cut the cabbage into quarters and discard the core portions. Slice the cabbage as thinly as possible by hand or with a food processor or mandoline.

2. Peel and core the apple. Slice it as thinly as possible.

3. Melt the butter in a frying pan and add the onion. Sauté the onion for 1 minute and add the cabbage and apple. Cook for 5 minutes longer, stirring, and add the salt, pepper, and brown sugar.

4. Add the water and vinegar and cook, covered, over low heat for ½ hour, stirring occasionally.

YIELD: 6 servings.   CALORIES PER SERVING: 74.

SAVOY CABBAGE WITH BUTTER

1 savoy cabbage (about 1½ pounds)
3 teaspoons salt
1 slice bacon, diced
2 tablespoons butter
1 cup chopped onions
Freshly ground black pepper (6 turns of the pepper mill)

1. Peel off each leaf of the cabbage individually and remove a large part of the core.

2. Pour 2 quarts of water into a kettle and add 2 teaspoons of the salt. Bring to a boil. Add the cabbage leaves and blanch for 1 minute. Leave the cabbage in the water and let it cool.

3. Drain the cabbage and cut each leaf into 4 pieces.

4. In a frying pan, sauté the diced bacon over low heat until it is crisp. Drain away the fat. Add the butter and onions and cook until the onions wilt. Lay the cabbage in the pan. Sprinkle on the remaining salt and the pepper. Cook, stirring, for about 8 minutes. All the moisture should have evaporated.

YIELD: 6 servings.   CALORIES PER SERVING: 78.

CARROT CUSTARD

6 to 8 carrots (about 2 pounds)
1 cup chicken stock (see recipe page 30)
½ teaspoon salt
Freshly ground black pepper (4 turns of the pepper mill)
½ teaspoon sugar
2 large eggs, beaten
2 tablespoons chopped fresh dill
Pinch of grated nutmeg

1. Preheat the oven to 375 degrees.

2. Trim off the ends of the carrots, then scrape them and slice them into rounds.

3. Put the carrots in a saucepan and add the stock, salt, pepper, and sugar. Cook, stirring often, until the carrots are tender but not soft. When done, most of the liquid should have evaporated.

4. In a food mill or processor, purée the carrots coarsely so there is still some texture. Transfer the purée to a mixing bowl and add the beaten egg, dill, and nutmeg. Blend well.

5. Pour the mixture into a 3- to 4-cup-capacity ring mold. Place the mold in a basin of boiling water, and transfer the mold and basin to the oven. Bake for about 30 minutes. Unmold and serve in wedges.

YIELD: 8 servings.   CALORIES PER SERVING: 64.

JULIENNE OF CARROTS AND SNOW PEAS

¾ pound carrots, peeled and trimmed
¼ pound snow peas, trimmed
1 tablespoon butter
2 tablespoons sesame seeds
½ teaspoon chopped garlic
1 tablespoon light soy sauce
2 tablespoons chopped chives or scallions

1. Slice the carrots into julienne strips, about 1½ inches long. Slice the snow peas into strips about ¼ inch wide.

2. Put the carrots into a saucepan and cover them with water. Bring to a boil and simmer for 4 minutes. Add the snow peas. Stir and cook for 2 minutes more and then drain.

3. Melt the butter in a nonstick frying pan and add the sesame seeds. Cook, stirring, until the seeds are light brown. Add the garlic,

carrots and snow peas, soy sauce, and chives. Sauté, stirring, for 1 minute. Serve.

YIELD: 6 servings   CALORIES PER SERVING: 65.

GLAZED CARROTS

1½ pounds carrots
½ teaspoon salt
Freshly ground black pepper (6 turns of the pepper mill)
1 tablespoon butter
½ cup finely chopped onion
½ cup water

1. Peel and thinly slice the carrots in rounds and sprinkle them with salt and pepper.
2. Melt the butter in a saucepan and add the onion. Cook, stirring, until the onion is wilted. Add the carrots and cook until they are slightly darkened. Then add the water. Cover and cook for about 15 minutes, or until the moisture has evaporated.

YIELD: 6 servings.   CALORIES PER SERVING: 62.

PARSLEYED SLICED CARROTS

1¾ pounds carrots, trimmed and scraped
½ teaspoon salt
Freshly ground black pepper (4 turns of the pepper mill)
½ teaspoon sugar
¼ cup water
2 tablespoons butter
2 tablespoons chopped fresh parsley leaves

1. Slice the carrots very thinly. Put them in a saucepan and add the salt, pepper, sugar, water, and butter. Bring to a boil, cover, and simmer for about 10 minutes, or until they are tender.
2. Remove the lid and cook the carrots until the liquid is reduced and the carrots are lightly glazed. Serve them with a sprinkling of parsley.

YIELD: 6 servings.   CALORIES PER SERVING: 92.

PURÉE OF CELERY ROOT

1½ pounds celery root, peeled and cut into 1-inch cubes
(about 4 cups)
½ pound potatoes, peeled and cut into ¾-inch cubes
(about 1 cup)
½ teaspoon salt
¾ cup milk
1 tablespoon butter
Freshly ground black pepper (6 turns of the pepper mill)
Pinch of grated nutmeg

1. Put the celery and potatoes into a saucepan and cover them with water. Add the salt and bring to a boil. Simmer for 20 minutes, or until the vegetables are tender.

2. Drain the celery root and potatoes and purée them in a food processor or force the mixture through a food mill or potato ricer. Return the purée to the saucepan. Bring the milk to a boil in another saucepan.

3. While the milk is heating, blend the butter, pepper, and nutmeg into the purée. Blend in the hot milk. Keep the purée warm until you are ready to serve it. (Celery root, like many other purées, does not suffer from being kept over low heat in a double boiler for a considerable length of time and thus can be made perhaps an hour ahead of time.)

YIELD: 8 servings.   CALORIES PER SERVING: 78.

CURRIED FRESH CORN AND TOMATOES

4 ears corn
1 tablespoon butter
½ cup finely chopped onion
1 teaspoon curry powder (preferably homemade,
see recipe page 265)
1 cup peeled, seeded, and diced ripe tomatoes
½ teaspoon salt

1. Using a knife, cut the corn kernels from the cobs. There should be about 3½ cups.

2. Melt the butter in a frying pan and add the onion and curry powder. Sauté briefly, stirring, until the onion is wilted. Add the corn, tomatoes, and salt. Stir and cover. Cook for about 5 minutes. Serve hot.

YIELD: 6 servings.   CALORIES PER SERVING: 125.

PARSLEYED CUCUMBERS

4 large, firm cucumbers
1 tablespoon butter
4 tablespoons chopped fresh parsley leaves
1 teaspoon salt
Freshly ground black pepper (6 turns of the pepper mill)
Juice of ½ lemon

1. Trim off the ends of the cucumbers and cut the cucumbers into 2-inch lengths. Quarter each section lengthwise. With a paring knife, carefully cut away the green skin and remove the seeds, leaving only the flesh.

2. Bring 1½ cups of water to a boil in a saucepan. Add the cucumbers and cook for about 1 minute. Drain.

3. Return the cucumbers to the saucepan. Add the butter, parsley, salt, pepper, and lemon juice and toss until the butter melts.

YIELD: 8 servings.   CALORIES PER SERVING: 33.

BRAISED ENDIVES

8 medium-sized Belgian endives
¼ teaspoon salt
Freshly ground black pepper (4 turns of the pepper mill)
¼ teaspoon ground cumin
Juice of 1 lemon
½ cup water
1 tablespoon butter
¼ cup chopped fresh parsley leaves

1. Wash the endives and trim the stem ends.

2. Put the endives in 1 layer in a saucepan just large enough to hold them (if it is too large the endives will burn). Sprinkle the endives with salt, pepper, cumin, and lemon juice. Pour in the water and add the butter. Cover the pan tightly. Bring the water to a boil and simmer for 30 minutes, or until the liquid has evaporated. Uncover the endives and brown them lightly on both sides. Sprinkle with the parsley and serve.

YIELD: 8 servings.   CALORIES PER SERVING: 32.

LENTIL PURÉE

1 pound lentils
1 small onion studded with a whole clove at each end
1 garlic clove
1 bay leaf
5 cups water
2 teaspoons salt
Freshly ground black pepper (4 turns of the pepper mill)
½ cup half-and-half
2 tablespoons butter

1. Pick over the lentils. Wash and drain them.
2. Combine the lentils, onion, garlic, bay leaf, water, salt, and pepper in a saucepan. Bring to a boil and simmer for 30 minutes. Drain.
3. Pour the lentil mixture into a food mill and pass it through into a saucepan. Discard any solids left in the mill.
4. Heat the half-and-half (but do not boil it) and add it along with the butter to the lentil mixture. Beat well to blend. Serve hot.

YIELD: 10 servings   CALORIES PER SERVING: 194

FRICASSEE OF WILD MUSHROOMS

½ pound porcini *and* chanterelle *mushrooms*
(or use only one type)
1 tablespoon olive oil
2 tablespoons butter
¼ cup finely chopped shallots
1 teaspoon chopped garlic
½ teaspoon salt
Freshly ground black pepper (6 turns of the pepper mill)
2 tablespoons chopped fines herbes *(tarragon, chervil, basil, thyme, parsley, alone or in combination)*

1. Clean, trim, and wash the mushrooms.
2. Heat the oil in a nonstick frying pan and add the mushrooms. Sautée over high heat until all the moisture has evaporated.
3. Add the butter, shallots, garlic, salt, and pepper. Sauté for 1 minute longer. Sprinkle with the herbs and serve.

YIELD: 6 servings.   CALORIES PER SERVING: 72.

FRESH PEAS WITH TARRAGON

2 pounds fresh peas, shelled (about 2 cups)
1 tablespoon butter
1 tablespoon finely chopped fresh tarragon
½ teaspoon salt
Freshly ground black pepper (4 turns of the pepper mill)

1. Bring 2 cups of water to a boil in a saucepan.
2. Add the peas and cook for 6 to 8 minutes. Drain and add the butter, tarragon, salt, and pepper. Mix well.

YIELD: 6 servings.   CALORIES PER SERVING: 60.

SAUTÉED SWEET RED OR YELLOW PEPPERS

4 large sweet red or yellow ("banana") peppers
(about 1 pound)
1 tablespoon butter
½ cup water
¼ teaspoon salt
Freshly ground black pepper (6 turns of the pepper mill)

1. Core, seed, and cut the peppers into ¼-inch-wide strips about 2 inches long.
2. Melt the butter in a saucepan and add the pepper strips, water, salt, and ground pepper. Bring to a boil and cover. Cook over high heat for about 5 minutes. Remove the cover and cook, stirring occasionally, until all the moisture has evaporated, leaving a glaze on the peppers.

YIELD: 8 servings.   CALORIES PER SERVING: 29.

GLAZED SCALLIONS

24 scallions
1 tablespoon butter
½ teaspoon salt
Freshly ground black pepper (4 turns of the pepper mill)
1 cup water

1. Wash the scallions and trim them. Cut off the ends and the tops. Spears of 5 inches in length should remain.

2. Place the scallions in one layer on the bottom of a large sauce-pan. Add the butter, salt and, pepper. Pour the water into the pan and bring to a boil. Cook, uncovered, over medium heat for 10 minutes, or until most of the moisture has evaporated.

YIELD: 6 servings.   CALORIES PER SERVING: 44.

SNOW PEAS WITH SESAME SEEDS

2 cups water
¼ teaspoon salt
1 pound snow peas
1 tablespoon butter
3 tablespoons sesame seeds
1 tablespoon chopped shallots
Freshly ground black pepper (6 turns of the pepper mill)

1. Pour the water into a saucepan and add the salt. Bring to a boil and add the snow peas to the pan. Blanch them for 1 minute and drain.

2. Melt the butter in a nonstick frying pan. Add the sesame seeds and brown them lightly. Add the snow peas, shallots, and pepper. Sauté for 1 minute and serve.

YIELD: 6 servings.   CALORIES PER SERVING: 82.

SNOW PEAS WITH SWEET PEPPER
AND POPPY SEEDS

2 cups water
¾ pound snow peas, trimmed and washed
½ sweet red pepper, cut into small squares (about ½ cup)
1 tablespoon butter
1 teaspoon poppy seeds
Juice of ½ lemon
¼ teaspoon salt
Freshly ground black pepper (4 turns of the pepper mill)

1. Bring the water to a boil in a saucepan. Add the snow peas and sweet pepper and cook for 2 minutes. Drain the vegetables.

2. Melt the butter in a nonstick frying pan. Add the poppy seeds, then the peas and sweet pepper. Add the lemon juice, salt, and pepper. Sauté for 1 minute, stirring. Serve immediately.

YIELD: 4 servings.   CALORIES PER SERVING: 82.

SPINACH PURÉE

1½ pounds fresh spinach, or 2 10-ounce packages
frozen leaf spinach
2 quarts water
1 teaspoon salt
Freshly ground black pepper (6 turns of the pepper mill)
2 tablespoons butter
Pinch of grated nutmeg

1. Trim the spinach and remove the coarse stems. Wash and drain the spinach, several times if necessary, to remove all the grit.

2. Pour the water into a kettle, add the salt, and bring to a boil. Drop the spinach into the water and cook for about 3 minutes. Drain the spinach and rinse it in cold running water. Drain again and, using a piece of cheesecloth or a dish towel, squeeze out all the moisture.

3. Purée the spinach in a food processor or blender.

4. Before serving, reheat the spinach in a saucepan, adding the pepper, butter, and nutmeg.

YIELD: 6 servings.   CALORIES PER SERVING: 57.

SPINACH LEAVES WITH NUTMEG

2 10-ounce packages fresh spinach
1 tablespoon butter
⅛ teaspoon grated nutmeg
¼ teaspoon salt
Freshly ground black pepper (6 turns of the pepper mill)

1. Peel away and discard any tough stems and blemished spinach leaves. Rinse well and drain the spinach.

2. Put the spinach in a saucepan and cook over medium heat, stirring constantly with a wooden spatula. When the spinach is wilted—in about 4 minutes—transfer it to a colander and drain it. Press the leaves with the back of a spatula to extract most of the liquid.

3. Transfer the spinach to a skillet, along with the butter, nutmeg, salt, and pepper. Cook, tossing and stirring, just to heat through.

YIELD: 4 servings.   CALORIES PER SERVING: 63.

STRING BEANS WITH SHALLOTS
AND TARRAGON

½ teaspoon salt
1 pound string beans, trimmed
2 tablespoons sweet butter
2 tablespoons chopped shallots
2 tablespoons chopped fresh tarragon,
or 2 teaspoons dried tarragon
Freshly ground black pepper (4 turns of the pepper mill)

1. Bring 2 cups of water to a boil in a saucepan. Add the salt and string beans. Bring the water back to a boil. (To prevent discoloration, do not cover the pan.) Simmer for 8 to 10 minutes. The beans should be tender but crisp. Drain.

2. Add the butter to the saucepan and then the shallots. Cook briefly, but do not brown. Add the tarragon and pepper. Sauté briefly and serve.

YIELD: 6 servings.   CALORIES PER SERVING: 63.

STRING BEAN PURÉE

1 pound string beans
1 tablespoon butter
2 tablespoons half-and-half
¹⁄₁₆ teaspoon or a pinch of grated nutmeg
Pinch of salt
Pinch of freshly ground black pepper

1. Cut off and discard the ends of the beans. Rinse the beans and drain them.

2. Pour 2 cups of water into a saucepan and bring to a boil. Add the string beans and cook until tender, about 10 minutes. The beans should still be slightly firm or *al dente*.

3. Drain the beans and purée them coarsely. This can be done either in a food processor or food mill, but a better texture will be obtained from the latter.

4. Combine the beans, butter, half-and-half, nutmeg, salt, and pepper in a saucepan, and place over heat. Stir rapidly with a wooden spoon while heating the purée through. Serve hot.

YIELD: 6 servings.   CALORIES PER SERVING: 48.

STRING BEANS WITH GARLIC

2 cups string beans, trimmed and cut into 2-inch lengths
1 tablespoon butter
1 teaspoon finely chopped garlic
¼ teaspoon ground cumin
Juice of ½ lemon
2 tablespoons chopped fresh parsley leaves
¼ teaspoon salt
Freshly ground black pepper (6 turns of the pepper mill)

1. Cut off and discard the tips of the beans. Wash and drain the beans.

2. Pour 2 cups of water into a saucepan and bring it to a boil. Add the string beans and cook until they are just tender, about 10 minutes. Do not overcook. The beans should be somewhat firm or *al dente*.

3. Drain the beans. Return them to the hot saucepan. Add the butter, garlic, cumin, lemon juice, parsley, salt, and pepper. Sauté, tossing, for about 1 minute. Serve hot.

YIELD: 4 servings.   CALORIES PER SERVING: 47.

BAKED TOMATOES WITH ROSEMARY AND GARLIC

4 tomatoes (about 2 pounds), skins removed
½ teaspoon salt
Freshly ground black pepper (8 turns of the pepper mill)
1 tablespoon olive oil
3 garlic cloves, cut into 16 slivers
1 tablespoon dried rosemary
2 tablespoons chopped fresh parsley leaves

1. Preheat the oven to 400 degrees.
2. Cut the tomatoes in half lengthwise. Hold the tomato halves in a dish towel and gently squeeze out the seeds and liquid.
3. Place the tomato flat side down in a baking dish. Sprinkle the halves with salt and pepper and brush them with the olive oil. With the tip of a pointed knife, make 2 small slits in each tomato and place a sliver of garlic in each. Sprinkle the tomatoes with the rosemary and bake for 8 to 10 minutes. Serve sprinkled with the chopped parsley.

YIELD: 8 servings.   CALORIES PER SERVING: 41.

BROILED TOMATOES PROVENÇALE

4 ripe tomatoes
1 tablespoon olive oil
1 tablespoon finely chopped garlic
½ teaspoon salt
Freshly ground black pepper (8 turns of the pepper mill)
2 tablespoons finely chopped fresh parsley leaves

1. Preheat the broiler.
2. Core the tomatoes and cut them in half.
3. In a flat, heatproof dish large enough to hold them, arrange the tomatoes cut side up, Distribute the oil over each tomato. Sprinkle them with garlic, salt, and pepper. Place the tomatoes 3 to 4 inches from the flame of the broiler for about 5 minutes. Remove them from the heat and sprinkle with the parsley before serving.

YIELD: 4 servings.   CALORIES PER SERVING: 60.

WATERCRESS PURÉE

8 bunches watercress
1 teaspoon salt
2 quarts water
2 tablespoons butter
Freshly ground black pepper (6 turns of the pepper mill)

1. Trim the watercress and remove the coarse stems. (The watercress should weigh about 1¼ pounds.) Boil it for 3 to 4 minutes in salted water. Cool the watercress in the water and drain it in a cheesecloth or dish towel, squeezing out all the moisture.

2. Purée the watercress in a food processor. Just before serving it, heat the purée in a saucepan with the butter and pepper.

YIELD: 6 servings.   CALORIES PER SERVING: 52.

ZUCCHINI BORDELAISE

1½ pounds small zucchini
2 tablespoons olive oil
½ teaspoon salt
Freshly ground black pepper (6 turns of the pepper mill)
2 tablespoons fresh bread crumbs
1 tablespoon butter
2 tablespoons chopped shallots
4 tablespoons chopped fresh parsley leaves

1. Rinse the zucchini and pat them dry. Trim off the ends, but do not peel them.

2. Heat the oil in a nonstick frying pan and, when it is hot, add the zucchini. Sauté the zucchini over high heat, shaking the pan and tossing the vegetable gently. Add the salt and pepper. Cook a total of 5 minutes.

3. Add the bread crumbs and butter to the pan. When the crumbs start to brown, add the shallots and toss the mixture for another minute. Serve the zucchini hot, sprinkled with the parsley.

YIELD: 6 servings.   CALORIES PER SERVING: 70.

MACEDOINE OF VEGETABLES

2 medium-sized carrots, scraped
2 medium-sized white turnips, scraped
1 medium-sized zucchini
1 celery stalk, scraped
1 tablespoon butter
¼ cup chopped scallions
1 cup fresh or frozen peas
½ teaspoon salt
Freshly ground black pepper (6 turns of the pepper mill)
2 tablespoons water

1. Quarter the carrots and cut them into strips about 1 inch long. There should be about 1 cup.

2. Cut the turnips into pieces the same size as the carrots.

3. Trim the zucchini, wash it, and cut it into the same size pieces as the others.

4. Slice the celery crosswise into thin pieces, about ⅛ inch thick.

5. Melt the butter in a saucepan and add the scallions and celery. Sauté briefly. Add the carrots, turnips, zucchini, and fresh peas (if fresh and not frozen are used). Add the salt and pepper. Pour the water into the pan and cover it tightly. Simmer, shaking and stirring so the vegetables cook evenly, for about ten minutes. If frozen peas are to be used, add them at the end of this cooking period.

YIELD: 6 servings.   CALORIES PER SERVING: 74.

MELANGE OF VEGETABLES

2 cups water
2 carrots (about ½ pound), cut in very thin julienne strips
2 inches long (about 2 cups)
½ cup snow peas, cut into thin julienne strips
2 tablespoons butter
2 white turnips (about ½ pound), cut into very thin
julienne to match the carrots
½ teaspoon ground cumin
½ teaspoon salt
Freshly ground black pepper (6 turns of the pepper mill)
2 tablespoons chopped chives or scallions

1. Bring the water to a boil in a saucepan. Drop in the carrots and snow peas and boil them for 1 minute. Drain.

2. Melt the butter in a nonstick frying pan. Add the carrots, and snow peas, turnips, cumin, salt, and pepper to the pan. Sauté, stirring, for 2 minutes. Add the chives. Stir and serve immediately.

YIELD: 6 servings.   CALORIES PER SERVING: 69.

..15..

Sauces

Getting rid of creamed and floured sauces is not so hard as it may seem. All through this book I have placed an emphasis on sauces in which the cook simply finishes off the preparation of a dish by pouring a liquid, such as wine, vinegar, or stock into the pan, dissolving any bits of solids that adhere to the pan, and then adding a touch of butter to give the sauce some smoothness. In this chapter are light basic sauces that are prepared apart from the central cooking process.

The Mushroom Sauce demonstrates how smooth a sauce can be even without cream. The Creole Sauce is beautiful looking. And the Fresh Tomato Sauce is not only delicious, it also can be made almost as fast from scratch as heated from a jar.

Aïoli is a cold garlicky sauce similar to a mayonnaise. It is so common in the south of France that it's simply placed on the table as a meal is served. Most traditionally, it is used to accompany poached fish surrounded by vegetables. But in Provence, they'll eat it with just about anything. For my taste, I enjoy it with boiled beef, poached chicken, and broiled fish, as well as with fish that's been poached. The sauce brings an energetic punch of life to all of these bland foods. The addition of apples, by the way, is typically Spanish, a touch of Catalan. To revert to the standard aïoli, simply remove the apple from this recipe.

AÏOLI WITH APPLES

1 apple (about 6 ounces)
2 teaspoons chopped garlic
½ teaspoon salt
1 egg yolk
1 cup olive oil
Freshly ground white pepper (8 turns of the pepper mill)

1. Peel and core the apple. Cut the apple into quarters. Then cut each quarter crosswise into ¼-inch-thick slices. Put the apple slices in a saucepan with 1 tablespoon of water. Cover and cook for 2 minutes. Drain and push the apples through a strainer. Allow the apples to cool.

2. Crush the garlic (with a mortar and pestle if one is available) along with salt until the garlic is smooth. Using a small wire whisk, blend the egg yolk with the garlic. Very slowly, pour the oil into the egg mixture, whisking continuously.

3. Add the apple purée, and white pepper to the mixture and blend them in.

YIELD: About 1½ cups, or about 18 servings.   CALORIES PER SERVING: 126.

PRESENTATION: Although some cooks will spread the sauce over the meat, I prefer to see it as a side dish, with about 2 tablespoons of the sauce placed at the perimeter of each plate. Covered, the sauce can be kept refrigerated for several days.

Beurre blanc is rich, and I can't deny it. But it is so flavorful that you simply don't need much of it to transport a dish into another realm. (The problem with this reasoning, of course, is that people always demand more of it.) The sauce, excellent for salmon steaks, is actually fine, too, for just about any broiled fish or meat, as well as steamed vegetables.

BEURRE BLANC

4 tablespoons butter, softened and cut into small pieces
2 tablespoons finely chopped shallots
1 tablespoon finely chopped fresh ginger
4 tablespoons dry white wine
3 tablespoons water
½ teaspoon salt
Freshly ground black pepper (8 turns of the pepper mill)

1. Melt 1 tablespoon of the butter in a small saucepan. Add the shallots and ginger. Sauté briefly without browning. Add the wine and water. Reduce the liquid to one fourth of its volume.

2. Stirring with a wire whisk, add the remaining butter, one piece at a time, until it is well blended. Add the salt and pepper.

3. Serve with broiled swordfish or any boiled or steamed seafood, notably lobster.

Optional step: After all the butter has been blended in, pour the sauce into a blender and mix at high speed for 30 seconds. Then return it to the saucepan to warm. This step is intended to make the beurre blanc extraordinarily smooth.

YIELD: 8 servings.   CALORIES PER SERVING: 54.

This is a variation of beurre blanc, made somewhat more acidic by the use of vinegar instead of wine.

GINGER-BUTTER SAUCE

4 tablespoons butter, softened
2 tablespoons chopped shallots
1 tablespoon grated fresh ginger
3 tablespoons red wine vinegar
3 tablespoons water
½ teaspoon salt
Freshly ground black pepper (8 turns of the pepper mill)

1. Melt 1 tablespoon of the butter in a small saucepan and add the shallots and ginger. Cook for 1 minute, without browning. Add the vinegar and water and reduce to one fourth of its volume.

2. Transfer the mixture to a food processor or blender and blend at high speed. Add the remaining butter and the salt and pepper and continue blending until very smooth. Serve hot, 1 tablespoon per serving, over fish or meat.

YIELD: 8 servings.   CALORIES PER SERVING: 54.

Caper Sauce is a pungent accent for leg of lamb, but it is also excellent with poached or broiled fish.

CAPER SAUCE

½ cup chicken stock (see recipe page 30) or lamb broth
2 tablespoons English mustard, prepared according to instructions on the back of the can
¾ cup plain yogurt
½ cup drained capers
1 egg yolk
2 tablespoons chopped fresh parsley leaves
Freshly ground black pepper (6 turns of the pepper mill)

1. Place the stock in a small saucepan. Reduce it by half over high heat. Add the mustard, yogurt, and capers. Whisk in the egg yolk. Bring the liquid to a boil.

2. Remove it from the heat and add the parsley and pepper.

YIELD: About 1 cup, or   CALORIES PER SERVING: 31.
about 8 servings.

If we need to eliminate all creamed and floured sauces, then we need adaptable sauces to replace them. This Creole Sauce fills the bill. It is a pungent, vegetable-laden sauce that will give spark to baked fish, broiled fish, broiled or steamed chicken, meat loaf, meatballs, hamburger, even vegetarian dishes, such as steamed zucchini or broiled eggplant.

CREOLE SAUCE

1 tablespoon olive oil
½ cup chopped onion
1 garlic clove, chopped
½ cup chopped celery
½ cup chopped scallions
1 cup sliced sweet red pepper
½ cup sliced sweet green pepper
1 cup sliced mushrooms
2 cups chopped canned or fresh tomatoes
½ teaspoon salt
Freshly ground black pepper (6 turns of the pepper mill)
1 dried hot pepper, or ¼ teaspoon hot red pepper flakes
4 tablespoons chopped fresh parsley leaves

1. Heat the olive oil in a saucepan and add the onion, garlic, celery, scallions, sweet red and green peppers, and mushrooms. Cook, stirring often, for about 5 minutes.

2. Add the tomatoes, salt, pepper, and hot pepper flakes and bring to a boil. Simmer for 10 minutes. Add the parsley. Serve with meat loaf, baked fish, or broiled chicken.

YIELD: 3½ cups, or about 15 servings.

CALORIES PER SERVING: 27.

Throughout this book, I have put forward recipes that often employ puréed mushrooms as a thickening and blending agent because mushrooms can be as successful as flour and cream. Here is a version of a mushroom sauce by itself to be used on broiled and steamed fish or poultry. It is fine with vegetables, too.

MUSHROOM SAUCE

3 tablespoons butter
4 tablespoons chopped shallots
½ pound mushrooms, sliced
½ teaspoon salt
Freshly ground black pepper (6 turns of the pepper mill)
¼ cup dry white wine
1 cup chicken stock (see recipe page 30)

1. Melt 1 tablespoon of the butter in a saucepan and add the shallots, mushrooms, salt, and pepper. Cook, stirring, for about 5 minutes. Add the wine and chicken stock and reduce by half over high heat.

2. Transfer the mixture to a blender and blend at high speed until smooth. Add the remaining butter and blend until very smooth, about 1 minute.

YIELD: 8 servings.   CALORIES PER SERVING: 56.

Sauce Rouille is the classic addition to fish soups and stews. It serves as a thickener and sharpens the flavors.

SAUCE ROUILLE

1 large potato (about ¼ pound)
2 teaspoons finely chopped garlic
1 egg yolk
1 teaspoon paprika
2 teaspoons cold water
¼ teaspoon salt
Freshly ground black pepper (6 turns of the pepper mill)
½ cup olive oil

1. Peel the potato and cut it into ¼-inch slices. Put the slices in a saucepan and cover them with cold water. Bring the water to a boil and then simmer for 5 minutes, or until tender.

2. Drain the potatoes and force them through a food mill or ricer.

3. Scrape the potatoes into a mixing bowl and add the garlic, egg yolk, paprika, water, salt, and pepper. Start beating with a wire whisk. Gradually add the oil to create a mayonaise emulsion.

YIELD: About 1 cup, or   CALORIES PER SERVING: 140.
about 8 servings.

We are so accustomed to canned tomato sauces that it can be a genuine shock to find out that wonderful tomato sauce can be made from scratch in virtually no time. The key here and in the recipe that follows this one is the high quality of the tomatoes.

FRESH TOMATO SAUCE

4 ripe tomatoes (about 1 pound)
1 tablespoon olive oil
¼ cup finely chopped onion
1 teaspoon chopped garlic
1 bay leaf
½ teaspoon dried thyme
½ teaspoon salt
Freshly ground black pepper (6 turns of the pepper mill)
2 tablespoons chopped fresh basil leaves

1. Drop the tomatoes into boiling water for 12 seconds. Then remove the skins. Cut out and discard the core. Chop the tomatoes. There should be about 3 cups.

2. Heat the oil in a small frying pan and add the onion. When the onion is wilted, add the garlic, tomatoes, bay leaf, thyme, salt, and pepper. Cook for about 20 minutes.

3. Remove the bay leaf. Pour the sauce into the container of a food processor. Blend. Remove the sauce from the processor and transfer it to a saucepan to warm. Add the basil just before serving.

YIELD: 2¼ cups, or   CALORIES PER SERVING: 21.
about 12 servings.

TOMATO AND HORSERADISH SAUCE

1 tablespoon butter
1 cup sliced onions
1 teaspoon chopped garlic
3 ripe tomatoes (1¼ pounds), cored and cut into small
cubes (4 cups)
1 bay leaf
4 tablespoons grated fresh horseradish
½ teaspoon salt
Freshly ground black pepper (6 turns of the pepper mill)
Dash of Tabasco sauce
½ teaspoon dried thyme

1. Melt the butter in a small saucepan (preferably a slant-sided *fait-tout*). Add the onions and garlic and sauté until they are wilted. Add the tomatoes, bay leaf, horseradish, salt, pepper, Tabasco, and thyme. Bring the mixture to a boil and simmer, covered, for 20 minutes.

2. Transfer the mixture to a food mill or processor. Blend until it is medium-coarse.

3. Serve hot with boiled meats, poached chicken, or with broiled or poached fish, pasta, or vegetables.

YIELD: 12 servings.   CALORIES PER SERVING: 26.

This salad dressing is much like many another vinaigrette. My own preference is to strive for some of the rich olive oil taste, but in a moderate way; so I mix the olive oil with peanut or vegetable oil. I also often like to cut down on the thickness of the vinaigrette (especially when there's a lot of mustard) so the same amount will go further and so it will be less caloric. To do that, I add the 3 tablespoons of water. This is a serviceable basic vinaigrette to which you can add any herbs that please you or, for that matter, garlic. To get a mild garlic flavor, I place a whole clove, peeled or unpeeled depending on the strength I'm looking for, in the dressing when it is finished and then simply let it sit in it.

VINAIGRETTE

2 tablespoons Dijon mustard
3 tablespoons red wine vinegar
¼ cup olive oil
¼ cup peanut oil
3 tablespoons water
Freshly ground black pepper (8 turns of the pepper mill)

1. In a mixing bowl, blend the mustard and vinegar well.

2. Combine the oils and pour the oil very slowly into the mustard mixture, whisking as you do, to create a kind of emulsion. Beat in the water. Add the pepper. There should be about ¾ cup. Store refrigerated for up to a week.

YIELD: About ¾ cup, or about 12 servings.　　CALORIES PER SERVING: 83.

GINGER VINAIGRETTE

1 tablespoon Dijon mustard
1 tablespoon grated fresh ginger
4 tablespoons chopped scallions
2 tablespoons chopped chives
½ teaspoon finely chopped garlic
2 tablespoons sherry vinegar or red wine vinegar
Freshly ground black pepper (6 turns of the pepper mill)
½ cup olive oil
3 tablespoons water

1. Put the mustard, ginger, scallions, chives, garlic, vinegar, and pepper in a mixing bowl. Blend well with a wire whisk.

2. Add the olive oil slowly, whisking well as you do. Add the water, blending well.

3. Serve with pasta salad or any other salad requiring a dressing.

YIELD: 12 servings.　　CALORIES PER SERVING: 84.

It is my conviction that the simplest preparation of fruit can take on an elegance of its own. Sauces like this raspberry sauce and the Cold Strawberry Sauce that follows certainly do.

RASPBERRY AND KIRSCH SAUCE

1 16-ounce package frozen raspberries
2 tablespoons kirsch

1. Purée the raspberries with the kirsch in a food processor.
2. Strain and serve hot or cold under ice cream, fruit, or sherbet.

YIELD: 1 cup, or about   CALORIES PER SERVING: 68.
  8 servings.

COLD STRAWBERRY SAUCE

1 10-ounce package frozen strawberries,
or 1 pint fresh, rinsed, and dried strawberries
(Fresh berries require ¼ cup of sugar added.)
Juice of 1 lemon

1. Place fresh or frozen strawberries in a blender or food processor. Add the lemon juice and sugar, if berries are fresh. Blend thoroughly for 20 seconds. Strain to remove the seeds, if desired.
2. Serve with fresh fruit, spooning the sauce onto the plate first and then placing sliced fruit in a pattern over it; toss with fruit salad as a binding ingredient; toss with fresh strawberries; use as a topping for sherbet or ice cream.

YIELD: 1¼ cups, or   CALORIES PER SERVING: 50.
  about 6 servings.

...*16*...

Desserts

To bring a relatively low-calorie approach to desserts, one has to discard a universe of magnificent cooking. Even if one is willing to retain some calories for the sake of sweetening the desserts, a great deal has to be relinquished. The puff paste and the creams and the custards are all gone. Thus, it is only here, in this chapter, that I feel some sense of loss. But after the despair passes, it is easy to get excited about the possibilities that remain. Fruit is still available, of course. And when pears are poached in wine and honey, things definitely begin to look brighter.

It is possible to do some baking, too, in a very disciplined fashion. So I have devised for this book a Thin Apple Tart, the crust serving as no more than a disk on which to rest slices of apple. And I have created a Cherry Tart in which the dough is a kind of bowl to hold virtually unadorned cherries.

There is an emphasis on sorbets, some of them employing egg white to make them creamy and fluffy. The sorbets offer a chance for delightful variation, with mangoes or bitter chocolate or cantaloupe.

I guess we'll survive.

APPLE BALLS WITH RED WINE

2 cups red Burgundy
1¼ cups sugar
1 piece cinnamon stick
2 strips orange peel
2 lemon slices
5 golden Delicious apples (about 2 pounds)

1. Bring the wine, sugar, cinnamon, orange peel, and lemon slices to a boil in a saucepan. Remove from the heat and allow to stand for 10 minutes.

2. Peel the apples. With a melon ball scoop, make about 4 cups of apple balls.

3. Place the apples in the saucepan, cover, and simmer for 7 minutes. The apples should be tender but not mushy. Refrigerate the apples overnight.

YIELD: 8 servings.   CALORIES PER SERVING: 187.

FRESH FRUIT SALAD WITH GRAND MARNIER

Juice of 1 lemon
¼ cup sugar
3 tablespoons Grand Marnier
2 tablespoons peach jam
1 cup seedless orange sections
1 cup seedless grapes
1 cup hulled strawberries
1 cup blueberries
1 mango, peeled and sliced
1 cup peeled sliced apple
1 cup peeled sliced pears

1. Combine the lemon juice, sugar, Grand Marnier, and peach jam in a mixing bowl.

2. Add the fruit and blend well. Chill until ready to serve. The fruit goes well with Tuiles (see recipe page 253).

YIELD: 8 servings.   CALORIES PER SERVING: 132.

BURGUNDY CHERRY COMPOTE

½ cup honey
1½ cups beaujolais or light Burgundy
¼ cup sugar
1 2-inch-long cinammon stick
1¾ pounds cherries, pitted (4 cups)

1. Combine the honey, wine, sugar, and cinammon in a wide saucepan. Bring it to a boil and reduce it to 1½ cups.

2. Add the cherries and poach them gently in the liquid for 5 minutes, shaking the pan occasionally. The point is to stop cooking the cherries before they begin to fall apart.

3. Pour the cherries into a bowl and skim off the foam. When the cherries stop steaming, place them in the refrigerator to cool. They can be served chilled by themselves, or warm or chilled over ice cream.

YIELD: 8 servings.   CALORIES PER SERVING: 176.

VARIATION: When the cherries have finished poaching, pour ¼ cup Cognac into the mixture; then tilt it toward the flame so that the flame reaches the fumes of the liquid and the Cognac catches fire. As soon as it flames, spoon it over ice cream. This is the classic cherries jubilee. At its best it is done at the table in a chafing dish.

ORANGE SLICES IN CASSIS

8 medium-sized navel oranges
¾ cup fresh orange juice
4 tablespoons cassis
1 tablespoon fresh lemon juice

1. With a tool called an orange zester, remove the surface of the skin of 3 of the oranges in long, very thin strips. There should be about ½ cup. Place the peel in a pan with cool water. Bring it to a boil and drain it immediately. Set aside.

2. Cut away the top and bottom of each orange. With the point of a sharp knife, remove the skin of all the oranges and all of the white membranes on the surface.

3. The idea now is to remove each segment of orange without any of the membrane that radiates out from the center. Take the knife and slice down on each side of each segment to free it from the membrane.

4. Place the segments in a bowl along with all the other ingredients. Toss gently. Cover the bowl tightly and refrigerate for 2 hours before serving.

YIELD: 6 servings.   CALORIES PER SERVING: 138.

POACHED PEARS IN RED WINE AND HONEY

8 Bartlett or Bosc pears (about 2 pounds)
Juice of 1 lemon
¼ cup sugar
½ cup honey
1½ cups dry red wine
½ teaspoon vanilla extract
2 whole cloves
3 whole black peppercorns
¼ cup cassis
½ teaspoon dried thyme, or 1 sprig fresh thyme

1. Peel and core the pears with a vegetable peeler (a corer might also facilitate this chore). Leave the stems attached. The pears can be whole, halved, or quartered.

2. Put the pears in a saucepan just large enough to hold them standing upright. Add the lemon juice, sugar, honey, wine, vanilla, cloves, peppercorns, cassis, and thyme. Bring just to the boil, then cover and simmer very slowly for about 30 minutes.

3. Lift the pears out of the pan. Stand them upright in a serving bowl. Strain the sauce over the pears and allow them to cool before serving. Baste the pears periodically with the wine sauce as they cool.

YIELD: 8 servings.   CALORIES PER SERVING: 180.

What we have here is a dream come true for people who have trouble making crust or who don't want to take the time. It's an apple pie, essentially, without a crust (although this mixture would do well, too, if placed in a crust after it was cooked). The part of the process that ensures the whole business won't fall apart after it is molded is the refrigeration. It must be cold to hold its shape.

POMMES EN GATEAU

¾ cup sugar
½ cup water
¼ cup rum
5 golden Delicious apples (2 pounds)
½ cup raisins
½ teaspoon grated lemon rind
Raspberry and Kirsch Sauce (see recipe page 244)

1. Put the sugar, water, and rum in a heavy saucepan and mix well. Bring to a boil and cook for about 5 minutes.
2. Peel, core, and slice the apples thinly. There should be about 7 cups.
3. Add the apples, raisins, and lemon rind to the pan and cook over very low heat for about 45 minutes. The apples should be translucent.
4. Butter a shallow fluted 3-cup mold. Transfer the apple mixture to it and allow it to cool. Refrigerate the mold for at least 3 hours. Warm the mold with a hot towel to help release the gateau. Unmold the gateau onto a serving platter and serve with the sauce.

YIELD: 6 servings.   CALORIES PER SERVING: 229.

PRESENTATION: Place some of the sauce on each plate. Place a wedge of the gateau in the center of the plate.

THIN APPLE TART

1½ cups Wondra flour, chilled
6 tablespoons cold butter, cubed
3 tablespoons plus 2 teaspoons sugar
4 tablespoons cold water
2 large apples (about 1 pound), peeled, halved,
cored, and sliced ⅛ inch thick
1 teaspoon butter

1. Preheat the oven to 450 degrees.

2. Put the flour, cubed butter, and 2 teaspoons of the sugar in a food processor. Start to blend and add the water. When the dough forms a ball, transfer it to a floured board and roll it immediately into a circle of about 13 inches. Press it into a circular 12-inch shallow black-steel or aluminum pie pan. (Usually these are called pizza pans, with a wall of only about ½ inch.) Trim away any dough rising up the wall of the pan. You want a simple, flat disk.

3. Sprinkle the dough with 1 tablespoon of the sugar. Place the apple slices on the dough in a circular, overlapping pattern. The pattern should be very precise, with only a slight overlap. First make the outer ring. Then make an inner ring; the center will tend to rise to a peak, but this will flatten while baking. If there is a hole remaining in the middle, fill it with some chopped apple. Sprinkle the apple with the remaining 2 tablespoons of sugar.

4. Bake the tart for 20 minutes. Place the tart under the broiler for 1 minute to help caramelize the top. The rims of the apple slices should be well browned. Remove the tart from the broiler and brush the top with the 1 teaspoon of butter. Serve hot.

YIELD: 8 servings.   CALORIES PER SERVING: 201.

One of the delightful developments of the new, lighter cooking is the growing awareness that fruit can be spectacular even when presented simply. This cherry tart is essentially a matter of preparing a pie shell to act as a bowl in which to bake cherries that have been slightly sweetened but are adorned in no other way. It is a remarkably good dessert. Incidentally, the crust contains only a bit less butter than I would ordinarily use, but I don't wish to ruin it for the sake of diminishing it by a few more calories. This tart needs to be served soon after it is made, within a couple of hours, anyway, or it will lose its color. One trick is to prepare the tart ahead of time, refrigerate it, and then bake it just before it is needed.

FRENCH CHERRY TART

1½ cups plus 2 tablespoons all-purpose flour
6 tablespoons cold butter, cut into small pieces
4 tablespoons cold water
3 tablespoons sugar
2 pounds fresh cherries, pitted (about 5 cups)

1. Combine 1½ cups of the flour, the butter, and water in a food processor and blend until the mixture begins to form a ball, in perhaps 30 seconds.

2. Using a rolling pin, roll out the dough into a circle 13 inches in diameter and ¼ inch thick.

3. Pick up the dough by rolling it onto the pin and then unrolling it over a 10½-inch black tart pan with a removable bottom. Press the dough gently into the pan, gathering it toward the wall of the pan to thicken the sides of the shell. Place it in the refrigerator for 10 to 15 minutes to allow it to relax.

4. Preheat the oven to 375 degrees.

5. Blend the 2 tablespoons of flour with 1 tablespoon of the sugar. Sprinkle the bottom of the tart shell evenly with the flour mixture. Place the cherries in the shell in a circular pattern. Sprinkle the cherries with the remaining 2 tablespoons of sugar and bake in the bottom of the oven for 45 minutes.

YIELD: 8 servings.   CALORIES PER SERVING: 262.

Like the Cherry Tart, this one is simple and as natural as can be. But apricots are not as sweet as cherries and, to my mind, they benefit from some additional sweetness. To achieve that, I've been adding a bit of brushed honey to the top. That's enough for a good dessert, but if you'd like a little more embellishment follow the optional suggestion and sprinkle toasted almonds over the top.

APRICOT TART

1½ cups plus 2 tablespoons all-purpose flour
6 tablespoons cold butter, cut into small pieces
4 tablespoons cold water
3 tablespoons sugar
2 pounds fresh apricots, pitted and halved
¼ cup honey
2 tablespoons sliced toasted almonds, optional

1. Combine 1½ cups of the flour, the butter, and water in a food processor and blend until the mixture forms a ball, perhaps 30 seconds.

2. Using a rolling pin, roll the dough into a ¼-inch-thick circle about 13 inches in diameter. Pick up the dough by rolling it onto the pin and then unrolling it over a 10½-inch black tart pan with a removable bottom. Press gently into the pan, gathering the dough toward the wall of the pan to thicken the shell's sides. Place the shell in the refrigerator for 10 to 15 minutes to allow the dough to relax.

3. Preheat the oven to 375 degrees.

4. Blend the 2 tablespoons of flour with 1 tablespoon of the sugar and sprinkle the bottom of the tart shell evenly. Place the apricots in the shell in a circular pattern and sprinkle the top with the remaining sugar. Bake in the bottom of the oven for 45 minutes.

5. Remove the tart from the oven, allow it to cool, and brush the top with the honey. Distribute toasted almonds over the top, if desired.

YIELD: 8 servings.   CALORIES PER SERVING: 271.

The word tuiles *is French for tiles, but the tiles it refers to are the Spanish variety. The cookies have the shape of those rounded tiles that characterize Spain and, for that matter, allow places like Coral Gables, Florida, to share some of that feeling. They are common as part of a team of cookies known in combination as petits fours that usually appears as the sweet punctuation to an opulent meal.*

TUILES

1 cup sugar
4 large egg whites
¼ teaspoon vanilla extract
⅔ cup all-purpose flour
6 tablespoons butter, melted
1 cup slivered blanched almonds

1. Preheat the oven to 400 degrees. Butter 2 baking sheets.

2. Combine the sugar and egg white in a mixing bowl and beat the mixture with a wire whisk for about 2 minutes, until it is foaming. Add all the remaining ingredients and blend well.

3. With a small spoon, drop the batter onto a baking sheet, leaving enough space to allow for the tuiles to spread. Bake for 10 to 12 minutes. While they are still hot, lift them off of the baking sheet and bend each cookie over a rolling pin so it takes the shape of a roof tile. Allow the cookies to dry in order to maintain their shape.

YIELD: About 36 cookies.   CALORIES PER COOKIE: 70.

PRESENTATION: These cookies beg to be served with a strong cup of coffee. They can be mixed with other cookies or served alone. (It is my experience that some people, understandably, want only the *tuiles.*)

This soufflé may seem heavier than it is. There is no milk or cream or flour. And it's very classy. To cut down on calories still further, use smaller cups.

SOUFFLÉ GRAND MARNIER

8 large egg yolks
⅔ cup plus 2 tablespoons granulated sugar
⅓ cup Grand Marnier
2 tablespoons butter
8 large egg whites
Confectioner's sugar for sprinkling on top

1. Preheat the oven to 450 degrees. Place 6 1¼-cup soufflé dishes in the refrigerator to chill.

2. Beat the egg yolks and ⅓ cup of the granulated sugar in a double boiler over hot water, whisking the mixture until it thickens to the consistency of heavy cream. Add the Grand Marnier.

3. Transfer the mixture to a mixing bowl placed in a larger bowl of crushed ice. Continue beating over the ice until the mixture has cooled.

4. Butter the bottoms and sides of the dishes, paying special attention to the walls. Use the 2 tablespoons of sugar to coat the insides of the dishes and return the dishes to the refrigerator.

5. Place the egg whites in a mixing bowl, preferably a copper one, and with a balloon whisk, beat them until they are stiff. Beat in the remaining ⅓ cup of sugar. With a large rubber spatula, fold the whites into the Grand Marnier mixture.

6. Spoon equal amounts of the mixture into the prepared dishes. The mixture should fill the dishes to a height about ¼ inch over the rim. With your thumb, create a channel around the periphery of the dish to allow for expansion. Place the dishes on a baking dish and bake for 7 minutes. Lower the oven temperature to 425 degrees and bake for 5 minutes longer. Serve sprinkled with confectioner's sugar.

YIELD: 6 servings.   CALORIES PER SERVING: 282.

A strawberry soufflé without flour is a recipe that I have often offered in books and elsewhere. Ever since I learned to make it, I have looked for other ways to use similar techniques. What I've done here is to transfer most of the technique to apples and to do away with the egg yolks as well as the flour. The reason one uses yolks and flour in a soufflé is to bind it and make it richer. But puréed fruits have a binding ability all their own.

APPLE SOUFFLÉ

5 golden Delicious apples
4 tablespoons butter
¾ cup granulated sugar
1 teaspoon grated lemon rind
3 tablespoons Calvados or apple jack
8 large egg whites
Confectioner's sugar for sprinkling on top, optional

1. Place 6 1¼-cup soufflé dishes in the refrigerator to chill.

2. Preheat the oven to 450 degrees.

3. Peel and core the apples. Cut them into quarters and slice each quarter very thinly. There should be about 4 cups.

4. Heat 2 tablespoons of the butter in a large frying pan and place the apples in it, along with ½ cup of the granulated sugar and the lemon rind. Cook over high heat, stirring, for about 10 minutes, or until all the liquid evaporates. Allow the apples to brown slightly and add 3 tablespoons of Calvados. Mix well.

5. Transfer the apples to a food processor and purée finely, about 1 minutes. Transfer the purée to a large mixing bowl.

6. Butter the bottoms and sides of the soufflé dishes, paying special attention to the walls. Return them to the refrigerator.

7. Place the egg whites in a very clean and dry copper or stainless steel bowl and, with a balloon whisk, beat them until they are stiff but still moist. Beat in the remaining ¼ cup of sugar. With a large rubber spatula fold the whites into the purée.

8. Spoon equal amounts of the mixture into the prepared dishes. The mixture should fill the dishes to about ¼ inch over the rim. With your thumb, create a channel around the periphery of the dish to allow for expansion. Place the dishes on a baking sheet and bake for 7 minutes. Reduce the oven temperature to 425 degrees and bake 7 minutes longer. Serve sprinkled with confectioner's sugar, if desired.

YIELD: 6 servings.   CALORIES PER SERVING: 249.

PRESENTATION: This looks fantastic to start with and then quickly loses its looks. The trick is to get the soufflé from the oven to the table quickly.

Sherbets are the traditional light desserts. The trick, these days, is to find some way of making them especially interesting. I think I've done that, with mangoes and cantaloupe and even chocolate.

MANGO SHERBET

4 mangoes (3¼ pounds for 4 cups purée)
½ cup sugar
4 tablespoons fresh lemon juice
1 large egg white, slightly beaten

1. Quarter the mango and remove the skin. Purée in a food processor.

2. Add the sugar and lemon juice and blend.

3. Pour the purée into an ice-cream freezer and follow the manufacturer's instructions. When the purée begins to freeze, add the egg white and resume freezing.

YIELD: About 6 cups, or   CALORIES PER SERVING: 108.
about 10 servings.

SORBET WITH BITTER CHOCOLATE

½ pound bitter chocolate
3 cups lukewarm water
3 ounces sweet chocolate, grated
¾ cup sugar

1. Melt the bitter chocolate slowly in the top of a double boiler.

2. Blend the water with the melted chocolate. Add the grated sweet chocolate and the sugar and blend well.

3. Pour the mixture into an ice-cream freezer and follow the manufacturer's instructions.

YIELD: 10 servings.   CALORIES PER SERVING: 215.

PINEAPPLE SORBET

1 4-pound ripe pineapple
½ cup sugar
5 tablespoons fresh lemon juice
1 large egg white, slightly beaten

1. Trim the top and bottom of the pineapple. With a knife, slice down the sides to remove the skin and any green flesh. Dig out any brown fibrous eyes. Quarter the pineapple. Remove any woody flesh; there will be a beam of hard pineapple along the peak of each quarter.

2. Purée the pineapple in a food processor. Add the sugar and lemon juice and blend.

3. Place the purée in an ice-cream freezer and follow the manufacturer's instructions. When the puree begins to freeze, add the egg white and resume freezing.

YIELD: About 6 cups, or about 10 servings.   CALORIES PER SERVING: 88.

NOTE: This is a tart sorbet relatively low in sugar and high in lemon juice. If it is too tart for your taste or not sweet enough, adjust the ingredients accordingly.

CANTALOUPE SORBET

2 ripe cantaloupes (2 pounds each)
¾ cup superfine sugar
4 tablespoons fresh lemon juice
1 large egg white, slightly beaten

1. Quarter the cantaloupes and remove the skin and pits. Slice the cantaloupes into ½-inch-thick pieces and put them in the food processor. Add the sugar and lemon juice. Purée the mixture. There should be 4 cups of purée.

2. Place the mixture in an ice-cream freezer and follow the manufacturer's directions. When the sorbet has begun to freeze, add the egg white and resume freezing.

YIELD: 8 servings.   CALORIES PER SERVING: 116.

KIWI SORBET

12 kiwi fruits (about 2 pounds)
¾ cup sugar
1 large egg white, slightly beaten

1. Peel the kiwis and slice them coarsely. Place in a food processor along with the sugar and purée finely. Be sure there are no lumps. There should be about 3 cups.

2. Transfer the mixture to an ice-cream freezer and follow the manufacturer's instructions.

3. Beat the egg white with 2 or 3 strokes of a whisk. When the mixture is half frozen, pour the egg white into it and resume freezing until done.

4. The sorbet can be garnished with thinly slice strawberries and mangoes arranged in a pattern around the periphery of the plate.

YIELD: About 1 quart, or about 8 servings.   CALORIES PER SERVING: 134.

PEACH SHERBET

3½ pounds ripe peaches
1¼ cups sugar
Juice of 2 lemons (¼ cup)

1. Bring 1 quart of water to a boil in a saucepan and add the peaches. Bring the water back to the boil and remove the peaches. Let them cool and then peel them and remove the pits. Place the peaches in a food processor along with the sugar and lemon juice.

2. Purée the peaches until fine and transfer the mixture to an ice-cream freezer and follow the manufacturer's instructions.

YIELD: 10 servings.   CALORIES PER SERVING: 150.

...*17*...

Miscellaneous

The category "miscellaneous" always puts me off and probably affects everybody else that way, too. It sounds like a grab bag of the inconsequential. But that is certainly no reflection of my own feeling about this group of recipes. Granted, they don't fit neatly into any of the foregoing sections, but they had to be in this book nevertheless.

The delightful rabbit dishes included here are among my favorites in all the world. And, as for the bread, anyone who has ever wandered into my kitchen knows that I am constantly baking it—the very same bread that appears here. The Oriental Curry Powder that I describe in this collection of recipes was a revelation to me, bringing curry back to life.

What people like to say about rabbit is that it tastes like chicken. Well, I suppose it does, a little. But that really doesn't do the dish much of a service. Rabbit tastes like rabbit, which is to say that a young rabbit (as required by this recipe) is likely to be extremely subtle in flavor, almost without any taste at all, with a touch of gaminess. It is, therefore, a kind of tabula rasa, as pasta is, waiting for the cook to make the sauces that will bring it alive as food. A mustard sauce does the trick.

RABBIT À LA MOUTARDE

2 tablespoons olive oil
1 2½-pound rabbit, cut into 12 serving pieces,
plus the liver
½ teaspoon salt
Freshly ground black pepper (8 turns of the pepper mill)
3 tablespoons Dijon mustard
½ cup plus 3 tablespoons dry white wine
1 large carrot, quartered and cut into 1-inch lengths
(1 cup)
12 peeled white onions
4 small red potatoes, cut in quarters (1 cup)
½ teaspoon finely chopped garlic
12 small mushrooms (about ½ pound)
1 bay leaf
½ teaspoon dried thyme
1 cup chicken stock (see recipe page 30)
½ cup whole plum tomatoes
¼ cup chopped fresh parsley leaves

1. Heat the oil in a Dutch oven. Sprinkle the rabbit pieces with salt and pepper and put them in the pot. Brown the rabbit lightly on all sides quickly for about 5 minutes.

2. Blend the mustard with 3 tablespoons of the wine. Drain all the fat from the Dutch oven. With a pastry brush coat all the pieces of rabbit with the mustard-wine mixture. Cook for 5 minutes while stirring.

3. Put the carrots, onions, and potatoes into a saucepan. Cover with water. Bring to a boil and then drain.

4. Add the garlic, mushrooms, drained vegetables, bay leaf, and thyme to the Dutch oven and cook for another 5 minutes. Add the remaining wine, chicken stock, and tomatoes and simmer, covered, for about 40 minutes, or until the rabbit is tender.

5. To thicken the gravy, uncover the pan and cook over medium heat for 5 minutes more. Garnish with parsley and serve.

YIELD: 4 servings.   CALORIES PER SERVING: 483.

PRESENTATION: Often this is served with boiled or mashed potatoes. My suggestion, in this instance, however, is to serve the rabbit with a Purée of Celery Root (see recipe page 224). Place the purée in the center of the dish with 2 or 3 pieces of rabbit covered in vegetables and gravy around the purée.

BRAISED RABBIT WITH RED WINE

6 sprigs fresh parsley
½ teaspoon dried thyme, or 2 sprigs fresh thyme
1 bay leaf
2 tablespoons oil
1 2½-pound rabbit, cleaned and cut into 12 serving pieces
½ teaspoon salt
Freshly ground black pepper (8 turns of the pepper mill)
½ pound small mushrooms
¾ pound small white onions (about 16)
1 tablespoon finely chopped garlic
1½ cups dry red wine
½ cup chicken stock (see recipe page 30)
1 tablespoon tomato paste

1. Prepare a bouquet garni by wrapping the parsley, thyme, and bay leaf in a piece of cheesecloth.

2. Heat the oil in a Dutch oven. Sprinkle the rabbit pieces with salt and pepper. Brown them lightly on all sides for about 5 minutes, stirring constantly. Drain off the fat and add the mushrooms, onions, and garlic. Cook the rabbit and vegetables for about 5 minutes, stirring constantly.

3. Add the wine, chicken stock, tomato paste, and bouqet garni to the pot. Bring it all to a boil and simmer for about 40 minutes, or until the rabbit is tender. To thicken the gravy, uncover the pot and cook over medium heat for about 5 minutes.

YIELD: 4 servings.   CALORIES PER SERVING: 428.

PRESENTATION: This dish can be served in the same manner as Rabbit à la Moutarde. As a simple variation, place 2 or 3 rabbit pieces in the center of each dish surrounded by 3 or 4 Parsleyed Potatoes or portions of Purée of Celery Root (see recipes pages 212 and 224).

Bread is an important part of many a meal, even among those trying to eat as lightly as possible. The rule to keep in mind when serving it is to never put butter on the table. Smearing bread with butter is an incredibly easy way to send the caloric count of a meal through the roof. Instead, in good French bistro fashion, expect guests to use the bread to finish off the sauce, which, in this book anyway, will tend to be relatively low in calories.

BAGUETTES WITH SESAME SEEDS

2 envelopes active dry yeast
2¼ cups warm (90-degree) water
6 cups unbleached all-purpose flour
1 tablespoon salt
2 tablespoons sesame seeds
2 ice cubes

1. Place the chopping blade in the food processor bowl. Add the yeast and ¼ cup warm water. Mix by turning the chopping blade by hand. Add all the flour. Blend for 5 seconds. Add the salt and blend for 5 seconds. While the blade continues to turn, gradually add the remaining water. Blend until the batter begins to form a large ball, 20 to 25 seconds.

2. Flour a board and knead the dough, forming it into a ball. Flour a large mixing bowl and place the ball of dough in it. Sprinkle the top with flour. Cover it with a dish towel. Let the dough rise in a warm place until it doubles in bulk. (The time required varies with environmental factors, but at room temperature of about 75 degrees it will take at least an hour.)

3. Turn the dough out onto a lightly floured board and punch it down. Make a new ball and put it back in the mixing bowl. Sprinkle it with flour; cover and let it rest again for 45 minutes.

4. When the dough rises about double again, remove it from the bowl, punch it down, and shape it into the loaf desired. This quantity is sufficient for 5 baguettes of about 18 inches in length, each stretched along the length of a tubular French bread pan. Allow the dough to continue to rise to 50 percent additional volume.

5. Meanwhile, preheat the oven to 425 degrees.

6. Brush the loaves lightly with water and distribute the sesame seeds over the top of each loaf. With a razor blade, diagonally score the surface of the loaves several times, making each incision about ½ inch deep.

7. Place the loaves in the oven and throw the ice cubes onto the oven floor. (The ice adds steam to help produce a thin crust.) Bake

for 30 minutes. Lower the oven temperature to 400 degrees and bake for 10 minutes. Transfer the bread to a rack and let it cool.

YIELD: 20 servings.   CALORIES PER SERVING: 147.

During my childhood, whole wheat bread was deemed crude, peasant-like. Now, of course, its time has come.

WHOLE WHEAT BREAD

2 envelopes active dry yeast
2¼ cups warm (90-degree) water
3 cups whole wheat flour
3 cups all-purpose flour
1 teaspoon salt

1. Place the dough blade in the bowl of a food processor and add the yeast and ¼ cup warm water. Turn the chopping blade by hand to gently mix the two. Add all the flour. Blend for 5 seconds. Add the salt. While the blade continues to turn, gradually add the remaining water. Blend until the batter begins to form into a large ball. This takes about 20 to 25 seconds.

2. Flour a board and knead the dough, shaping it into a ball. Flour a large mixing bowl and place the ball of dough in it. Sprinkle the top with flour. Cover it with a dish towel. Let the dough rise in a warm place until it doubles in bulk. (The time required varies with environmental factors, but if the temperature is 75 degrees it will take at least an hour.)

3. Turn the dough out onto a lightly floured board and punch it down. Make a new ball and put it back into the mixing bowl. Sprinkle it with flour, cover it, and let it rest again for 45 minutes to an hour.

4. When the dough doubles again, remove it from the bowl, punch it down, and shape it into a loaf of the shape desired. This quantity is sufficient for 2 loaves 24 inches long, stretched along the length of a tubular French bread pan. Let the dough continue to rise until it increases by 50 percent of its volume.

5. Preheat the oven to 425 degrees.

6. With a razor blade or sharp knife, diagonally score the surface of the loaf several times, making each incision about ½ inch deep.

7. Place the loaves in the oven and throw a couple of ice cubes into the oven to ensure a crisp crust. Bake for 30 minutes. Lower the oven temperature to 400 degrees and bake an additional 10 minutes. Transfer the bread to a rack and let it cool.

YIELD: 20 servings.   CALORIES PER SERVING: 132.

GARLIC CROUTONS

3 garlic cloves
2 tablespoons olive oil
2 cups commercially available sliced white bread
(it should be the high-quality firm-textured bread),
trimmed of crust and cut into ¼-inch cubes

1. Peel the garlic and crush each clove slightly with the side of a knife.

2. Heat the oil in a nonstick frying pan and add the garlic and bread cubes. Cook, stirring and shaking the pan, until the bread is golden brown. Drain. Remove the garlic. Serve with fish soup or Gazpacho.

YIELD: 12 servings.   CALORIES PER SERVING: 35.

CROUTONS

½ loaf French or Italian bread
1 garlic clove
2 tablespoons olive oil

1. Rub the crust of bread all over with the garlic.

2. Cut the bread into ⅛-inch-thick slices and arrange the slices on a baking sheet. Sprinkle with the oil.

3. Broil the slices until golden on both sides.

YIELD: About 12 croutons.   CALORIES PER SERVING: 75.

This recipe was inspired by a letter I received in November 1982. I had written in the newspaper that curried dishes were beginning to lose their appeal for me. A reader, Gail Duke of Minneapolis, tried to help by sending me her solution, which was her own recipe for curry powder. I took the suggestion, adapted it to my own taste, and curried dishes have regained their appeal.

ORIENTAL CURRY POWDER

4 tablespoons ground tumeric
3 tablespoons ground coriander
2 tablespoons ground cumin
1 tablespoon white peppercorns
1 tablespoon whole cloves
2 tablespoons ground ginger
1 tablespoon ground cardamon
2 teaspoons cayenne pepper
1 tablespoon ground mace
1 tablespoon dried **fine herbes** *(commercially packaged thyme, oregano, sage, rosemary, marjoram, and basil)*
1 tablespoon fenugreek

Place all the ingredients in a grinder and grind them into a very fine powder. Store the powder in a glass jar with a tight lid.

YIELD: 1 cup.   CALORIES PER TEASPOON: 7.

Very often I prepare an egg dish that is sort of a naked eggs florentine. It's florentine because the egg is accompanied by spinach, naked because it does not have the rich cheese sauce customarily placed on top. It is a very satisfying dish and handsome, too, so long as it is prepared with enough care to keep the egg yolks whole.

BAKED EGGS WITH SPINACH AND GRUYÈRE

*2 pounds fresh spinach
1 tablespoon butter
½ teaspoon salt
Freshly ground black pepper (8 turns of the pepper mill)
1 garlic clove, peeled
Pinch of grated nutmeg
8 large eggs
½ cup grated Gruyère cheese*

1. Preheat the broiler.

2. Pick over the spinach and discard any tough stems or blemished leaves. Wash thoroughly. There should be about 12 cups of spinach.

3. Bring ¼ cup water to a boil and place the spinach in it. Stirring, cook for about 1 minute, or until the leaves wilt. Drain the spinach in a collander, pressing the leaves to remove all moisture.

4. In an 11-inch nonstick frying pan, melt the butter and add the spinach, salt, 4 turns of the pepper mill, garlic, and nutmeg. Heat through, stirring, for 1 minute.

5. Make a small indentation in the spinach for each egg. Break the eggs over the spinach, allowing the whole yolk to settle into each indentation. Sprinkle with the cheese and 4 turns of the pepper mill. Place the pan about 4 inches from the source of heat in the broiler. Broil for 2 minutes, or until the eggs are partially cooked. The yolks should remain runny.

YIELD: 4 servings.   CALORIES PER SERVING: 303.

PRESENTATION: The knack is in keeping the yolks from breaking. First spoon out some of the spinach and place it in the center of a plate. Then scoop out the yolk and some white along with some of the spinach. Place 2 eggs on each mound of spinach.

Index